Dear Jim
Thank you for all
the fine years of
great service. Best wishes
to you & your family.
Peace,
Mary Jo.

Moving Meditation

EXPERIENCE THE GOOD WITHIN

MARY JO RICKETSON

WestBow
PRESS
A DIVISION OF THOMAS NELSON

WestBow Press books may be ordered through booksellers or by contacting:

WestBow Press
A Division of Thomas Nelson
1663 Liberty Drive
Bloomington, IN 47403
www.westbowpress.com
1-(866) 928-1240

Because of the dynamic nature of the Internet, any web addresses or links contained in this book may have changed since publication and may no longer be valid. The views expressed in this work are solely those of the author and do not necessarily reflect the views of the publisher, and the publisher hereby disclaims any responsibility for them.

Any people depicted in stock imagery provided by Thinkstock are models, and such images are being used for illustrative purposes only.

Certain stock imagery © Thinkstock.

ISBN: 978-1-4497-2468-9 (sc)
ISBN: 978-1-4497-2467-2 (ebk)

Library of Congress Control Number: 2011914873

Printed in the United States of America

WestBow Press rev. date: 11/07/2011

In Appreciation

I am deeply grateful to the many people who have made this project possible. I want to acknowledge and express a heartfelt appreciation for all those who have come before us for their wisdom, understanding, and willingness to share their knowledge and experience. The many quotes in this book are the smallest fraction of all that has been handed down to us.

Thank you to all I have been fortunate to know in this lifetime. You have all made a difference. Thank you to my colleagues, clients, and students for all the work we have shared in together. I have benefited greatly from your presence and the stories you share openly with love. I feel love, respect, and gratitude for you all. Thank you to Nancy Cinamon-Murray, who completed the first edit of the work to ready it for submission.

To my family I owe the deepest thanks and love. I thank my husband and our two children, who lift and inspire me every day with their love and support. I thank my parents, who have always been there for me and my family. They are the foundation we rest on and count on. I thank my brothers and sister and their beautiful families. Thank you to all my family—aunts, uncles, cousins, grandparents, and my wonderful family on my husband's side—so many have offered love and support.

Most importantly, I thank God for all of you and for making all things possible in love.

CONTENTS

Introduction

"What lies before us and what lies behind us are small matters compared to what lies within us. And when we bring what lies within us into the world, miracles happen."

—Ralph Waldo Emerson

"We shall be God's temples, and God will be the God within us."

—Saint Ignatius of Antioch

"Do you not know that your body is a temple for the holy Spirit within you, whom you have from God, and that you are not your own."

—1 Corinthians 6:19

"Do not let your hearts be troubled or afraid."

—John 14:27

"I am with you always."

—Mathew 28:20

We all have within us a potential to experience optimal well-being in mind and body. This potential, the Good Within, can be recognized and realized through the work of Mind-Body Training (MBT). Our work is a moving meditation, a daily practice of exercises that trains the mind to be fully present in the body. The mind-body becomes the instrument to consciously experience our true nature and inherent potential.

The training is grounded in the scientific principles that promote optimal well-being in mind-body. By grounding our work in science and what can be experienced in the visible world, we become more able to deepen our awareness of what is unseen, the Good Within. Through our training, we realize an eternal truth about our being. We are inherently, infinitely, and equally Good Within because we are of God.

The exercises are designed to help us remember our true nature and inherent goodness. As we move in the exercises, our work to realize the Good Within is ultimately an effort to know and feel God's presence in mind-body. We experience this presence as a vital energy that moves and inspires us. We feel stable and strong. We are willing to persevere while maintaining a sense of ease, a flow to our movements that some call grace. Our attention is focused, and we are ready and able to respond to all life offers. By moving with greater awareness of the Good Within, we recognize our potential to know optimal wellness in mind-body.

Our awareness of the mind-body as a precious gift unleashes its potential as an instrument to know and feel God's goodness and love within ourselves, within others, and in all of creation.

We may have doubts about our and others' inherent goodness based on what we see with our eyes. We may believe that optimal well-being is out of our reach. We may fear that we will never realize our potential or that the goodness we do know will be taken from us. This mindset of disbelief and fear is not a testimony to our true and full nature. It is the result of the limited vision of the ego, the small self that is unaware of its union and oneness with God. We feel small and alone when we forget that God is with us always. In this state of perceived separation from all that is good, fear arises. The fear is uncomfortable and gets our attention. It brings the mind to the present moment in touch with the body. In this moment of union in mind-body, we have an opening to remember: God is as close as the breath of life we feel moving within us. Mind-Body Training can help us remember God is within us and all around us, both near and far.

As we work, we are better able to let go of the false beliefs that have, in the past, been barriers to our ability to trust in a loving and living God. Our work together in the exercises is not about how much weight we can lift, how many sit-ups we can do, how fast we can run, or how much we weigh. No effort on our part can add to or take away from what is already given, whole and complete, within us. No effort on our part can bring us closer to God, save us from suffering, or restore peace in our hearts. God does not ask us to bear this burden. God is already close. He is within us. His peace is already ours, given in the gift of life. Our efforts do not change God, who is within. God is unchanging and everlasting love. Our efforts change us so we become more able to give willingly of ourselves to understand our relationship to God. In God we realize an inner source of vital energy, our ability to relate to others, a strong and free will, an open heart, and a conscious spirit with clear vision. This is already ours. The exercises are the tools to help us to remember and live this truth.

We exercise and discipline the mind-body to know ourselves, others, and our world as God knows us. All knowledge is the way we discover, describe, and understand God. We are not creators of the universe or anything in it. Our efforts are to discover the tools to see and understand the universe as it already is. We see and understand more clearly our purpose and place in this world as we are able to live in the truth and light of God's goodness and love. Our work is to see and feel the Good Within as it manifests in thought, word, and action. We work to build and strengthen a relationship with God that is personal and current. We allow God to be the one source of life and love, to comfort, to guide, and to support us. As we come to know

God, we come closer to the experience of our true nature and see God at work in all beings and all things. Our relationship with God is strengthened in knowing ourselves and others fully.

God's goodness is our inherent and true nature. We are not God, but we exist in space and time as one small but vital part of the infinite goodness that is God. We are each called to do our part by fulfilling our purpose to bring the Good Within to life.

In the exercises, you will be introduced to a self you may already know somewhere deep within but may have forgotten or lost touch with consciously. You will get to know yourself and others as God knows you, as God created you, in God's image and likeness. You are a child of God.

Our work is to bring to life the seven gifts of God's goodness within. The seven gifts are:

1. Vitality
2. Balance
3. Strength
4. Endurance
5. Flexibility
6. Focused attention
7. Coordination

We bring these gifts to life by using seven tools that optimize our learning:

1. Reading
2. Writing
3. Speaking
4. Movement
5. Visualization
6. Prayer/meditation
7. Observation/reflection

In your daily practice, you may call on one or more of the tools. The work awakens the seven gifts not independent of each other but as one whole within you.

Chapter 1 describes the science behind the mind-body connection and how we can use our conscious awareness of the oneness of mind and body to transform our lives by bringing the Good Within to life. We learn to be fully present in each moment as the means to realizing our full potential.

Chapter 2 provides the inspiration for our work and a clear vision of how our faith, united with observable fact, becomes a powerful motivator. The seven gifts of God's goodness are identified and described in mind-body. Mind-Body Training can show us how to utilize the amazing gift of mind-body and realize our potential to know optimal well-being.

Chapter 3 discusses the information we need to begin our work, including suggestions to optimize our practice and to experience the many benefits of Mind-Body Training. The principles that guide our movements are outlined, along with a brief description of how we can use each of the tools to further our learning and growth.

Chapter 4 provides suggestions for developing a daily practice of Mind-Body Training that best suits our needs. The individualized plan will include seven ways to bring the Good Within to life:

1. Cardiovascular (aerobic) training
2. Core and strength training
3. Flexibility training (yoga postures)
4. Adequate rest/prayer/meditation
5. Life-giving nutrition
6. Family/community/church
7. Written goals and a plan of action

Keeping these essential components of your training in focus allows you to begin with the end in mind. As you begin the work in the exercises, you will recognize the unique and essential aspects of a way of life that promotes optimal well-being.

Chapter 5 includes forty exercises divided into three easy-to-manage categories of movement: the warm-up, core and strength training, and flexibility training. The exercises are presented in a format that includes a title, statements to convey the essence of the message, an intention or focus, and suggestions for practice in mind-body both "on the mat" and "off the mat" in everyday life. Pictures of the exercises with detailed instruction are also provided.

Chapter 6 contains the exercises that constitute our continued daily practice. We can work with one exercise per day or focus on the exercise for a week or longer. Mastery comes with practice and patience. Work at your own pace. You will repeat the exercises again and again. Let every time be new—a new level of awareness, a new perspective, and a new depth or intensity.

Chapter 7 is a little story of great love. When I first conceived the topic for this book, I imagined seven chapters. Seven represents wholeness in the union of its component parts "three" and "four," which is symbolic of the union between God and man. As the material came together, there were only six chapters, until one day before I submitted the final manuscript for proofreading, chapter 7 came into being.

Appendix A outlines exercise routines for varying levels of physical ability and desired intensity. Appendix B lists all the exercises, and appendix C summarizes the seven gifts and the benefits in mind-body. Appendix D is a list of additional readings on related topics.

I hope you will come to love this work as you sense the vital energy and goodness that it awakens in you.

Mind-Body Connection

"But as it is, there are many parts, yet one body."

—1 Corinthians 12:20

"Nothing in life is to be feared. It is only to be understood."

—Madame Curie

"If we all did the things we are really capable of doing we would literally astound ourselves."

—Thomas Edison

"Whoever believes in me will do the works that I do, and will do greater ones than these, because I am going to the Father."

—John 14:12

Mind-Body Science

Through research performed in the last twenty years, we now have ample scientific evidence for the existence and power of the mind-body connection. Numerous studies with both animals and humans have increased our understanding of the mind-body link, demonstrating it to be a powerful tool for improving the quality of our lives. Mind-body exercises and strategies can enhance our ability to deal with stress, help us to prevent and heal illness, improve performance at work, in school, and in athletics, increase creativity, reduce tension, anxiety, and depression, and promote a state of mind-body that fosters healthy relationships.

Mind-Body Training shows us practical ways to harness the powerful force of the mind-body connection and bring the Good Within, our inherent potential for well-being, to life. We are at our best when our mind and body are working together so that our thoughts and actions become aligned to the truth of our being. We become increasingly aware of what we are truly capable of achieving in mind-body.

Larry Dossey, MD (1989), a leading physician in the field of mind-body medicine, states "The mind steadfastly refuses to behave locally, as contemporary scientific evidence is beginning to show. We now know, for example, that brain-like tissue is found throughout the body" (p.174). Michael D. Gershon, MD (1998), in his book *The Second Brain*, provides evidence to support his theory that your gut has a mind of its own. We have all had a "gut feeling" about something. Gershon has shown that this gut feeling is actually intelligence at the cellular level. The same nerve cells that exist and process information in the brain also exist in our digestive systems. The enteric (meaning "of the body") nervous system operates both independently of and interdependently with the central nervous system, which is made up of the brain and spinal cord.

What does all this mean for you and me? It means that what we think and perceive with the mind is directly linked to our experiences and the feelings we have in the body. In other words, in mind-body medicine, our thoughts and emotions affect our health. How we perceive the world in which we live and our own selves in that world plays a significant role in our health and happiness. If we think predominantly negative thoughts and fail to see the mind-body as it truly is, over time we will feel stressed and our bodies may manifest this stress as disease ("dis-ease"). When we understand how amazing and resilient the mind-body is, we can find comfort in knowing and feeling that both health and happiness are possible because they reflect our inherent and true nature.

One of the most important truths for us to recognize is that disease does not reflect our mind-body's *inability* to deal with stress. To the contrary, disease is the mind-body's attempt to relieve stress and restore equilibrium. For example, if we are stressed and go for extended periods without adequate sleep or nourishment, the immune system may respond by manifesting a cold. In the light of mind-body science, the cold becomes an asset. The cold gets our attention, reveals an imbalance, and encourages us to respond in ways that restore equilibrium. The cold allows the body to release unneeded tension and toxins through the symptoms of sneezing, having a runny nose, coughing, feeling pain, and running a fever. If we drink plenty of water, balance work with adequate rest, and nourish the mind-body, in two or three days, we will feel much better. Our balance and strength will be restored. When we "fight" the cold with all sorts of remedies to stop the sneezing and coughing and fail to make the necessary adjustments to restore balance, we will more than likely prolong the cold and inhibit the effectiveness of the body to restore the natural state of health. Understanding the mind-body connection will help us to see that the stress of disease has the potential to work for us to restore balance and promote healing. This understanding will also help us to use medicine more effectively when needed.

In 1992, a review by two National Institute of Health scientists in the *Journal of the American Medical Association* noted the role of stress in autoimmune diseases, coronary artery disease, gastrointestinal disorders, chronic pain, and a range of other medical, as well as psychiatric, disorders (Chrousos and Gold, 1992). In all of these disorders, research indicates that the effect of stressful life events on morbidity and mortality is mediated by over-activation of the "fight or flight response." We overreact when we perceive the world around us as a frightening place that threatens our well-being. This fear activates the fight or flight response, and we fight against or run away from the perceived threat. In the example above, we may increase our stress load when we perceive the cold as "bad" and try to fight it rather than letting it run its natural course.

The stress response is initiated through the autonomic nervous system and includes physiological changes such as increased blood pressure, respiratory rate, heart rate, oxygen consumption, blood flow to the muscles, perspiration, and muscle tone. Further research has shown that the effects of stress reach far beyond the physical.

Robert Sapolsky, PhD (2004), provides evidence in his book, *Why Zebras Don't Get Ulcers,* that stress can impact the brain and our ability to learn, including memory. Other psychological effects of stress include a feeling of loss of control and predictability, lack of outlets for frustration, inadequate sources of social support, and the general perception that life is worsening. In studies with rats, Sapolsky stressed the rats by administering electrical shocks. The shocks were of low intensity and not powerful enough to cause any physical damage to body tissues. He found, however, that under stress "the rats cannot learn the task. It does not learn to cope. On the contrary, it has learned to be helpless . . . They have actually learned not to bother paying attention" (p. 39). He also reports that the rats over-generalize. Rather than feeling, "When I am getting shocked, there is nothing I can do and it feels terrible, but it is not the whole world. It isn't true for everything," with learned helplessness the rat seems to behave as if, "There is nothing I can do ever." Even when control and mastery are potentially made available to it, the rat cannot perceive the new opportunity.

Mind-Body Training provides the knowledge, methods, and tools that teach us to overcome stress and its harmful effects by recognizing, developing, and preparing the mind-body to process and respond to stressful life events more effectively. With training and practice, we learn that we can choose our response to stress rather than react in ways that teach us to exhibit helplessness.

Mind-Body Training purposefully challenges us to recognize the seven gifts of God's goodness: *vitality, balance, strength, endurance, flexibility, focused attention, and coordination.* These gifts will enable us to respond to stress in ways that further our learning and growth. We come to believe, "I am willing and able" rather than, "I am helpless or unable to respond."

If we look back on the physiological changes that occur in the body under stress, we will notice that these are the same changes that occur with physical exercise and include increased blood pressure, respiratory rate, heart rate, oxygen consumption, blood flow to the muscles, perspiration, and muscle tone. Why is it that in one case, when we perceive an event as stressful, these changes weaken the mind-body, and on the other hand, in the case of regular exercise, the same changes in the body can strengthen and protect us from the harmful effects of imbalances that lead to disease?

The difference is in our state of readiness or preparedness in mind-body to respond to the stress and whether we perceive it as good or bad. Stress can work for us or against us. The choice is ours. If we are willing to do the work in mind-body to feel prepared, if we believe that we can handle what comes our way, we will be more able to respond effectively. When we choose effective responses, we build confidence and continue to further our capacity to learn and grow. Mind-Body Training develops in us "response-ability" by purposefully stressing us in ways that foster awareness of the present moment as the means to choosing more effective responses. When the mind is fully present in the body, we become "response-able." We feel prepared and able to respond. The stress is no longer perceived as a threat to us but an opportunity to strengthen our ability to respond in ways that bring goodness to life.

On the other hand, if we feel we cannot handle the stress and perceive it as a threat to our well-being, we will react accordingly. Our "reaction" is not a chosen response because it is set off by the sympathetic nervous system, which is autonomic and not within our control. Adrenaline is pumped into our system, triggering the changes associated with fight or flight. When we over-activate fight or flight, we live constantly on edge. In the case of exercise, it would be similar to never being able to get off the treadmill.

Remember, all of this is good and as it needs to be to ensure our survival. The autonomic reaction to a perceived threat is life-giving. When we truly are in danger, this autonomic reaction can save our lives. There is no time to think, and the mind-body reacts instantly to ensure its survival. Over-activation of the sympathetic nervous system, as mentioned before, can lead to imbalances that result in stress-related diseases. The key is in our perception. When we look out into the world, do we see a world that frightens us, or are we open to the possibility that we can learn to respond to this world in ways that bring the Good Within to life?

We can begin to shift our perception by recognizing that the Good Within is not a thing we have to work to attain or try to control. It is our inherent and true nature. We are made up of hundreds of trillions of cells, and within us there are thousands of chemical and electrical reactions in every second to sustain life. These inner processes are not controlled by us but by an inner knowing—intelligence at the cellular level. In her book *Molecules of Emotion*, Candance Pert (1999), a noted biophysicist at Georgetown University, commented on this intelligence within:

> So, if the flow of our molecules is not directed by the brain, and the brain is just another nodal point in the network, then we must ask—where does the intelligence, the information that runs our bodymind, come from? We know that information has an infinite capability to expand and increase, and that it is beyond time and place, matter and energy. Therefore, it cannot belong to the material world we apprehend with the senses, but must belong to its own realm, one that we can experience as emotion, the mind, the spirit—an *inforealm*. This is a term I prefer because it has a scientific ring to it, but others mean the same thing

8

when they say field of intelligence, innate intelligence, the wisdom of the body. Still others call it God (p.310).

Pause for a moment. Take a deep breath in, and when you exhale, feel the body relax as you let go of unneeded tension or tightness. Consider the possibility that the innate intelligence that runs the mind-body, that runs every mind-body, also runs the world and the universe. Begin to respond to the world believing and trusting in the Good Within you, in others, and in all that is. Trust in a kind and loving God.

"The world is not to be put into order, the world is order incarnate. It is for us to harmonize with this order."

—Henry Miller

"Science without religion is lame. Religion without science is blind."

—Albert Einstein

Present Moment Training

The most vital aspect of our work is to discipline the mind to stay fully present in the body. The body is always present. We cannot take the body back to the past or ahead to the future. The mind, however, is rarely consciously present. Research has shown that approximately 90 percent of our thoughts in a given day are thoughts of the past or future. The key to our becoming more "response-able" is to train the mind to stay fully present, to be at one or in union with the body. In essence, we are inviting the mind home, for the body is home to our consciousness.

When the mind is stuck in the past or worried about the future, we feel stress and tension. This tension is an uncomfortable feeling and is literally the body's attempt to get the mind's attention. The tension and stress we feel do not have to be debilitating. They have the potential to be life-giving if we are willing to perceive them in light of the truth. The discomfort we feel draws our attention to the body and brings us to the present moment because the body is always present. We only have to train the mind to be in the space of union, to be willing to stay fully present in the body. When the mind is wholly present in body, the mind-body becomes the instrument to know and feel the Good Within, which is ever-present. We learn to train the mind-body to be the opening to perceive what is already present, whole, and complete within us. God is with us always. We only have to train the mind-body to perceive it.

Fear is our greatest obstacle to living in the present moment. It can also be the opening to peace, faith, grace, and all that is good. I recall a time in my life when I was afraid I was going to die. I was in an airplane, and the ride became turbulent. As my mind raced ahead to the future, I imagined the plane crashing, and these thoughts triggered an emotional and physical reaction in me. I gripped the seat. I felt a sense of loss of control, and my muscles tightened to compensate. My heart was racing. I did not want this turbulence. I wanted smooth and calm. I was fighting against the movement by trying to hold tightly. I thought of my training and took a deep breath. I reminded myself to let go with each exhalation, to relax and soften. I reminded myself to stay in the body, feel the movement, and stay with what is. If you have been given movement, it is best to go with it. In that moment of realization, the turbulence that I initially perceived as life threatening felt totally different. When I stayed present and noticed the actual sensations in the body, there was nothing inherently unpleasant about it. In fact, if I had told my husband, who was sitting next to me, who flies frequently, that I was afraid I was going to die, he might have laughed and said, "It's only a little turbulence; nothing to be afraid of." Interestingly, not a minute later, the turbulence stopped and it was smooth sailing.

Those few moments of suffering were the result of what can happen when the mind gets ahead of the self, out of touch with the body. The body grounds us, and when we "keep our wits about us" by keeping our attention in the present moment, we give ourselves the best chance to respond effectively. When we are not accustomed to being at 37,000 feet in the air, we can feel a loss of control that frightens us. Staying present and in touch with the body grounds us in reality. Much that we fear is imagined in the mind with no basis in reality.

Learning to be fully present and accept what is takes time and practice. We work to discipline the mind to stay present moment to moment while at the same time honoring the limitations of our humanness. The mind is at times short-sighted, limited, finite, small, and self-centered. We do not have to shun, judge, or condemn this side of ourselves but learn to accept and even embrace these limitations as we practice self-control in mind-body through our thoughts, words, and actions. Buddha spoke of the importance of self-control: "More than all your enemies, more than all those who hate you, an undisciplined mind does greater harm."

Present moment training is vital because when the mind is wholly present in union with the body, we are aligned to God, who is ever present. When we wander for too long or too far from center with thoughts of the past or future, we create an imbalance that results in tension. We can remember the past and honor all those who have come before us, and we can look ahead with hope to the future, keeping in mind that the present moment is the place in space and time of union, past and future. Training the mind to stay present helps us to reduce tension and stress as we realize we do not have to analyze, relive, or be confined by our past or worried over the future. The present moment holds the past and future within us, perfectly ordered.

Our past, back to the first man and woman, is held in our DNA, our genetic code. It defines our humanness. Every event in our individual and collective history is held in the body, in the brain, tissues, and other organs. The body remembers sometimes what the mind has forgotten. When we understand that all of the past is held in the present moment, not by us, but within us as the Living God, we are more willing to let go of the past and live fully in the now. It can all work for us in the present. The past can also hold us back from realizing our potential if we refuse to let it go and live now.

Similarly, the future, as potential, is within us. If we are able to stay God-centered rather than self-centered, our worries of the future fade as we abide in the space of love and trust in God, as we abide in the body here and now. Trust in God does not mean we will never feel stressed or afraid. It means when we feel stressed or afraid, we are able to stay present, to feel God's presence, and to respond to the stress in ways that promote life.

An Amazing Gift

"In the beginning God created the heaven and earth . . . so God created man in his image, in the image of God created he him, male and female created he them . . . And God saw everything that he had made, and behold, it was very good."

—Genesis 1

"Lord, I love the house where you dwell, the tenting place of your glory."

—Psalm 26:8

"Those who have failed to work toward the truth have missed the purpose of living."

—Buddha

The mind-body is truly an amazing and precious gift. Pause for a moment and recall the circumstances of your birth. Your parents played an important role in bringing you to this earth, but they did not create you. They did not plan, order, and form your brain and spinal cord, your heart and lungs, your arms and legs. God created you, and God created you in the image and likeness of God. All that God created is very good, and that includes you.

"Then God said: Let us make man in our image, after our likeness."

—Genesis 1:26

From the moment of conception, forty-six chromosomes (twenty-three from the male and twenty-three from the female) with thirty thousand genes came together to determine all your physical characteristics. Even more amazingly, intelligence and personality were already in place within your genetic code. At conception, you were essentially and uniquely you; from a single cell to a tiny human being in forty weeks.

Your heart started beating at eighteen days old when you were only 0.1 inches long. Your brain was functioning at forty days and you were .75 inches long. You could hear sounds inside your mother's womb that an adult cannot hear. Your brain was more active during fetal development than at any other time in your life.

Although we have no memory of this worldly birth, what we can remember now is that what is seen on the surface is only a small fraction of all that we are. Our true nature—our wholeness—is experienced in consciously aligning our being with the truth. We are inherently and infinitely Good Within because we are of God. What I know, what you know, what the smartest people all around the world know, and even our collective knowledge throughout all of history is still next to nothing when it comes to the infinite universe we live in when it comes to God. If we insist on relying solely on what we know, we will likely live in a perpetual state of imbalance, tension, and fear. What we can see and understand is the smallest fraction of all that is. We recognize this boundary, our humanness, as a gift and not as a burden or limitation, and we continue to work to increase our knowledge and understanding mindful that a finite brain cannot fully grasp infinity. We can begin to let go of our need to comprehend and control that which is beyond us and more simply align ourselves with what is—with God.

God reminds us of this truth in everyday miracles, great and small, and works through us in the most wondrous ways. A dear friend shared this story. In her late thirties, she was the mother of two young boys when she became pregnant with twins. Early in her pregnancy, the doctors discovered a life-threatening condition in one twin known as hydrocephalus. The doctor told her and her husband that the CAT scan revealed there was so much water surrounding the brain that she could not see the baby's brain. The doctor cautioned the parents that the child would likely to be physically and mentally handicapped and might not survive beyond birth. She also informed them that the second fetus, an identical twin, would be likely to have similar problems. The medical recommendation was abortion of both fetuses.

The parents struggled with a decision. The mother consulted a trusted advisor and friend who is a priest. He said to her, "Things are not always as they seem." In that moment, a feeling of peace overwhelmed her, and she decided to carry the babies to term. Months later, the delivery room was filled with doctors and medical personnel expecting to revive two high-risk infants. Tears and cheers filled the room as the doctor delivered two beautiful, healthy baby girls; in his own words, it was "a miracle."

If we choose to work alone, we are severely limited by our human vision. With God, all things are possible. Through our work, we train the mind-body to make every effort to accept what is and strengthen our belief that our body, our world, and our universe is a place that has the potential for us to know and feel goodness in its many forms—health, success, abundance, peace, love, and happiness.

If we believe that we are made in the image and likeness of God, then God reveals God to us, through us in mind-body. We open the mind and heart to recognize and receive the seven inherent gifts of God's goodness: *vitality, balance, strength, endurance, flexibility, focused attention, and coordination.*

In our bones and blood is the gift of *vitality.* Our bones provide the framework for the moving body, protect soft organs, and are the source of red blood cells that carry life-giving oxygen to all parts of the body. All that we are rests on and in the bones. The bones are as strong as steel but five times lighter. The red blood cells that carry oxygen to all the body tissues and organs form the basis of the life-giving blood and are derived from the bones. Vitality reveals our true nature and our inner source of energy, drive, and motivation. We feel grounded, connected to an inner source that energizes and sustains us in each present moment.

The gift of *balance* is embodied in our reproductive and excretory systems. The reproductive system is located in the body's center of gravity, the pelvis. The right and left hips are aligned over center, the spine. Reproduction is a creative act that brings together opposites in union—the male and female, twenty-three chromosomes from each—united to become one new life. In the excretory system, the body maintains the balance between our internal and external environment, between what is to be retained and what is to be let go. Balance reveals the dual nature of our earthly existence as two become one in a union that yields creative and productive expressions of life: male/female, yin/yang, day/night, work/rest, full/empty, good/bad, light/dark, positive/negative, contraction/relaxation, right/left, within/without, and seen/unseen. Every opposite has a point of union where the two touch or meet to realize oneness. Balance in our lives promotes stable and healthy relationships and environments.

Our digestive and endocrine systems reveal to us the gift of *strength.* Our digestive system is thirty feet in length from opening to opening and digests, assimilates, and distributes life-giving food and water to all parts of the body, including the brain. In an average lifetime, we will digest fifty tons of food. Imagine the amount of work done by our digestive system to transform the food we eat into the cells, tissues, and organs of the body, providing us with the energy we need to move and grow. The endocrine system works in conjunction with the digestive system to provide the hormones that self-regulate and control the inner processes without any thought or effort on our part. Strength sows the seeds of self-discipline and a strong will that is grounded and balanced. We experience self-control and self-mastery.

The cardiovascular system—the heart and blood vessels—reveals to us an open heart in the gift of *endurance.* The cardiovascular system is central to the body and is located in the chest protected by the rib cage. The heart will beat 101,000 beats and pump more than 75,000 pints of blood in a single day. In an average lifetime, the heart will beat 2½ billion times. If laid end to end, the interior network of blood vessels and capillaries that carry the blood to all body tissues and organs would be one hundred thousand miles in length, long enough to travel around the world four times or halfway to the moon. A strong heart is an open heart. When the heart is open and the blood is flowing easily through the blood vessels, we are able to endure. Endurance is being able to go the distance. It allows us to persevere, to love, and to show patience, compassion, and forgiveness.

The respiratory and muscular systems embody the gift of *flexibility.* Through the lungs the respiratory system carries the breath of life. In a single day, 2,200 gallons of air will flow into the lungs, drawing about ninety-four gallons of oxygen to be delivered to the body, expelling seventy-eight gallons of carbon dioxide. The lungs, however, can only do their job because of the muscles at the core that contract and relax, causing the lungs to inflate as we breathe in and deflate with each exhalation. Again, without any conscious effort on our part to control the breathing, the body maintains this beautiful balance and flow of life energy. Flexibility awakens in us a sense of ease, peace, flow, and grace. We are resilient and adaptable.

The central nervous system consists of the brain and spinal cord and embodies the gift of *focused attention*. The central nervous system (CNS) is a control center of the mind-body, providing direction and guidance to best utilize resources and energy. The brain receives and sends messages to all parts of the body along a network of nerve fibers. The messages are sent as tiny electrical impulses that can move at speeds up to three hundred feet per second. You were born with 100 billion brain cells or neurons. The brain receives about nine gallons of blood every hour to do its work. The brain needs a great deal of energy, and although it only weighs 2.5 percent of the whole body, it uses about one-fifth of all the energy produced in the body. The gift of focused attention leads to unwavering faith, lasting values, and clarity of vision. We see and live the truth.

The last gift of *coordination* brings all the parts together as one whole. We look at the parts in isolation at times for our own ease of understanding. In reality, they do not exist separately but function as one whole. Coordination is a harmonious interaction in the present moment—in a word, fulfillment.

The mind-body is truly amazing. We are each a living miracle. Take up the body; embrace the beauty and wonder of the gift given. Learn to use this gift in ways that bring love and goodness into our world.

The Foundation for Optimal Well-Being

"You formed my inmost being; you knit me in my mother's womb. I praise you, so wonderfully you made me; wonderful are your works."

—Psalm 139:13

"So strengthen your drooping heads and your weak knees. Make straight paths for your feet, that what is lame may not be dislocated but healed."

—Hebrews 12:12

"When you are inspired . . . dormant forces, faculties, and talents become alive, and you discover yourself to be a greater person by far than you ever dreamed yourself to be."

—Patanjali

"Keep your eyes on the stars, and your feet on the ground."

—Theodore Roosevelt

The foundation for optimal well-being is based on four guiding principles that give meaning and direction to our training in mind-body.

1. All beings, because they are of God, are inherently, equally, and infinitely Good Within. This is our true nature.
2. Our purpose in life is to recognize and realize the Good Within, to experience our true nature, and to learn how to bring this good forth into the world.
3. No matter the particular circumstances of our individual lives, we each have within by divine design all we need in exact measure to fulfill our purpose. We develop the ability to bring good into the world by giving to others in our own unique way.

4. The mind-body is the instrument of goodness manifested. It is how the Good Within moves through us and into the world. *We can only realize the Good Within, our potential, when the mind-body is working as one in the present moment. Now is the time.*

Our method is simple and consistent. The exercises challenge us in specific ways to awaken the seven gifts of God's goodness within by following a three-step learning process:

1. **Prepare:** The training prepares and readies the mind-body to recognize and realize our true nature and inherent potential.
2. **Receive:** The mind-body is open and receptive to information from both the outer world of the senses and the inner world of thought, feeling, imagination, and intuition.
3. **Respond**: We learn to move with purpose and respond effectively to all that life brings as we become "response-able."

Mind-Body Training utilizes the tools that optimize our learning experiences. The work is fun; it challenges us, raises our curiosity, and engages the mind-body. The exercises build confidence, and we feel resourceful and energized. We improve our ability to focus and to use our vital energy to master new skills with greater ease and understanding.

The seven tools of Mind-Body Training support and promote optimal learning experiences.

Reading is for the mind what exercise is for the body. It is essential for optimal growth and well-being. When an individual learns how to read, he or she learns a necessary skill for life. Reading is an exercise in preparing, receiving, assimilating, integrating, and responding to information from both the outer world, the printed word on the page, and our inner world, the information behind the eyes, in the mind. The skills we build through reading prepare us to receive and respond to information throughout a lifetime.

Writing is a tool for learning how to express ourselves. When we write, our thoughts become matter as words on the paper. Each time we sit to write, we are training the mind-body to work together to bring our thoughts and ideas into being so that we begin to realize that we do matter. Learning to write can make a difference in how we perceive and express ourselves.

Speaking is a form of communication, from the root word "commune," to come together. We use our voice to make connections with others. We reveal through the words we choose who we are and our beliefs about the world we live in. When we speak, we can become more aware of how our words reflect our deeply held assumptions and beliefs. We can learn that what we say is often in line with what we do. We can learn to choose our thoughts, words, and actions mindfully.

Movement is the essence of life and optimal well-being in mind-body. Through movement we have the opportunity to recognize and realize our inherent goodness in the seven gifts. The exercises stimulate and awaken in our awareness the gifts of *vitality, balance, strength, endurance, flexibility, focused attention, and coordination.* The mind-body was designed to move and grow.

When we move in the ways God intended, we feel lifted and energized because we are fulfilling our purpose. Research has identified the benefits of regular movement or exercise and how it improves the performance of every system in the mind-body. In recent years, scientists have reported that regular exercise may keep the brain sharp as we age, improving and protecting such cognitive processes as memory, sensory acuity, reaction speed, learning abilities, practical intelligence, and emotional control. Learning is movement in mind-body.

Visualization is the mental exercise of using positive imagery or mental pictures to produce desired outcomes. The mind-body learns to make real what can be first vividly imagined. It is important to stay focused on the images that pertain to those words and actions for which you are able to assume responsibility. For example, it will do you little good to imagine someone giving you a million dollars. You have no control over others. A more effective visualization would be to see yourself doing something to earn that million. You do have the power to choose your thoughts, words, and actions. Visualization is a powerful tool for learning and change. It is being used successfully in the fields of business, health care, education, athletics, and the creative arts.

Prayer and meditation train the mind to focus with attention and will. We develop discipline of thought and increase our ability to use the mind-body purposefully. In prayer and meditation we have the opportunity to practice present moment awareness. This can nourish the mind-body in many ways. Some of the scientifically proven benefits include deep rest, relaxation, emotional ease, increased energy, improved immune function, improved learning, decreased anxiety and tension, and increased self-esteem. Prayer and meditation draw us closer to God, closer to our true nature, which is optimal well-being in mind-body. Optimal well-being does not mean we will never get sick. It does allow us to recognize illness as part of the healing process that has the potential to restore equilibrium and health.

Observation and reflection can sharpen our senses and increase our awareness of self, others, and our environment. Increased awareness becomes a powerful and effective learning tool by increasing our capacity to process information. Observation empowers us to take a moment and be open to perceive and receive information that is essential for effective responses. Reflection allows us to see again the thoughts, words, and actions and the outcomes associated with our choices. This information is useful so that we become more able to choose effective responses as we learn and grow.

Imagine all this working for you. Imagine feeling energized, balanced, and strong. See yourself being able to go the distance and feel a sense of ease in your movements. Know that you can focus your attention to bring the many aspects of your training together. There is so much good to see in this world. I have been witness to many people who have changed their lives in remarkable ways through the practice of Mind-Body Training. The work is a celebration of the person and his or her inherent goodness and valued purpose. It is the realization of this truth that leads to great accomplishments, success, peace, and happiness.

Imagine:

- Increased energy and being able to do things you once thought impossible, increasing your strength by a factor of four, and being able to do three times as much work in the same amount of time.
- Complete recovery from significant heart disease, transitioning from an inability to perform the normal activities of daily living to being able to run two to three miles every day, along with weightlifting and yoga.
- Bringing your blood pressure under control and discontinuing your medication.
- Going from being afraid you might have to quit your job because of debilitating pain to putting in a full day with ease.
- Commitment to a way of life that allows you to lose thirty pounds and feel stronger and better than ever.
- Overcoming anxiety and depression and feeling a restored sense of self-control.
- Sleeping restfully each night and waking up energized and thankful for the new day.
- Improving your performance at work and landing a new position that suits you beautifully.
- Improving your performance on exams by feeling relaxed, readied, rested, and prepared.
- Playing your sport at peak performance with focused attention and coordination.
- Being able to stay calm and focused when facing a difficult situation.
- Utilizing Mind-Body Training to overcome recurring migraine headaches.
- Working through the aches and pains you thought might stop you to find strength and determination to move forward.
- Being able to make difficult decisions and put thoughts into action.
- Working through challenges, obstacles, fear, and self-doubt to experience increased confidence.
- Being able to relax, be still, and feel the mind-body heal.
- Being able to see the child who poses many challenges in the family as a blessing.
- Finding joy and a sense of fulfillment in your work.
- Strengthening relationships by working together.
- Following a dream, reaching a goal, and remembering all that you can do.
- Using what you have learned to reach out to others.
- Standing tall, breathing deeply, and staying in touch even when you feel a bit numb.
- Holding on when you have to and accepting weakness as the opening to a new definition of strength.
- Being willing to endure and stop when you have to, and giving yourself permission to go when you feel ready.
- Believing without evidence or proof.
- Rejoicing in the accomplishments and goodness of others.

- Breathing a sigh of relief when you realize the fear that gripped you was only imagined, not real at all.
- Being a witness to the good in every family member.
- The innocence of all children.
- Trusting yourself and others.
- Letting go of the past.
- Finding yourself just as you are and knowing that you belong. You are vital.
- The joy of realizing the size of the hurdle you just cleared.
- The excitement in exploring all things new.
- Remembering the love and light within when all else fails.

Imagine what is possible when you begin to see the Good Within yourself, others, and all that is.

"Imagination is more important than knowledge."

—Albert Einstein

Beginning the Work

"Let us not grow tired of doing good, for in due time we shall reap our harvest, if we do not give up."

—Galatians 6:9

"It is he who gives to everyone life and breath and everything . . . He is not far from any one of us. For in him we live and move and have our being."

—Acts 17:25

"What is learned . . . depends far less on what is taught than on what one actually experiences in the place."

—Edgar Friedenberg

Begin with the end in mind. We are working toward a way of life, a daily routine that awakens the Good Within and helps us to remember our true nature and inherent potential. As you prepare to begin the work, consider moving in the seven ways described below. In time and with practice you will be able to establish a daily routine that encompasses each of these practices.

1. **Cardiovascular (aerobic) training:** *Aerobic* means with oxygen. In aerobic movement, we train the mind-body to keep the flow of oxygen-rich blood moving freely to all cells, tissues, and organs, including the brain. With training, the heart and blood vessels remain open, supple, and strong and capable of optimal oxygen delivery and utilization to all parts of the body. As a result, our whole being is nourished and sustained. Cardiovascular training includes walking, running, swimming, rowing, biking, aerobic dance, and other movement in which the heart rate is elevated for a sustained period of exercise. Cardiovascular training

is the single most important aspect of our physical training because it keeps the heart open and strong.

2. **Core and strength training:** All movement in the body originates at the core. The core muscles include the abdominals, gluteus maximus (the buttocks), and erector spinae (lower back to the base of the skull). When we develop core strength, we develop a foundation for all movement. The strength and stability allow us to move with greater ease and will enable us to do things we once thought impossible. Core and strength training will exercise the abdominals, gluteus maximus, and back muscles to promote alignment, strength, and stability. In balance we must also be able to relax the muscles at the core to prevent undue tension and tightness.

3. **Flexibility training (yoga postures):** Flexibility training teaches us to move with greater ease. Yoga is an ancient philosophical discipline that is beautifully designed to awaken the life energy within and allow us to feel a sense of ease or flow in all our movements. Swami Rama (1979) describes yoga in his book *Lectures on Yoga:*

> The central teaching of yoga is that man's true nature is divine, perfect and infinite. He is unaware of this divinity, however, because he falsely identifies himself with his body, mind and objects of the external world. This false identification, in turn, makes him think he is imperfect and limited, subject to sorrow, decay and death because his mind and body are subject to the limitations of time, space and causation. Through the meditative methods of yoga, however, man can cast off this ignorance and become aware of his own true Self which is pure and free from all imperfections. The Sanskrit word yoga comes from the root *yuj,* meaning to join together, or unite; and yoga represents the union of the individual self, or atman, with the supreme universal Self, or Paramatman. This is the union of man with absolute reality . . . Yoga is a practical, systematic and scientific quest for perfection (p. 5).

In our practice, we will use the yoga postures to stretch and strengthen the mind-body as a way to recognize and realize our true nature. Stretching benefits us on the physical, mental, emotional and spiritual levels. In *The Genius of Flexibility (2005)* Bob Cooley states "Nothing is a substitute for stretching. Within minutes after stretching, *everyone* feels better. There is something inherently healing and pleasurable about stretching. Stretching teaches you how to handle the most intense situations" (p.27).

4. **Adequate rest:** Nothing can bring you down faster than lack of sleep. Adequate sleep can lift, energize, and restore equilibrium.

5. **Life-giving nutrition:** Food is the fuel that keeps the mind-body running. Through our training, we will learn to make choices that nourish the mind-body and sustain life. Our choices will be based on the simple practice of choosing foods as close to their natural state as possible and practicing moderation.

6. **Family/community/church:** All ways of being together to promote unity, strength, and love in action.

7. **Written goals and a plan of action:** While not absolutely essential, written goals and a plan of action can provide needed guidance, direction, and purpose for all our movements. The goals with an action plan become the map for the journey, enabling us to see the bigger picture. We get a much better sense of where we are, where we want to go, and how to get there.

As we begin the work, we will come to see how each of these practices becomes a way of life that optimizes our learning and growth and allows us to recognize and realize God's goodness in our lives. We can work with the fears and challenges by seeing them as opportunities to draw on the gifts we have been given. We use the tools of reading, writing, speaking, movement, visualization, prayer/meditation, and observation/reflection to enhance our practice. Try to use all the tools in the time and space that best suits you.

Reading the material alone will be less effective, for while the mind is engaged, the body is inactive. It is most helpful to also *feel and experience* the life energy, thus engaging the whole self. Our work in the exercises becomes an exploration of mind and body of both what is seen and unseen. Meaning is found not only in the words but also in the movement. What we seek is to know and feel God's goodness and love. To know it is our objective. To be it and to live it is our purpose.

Work to establish a daily practice. Take one moving meditation at a time. Choose a time to practice each day, perhaps in the morning or early afternoon. Choose a time that works best for you. You can work with the meditation for one day, a week, or even longer. Allow yourself the freedom to vary your practice and promote adaptability and resilience. In time, you will bring together the exercises and postures that constitute your daily practice. Suggested routines are outlined in Appendix A for your reference.

You will need a yoga mat and light weights (one—to five-pound dumbbells) to begin. Each moving meditation will be presented in a similar format:

- **Title:** The title is your mantra or focus for the period of practice. If you become distracted or lose interest, use the words repeated aloud or silently to yourself to keep you on track as needed.
- **Quotes:** The quotes from the Bible and other sources convey the essence of our practice. You can memorize them to establish in mind the thoughts you want to guide your actions.
- **Intention:** We consider the state of mind, the thoughts and beliefs that will best support our practice.
- **On the mat:** The specific exercises are described as ways to awaken the gifts within mind-body.

- **Off the mat:** We consider ways in which we can integrate our practice on the mat into everyday life.
- **Pictures/instructions:** Two photos are provided for every pose, along with instructions for carrying out the exercise.

As you practice, you will undoubtedly experience distractions and resistance to the work. Do not be tempted to judge these distractions as something to be avoided. They are an essential element of the work. Most commonly, time constraints, fatigue, boredom, travel, illness, or injury can feel like insurmountable obstacles. Learn to see, understand, and even welcome the distraction as a means to discipline the mind-body. When you feel distracted or meet resistance, breathe in deeply, and as you exhale, feel the sensation of letting go. Let go of the distraction or the tightness and direct your attention to the work again and again, happily.

This ability to focus amid the distractions reminds me of playing baseball as a kid. When the batter stepped up to the plate, the opposing team and fans would start the chant, "Batter, batter, batter . . . swing!" We would make as much noise as we could to try and distract the batter. Now, in some places this behavior is considered unacceptable. Are we afraid our children cannot handle a few distractions? Are we afraid they cannot focus and do well if there is opposition or resistance? They are certain to fail if they do not learn to discipline the mind to stay focused amidst the distractions. The yells of the opposing team do not have to weaken or offend the batter. They can just as easily be a stimulus to teach the batter to focus more intently and strengthen his ability to get the job done. There will always be distractions. It is best if we learn to deal with them.

In your work, be mindful of these suggestions that can optimize your experience:

- Come to the work with an open mind and open heart. Enjoy and have fun being challenged in purposeful ways.
- Set aside a specific time each day dedicated to the practice.
- Create a space to work that is big enough for you to move freely.
- Begin slowly. Be mindful to practice at a level and intensity that suits you. Consult with your physician if you have any medical condition or physical limitations. Be attentive and respectful to any limitations (physical, mental, emotional, psychological, and social). Rather than seeing the limitations as a barrier, see them as safe boundaries that can be explored.
- If you experience discomfort or pain in any of the exercises, stop doing the exercise and become the observer. Do not assume that something is wrong. The discomfort is your body's way of getting your attention. Reread the instructions carefully and check your alignment and technique to modify in ways that allow you to move without the discomfort or pain. If the pain persists, discontinue the exercise until you can consult a doctor, physical therapist, fitness instructor, or personal trainer who can provide you with additional information to resolve the issue.

- Practice before meals. Hydrate well with water. If you feel hungry before your practice, eat something light, a piece of fruit or a drink of juice. After your work, nourish yourself with moderate portions of wholesome, natural foods high in life energy. Most often, supplements like vitamins are not necessary.

- Wear loose, comfortable clothing. Athletic shoes can be worn for the warm-up, core, and cardio training. Bare feet are recommended for yoga. You can do all the work in bare feet if you have a padded mat or soft surface to work on. Bare feet on hard floors can be more difficult and can cause undue stress on the joints and soft muscle tissue.

- Consider forming a small group, even one other person you can work with, not necessarily in the same time or place. It adds to your practice to have someone to share the experience with and to learn from each other.

- No prior experience is necessary. You can ease into the practice by paying attention to your level of exertion and working within your own personal boundaries. The work is easily adaptable to varying levels of physical ability. Notable progress can be made by gently working to the edge of your ability.

- Let your practice grow. You do not have to force it with unreasonable demands on your time or mindless adherence to unforgiving regimens. You will know you are on the right track because you will feel good.

- *Every exercise is adaptable to varying levels of ability and circumstance.* If you feel unable to do the exercise wholly in body, pause, close your eyes, and imagine. Visualize yourself doing the exercise in as much detail as possible. Feel the pose being formed within you. Have someone read the instructions aloud to you. Let the words come to life within you. Let it move you.

- *Most importantly,* as you come to the work, relax. Breathe easy, feel the muscles being softened, and notice the weight of your body. Feel the touch of your feet or other body part to the floor. Gravity grounds you. There is no effort to hold on as you begin. When you initiate the movement to perform the pose, be mindful of the cues that assure proper alignment and technique and then allow the body to do what it already knows how to do. The muscles and bones are formed to move. Trust this inner knowing. Every system in the body will do its part. Do not try to micromanage every movement. It is not possible or desirable and will only create undue tension and anxiety.

The Exercises and Postures

"For the Kingdom of God is not a matter of talk but of power."

—1 Corinthians 4:20

"Out of clutter, find simplicity. In discord, find harmony. In the middle of difficulty, lies opportunity."

—Albert Einstein's *Rules of Work*

"God is near us at all times. God is available, a silence in the midst of chaos, a voice in the midst of confusion, a promise at the center of tumult."

—Joan Chittister

"Let us not grow tired of doing good, for in due time we shall reap our harvest, if we do not give up."

—Galatians 6:9

The exercises are pictured and described on the following pages. There are forty exercises in total. Remember to work at your own pace. Begin with one exercise per day. As you become more familiar with the training, you may decide to do several exercises at a time. Refer to Appendix A for suggested exercise routines once you become familiar with all the exercises. Ultimately, work to establish a daily practice that suits you. The details for developing your daily practice will be provided along the way. Begin with the end in mind. Remember, our work includes:

Seven essential ways to move:

1. Cardiovascular (aerobic) training
2. Core and strength training
3. Flexibility training (yoga postures)
4. Adequate rest/prayer/meditation
5. Life-giving nutrition
6. Family/community/church
7. Written goals and a plan of action

Seven tools to optimize learning:

1. Reading
2. Writing
3. Speaking
4. Movement
5. Visualization
6. Prayer/meditation
7. Observation/reflection

Seven gifts of God's goodness to awaken within us:

1. Vitality
2. Balance
3. Strength
4. Endurance
5. Flexibility
6. Focused attention
7. Coordination

The forty exercises are divided into three categories of movement:

1. Warm-up series
2. Core and strength training with weights
3. Flexibility training (yoga postures)

Let's begin.

WARM-UP SERIES

1. PRACTICE: Be present

"Do not worry about tomorrow, for tomorrow will worry about its own things."

—Matthew 6:34

"If we lose the present moment, we lose life."

—Buddha

"For where your treasure is, there will your heart be also."

—Matthew 6:21

"More than all those who hate you, more than all your enemies, an undisciplined mind does greater harm."

—Buddha

Intention: We begin with the intention to gently discipline the mind to be present. When we are able to see each moment as a gift, we will be much more able and willing to stay fully present to all that life has to offer. Now is the time. We can only act in the present moment. We cannot take our bodies back to the past or ahead to the future. We must be present to realize our potential and to realize the goodness in life—health, happiness, peace, abundance, and success. It is within us and all around us. Be present. Stay focused on the infinite positive possibilities presented to you in each moment.

On the mat: Mountain pose is our foundation. We feel our feet on the mat, and this is our grounding point in all the standing exercises. We draw attention to the midline and feel centered. We strengthen and stabilize the self with attention to the muscles at our core when we engage the abdominal muscles. The spine is lengthened, and the heart center is open, soft, and lifted. We take a deep breath in and come wholly into the body. We focus our attention. We are ready and able because we are one in mind-body, fully present.

Off the mat: It is not possible for us to be fully present in every moment. Only God is ever-present. The human mind is meant to wonder. It is healthy and restorative at times. Purposeful wonderings can lead to new insights and productive trains of thought. Aimless or excessive wondering weakens the mind and the body. The key is disciplining the mind so we can choose when and where to focus our attention. Our training in mind-body can also help us determine the what, how, and why of our focused efforts.

It takes practice and patience. Each and every moment can be an opportunity to discipline the mind to be present. What is in the present that is so desirable? If we can discipline the mind to stay fully present in the body, the mind-body becomes the opening to experience all that is good within us and all around us.

Exercise 1: Mountain pose

Mountain pose

Mountain pose is the foundation for all the exercises. Take time to become familiar with the details of the pose described below. Developing this strong foundation will optimize your results. Begin each standing exercise in mountain pose.

1. Begin by bringing your full attention to the work. Prepare the mind-body.

2. Grounded: Feel both feet on the floor, heels aligned to the toes, facing forward. Relax, soften, and feel the weight of the body. Gravity grounds you.

3. Centered: The right and left side of the body are aligned over the midline, the spine. This is one dimension of center. Feel this center at the level of the hips. We experience the self in three dimensions. Center yourself R/L through the spine, front to back, rock from heels to toes and top to bottom, and stand tall.

4. Strong: Grounded through the touch of the feet, centered in three dimensions through the space of the hips, come from the hips into the belly. Gently draw the belly button toward the spine, engaging the abdominal muscles. Feel the strength and stability deepen as you draw into your core. The abdominal muscles are engaged but not holding or tight; poised, not rigid. Over-tightening at the core can restrict or block the flow of the breath.

5. Open heart: From the foundation of being grounded, centered, and strong, breathe in as you lengthen the spine and lift into the space of open heart at the level of the chest on the sternum (breastbone). The shoulders will open in alignment to the hips as you feel the heart center expand and lift gently. The lower body, the foundation, is stable and strong. The upper body is open, soft and relaxed, and aligned to the root (feet)

and center (hips). Bring the hands to center, at the level of the heart center, with the palms touching in prayer position.

Prayer position

6. Flow and flexibility: With the hands in prayer position, breathe in through the nose, and feel the lift of the breath in the body. Exhale slowly, letting go and noticing the muscles relaxing as they fall back to gravity. Follow the flow of the breath. Be the one who is grounded and relaxed.

7. Focus: Draw your attention to a focus point at your center. Focus points closer to you and lower to the ground will provide more stability in the exercises. Focus points further away and higher are more challenging. Keep your attention one-pointed and without strain.

Mountain pose is your foundation. When we begin to add movement in the exercises, remember ABC for easy reference:

Alignment: Maintain alignment in the exercises. The joints (ankles, knees, hips, shoulders, elbows, and wrists) are your reference points. Stack the joints and keep them aligned over center.

Breathe: Establish a flow of movement with your breathing. Never hold your breath in the exercises. When lifting weights, exhale with exertion.

Control: Control your movements through the full range of motion. **Hold all the stationary poses for thirty to forty seconds as you are able.**

2. PRACTICE: See the oneness

"That they may all be one, as you are in me and I am in you."

—John 17:21

"All life is one. The world is one home. All are members of one human family. All creation is an organic whole. No man is independent of this whole. Man makes himself miserable by separating himself from others. Separation is death. Unity is eternal life."

—Swami Sivananda

"The eye cannot say to the hand, 'I do not need you,' anymore than the head can say to the feet, 'I do not need you.' And even those members of the body which seem less important are in fact indispensable."

—1 Corinthians 12:21-22

"Peace comes within the souls of men when they realize their oneness with the universe."

—Black Elk

Intention: The parts of our body, although distinguishable from each other, are not separate but part of one whole. Similarly, we are each a vital part of one whole that is this universe. We are each a part of one mystical body. Our body, our world, and our universe reveal this truth again and again; every opposite, which seems to separate and distance, in reality is part of one whole. The opposites exist on a continuum that is unbroken.

On the mat: Acknowledge that every part of you has a place and purpose. In the exercises, it can be useful to isolate our attention on the specific parts and movements of the body as we are learning. Be mindful that in reality the mind-body functions as one whole. If we isolate our attention alone on the parts, we may lose sense of the whole. We cannot possibly put our attention on all the different parts and aspects of our practice. See and feel the oneness in mind-body, and let it move you.

Off the mat: Practice viewing life from the perspective of oneness. Rather than "what is good for me," consider holding in mind today the thought "what is good for all." Notice your tendency to fall back to the perspective of separateness. It's easy to do because everything we see with our eyes alone can lead us to that conclusion. Remember to see the oneness.

Exercise 2: Deep-breathing exercises

1. Begin in mountain pose.
2. Breathe in, and with the palms facing upward, extend both arms overhead, bringing the palms to touch at center.
3. Exhale, release the arms, palms down, and let the arms slowly return to center at your sides.
4. Repeat, allowing the movement to flow, aligned to the flow of the breath.
5. Breathe in, arms lifting, spine lengthening, and reaching high. Breathe out, slowly letting go, relaxing, softening the muscles and letting the arms flow back to gravity.
6. Stay fully present to the vital energy within you. Vitality reveals our true nature and inner source of energy, drive, and motivation.
7. Repeat three times.

Deep-breathing exercises

1. Mountain pose.
2. Breathe in, bringing the arms overhead to touch the palms at center.
3. Open the palms to face forward.
4. Exhale, bend at the elbows, and draw the elbows toward the floor, using the muscles in your back and shoulders to gently pull the shoulders back, opening the heart center.
5. Postural pose improves posture by improving alignment to center, opening the heart, lengthening the spine, strengthening the back, and bringing the shoulders in alignment to the hips.
6. Repeat three times.

Postural pose

3. PRACTICE: Stress with purpose

"Peace comes not from the absence of conflict but from the ability to cope with it."

—Anonymous

"God is our refuge and our strength, who from of old has helped us in our distress."

—Psalm 46:1

Intention: All exercise is a form of stress that challenges us in mind-body. Exercise is stress with purpose. In Mind-Body Training we are learning to stress the self in a safe, effective way to awaken and grow within us the qualities of vitality, balance, strength, endurance, flexibility, focused attention, and coordination. We come to the work mindful that as we move in the exercises, we are learning to respond to the stress in a positive and productive way. From this perspective, stress with purpose is life-giving.

On the mat: We have the opportunity to practice on the mat how to meet stress with purpose. We can learn to see stress differently from a new perspective. We learn that we can choose how to respond to the stress rather than react. We choose our response in a state of mind-body that is prepared, willing, and able. Believe in yourself. Remember, "I am able."

Off the mat: With practice, we can learn to meet stressful situations with a greater sense of ease because we are more aware of our true nature and we understand we are never alone. Through our work in mind-body, we can say, "Okay, here it is—stress. I feel it. I sense it." And then we remember, "I am willing and able. I know and feel I can handle this." Get grounded with both feet on the floor. Center yourself. Engage your core and feel connected to your inner source. Open your heart and feel the flow of the breath. Take a deep breath in, and when you exhale, notice the sensation of letting go. Focus your attention on all that is good and then respond. It will come together beautifully for you.

Exercise 3: Knee-up

1. Mountain pose.
2. Shift your weight to your right foot and lift the left heel.
3. Prepare to take the weight of the body on the right leg.
4. Engage the abdominals for strength and stability. Lengthen the spine, lift into the heart center, and feel the flow of the breath.
5. Focus your attention, and when you feel ready, lift the left knee, aligned to the hip, drawing your left hand to rest on the knee.
6. Hold for thirty to forty seconds.
7. Repeat on the other side.
8. Vary the practice by beginning on the left side, holding for varying lengths of time, and/or adding the movements of the arms overhead with deep breaths as in the deep-breathing exercises.

Knee-up

1. From knee-up position, release the knee and draw the right foot up and behind you. Maintain alignment of the knee to the hip.
2. Take a hold of the foot near the ankle and draw the heel toward the hip. Notice the stretch of the quadriceps, the muscles on the front side of the upper leg. The tension is felt in the muscles, not the joints.
3. Feel centered and stable, and lift the left arm overhead aligned to the shoulder.
4. Lengthen the spine and lift into the heart center. The body is long, and the arm is reaching to the ceiling. Keep the pelvis level by gently tucking the tailbone with the abdominal muscles engaged.
5. Focus your attention and hold for thirty to forty seconds.
6. Repeat on the other side.
7. More challenging is to lift your focus to a point on the ceiling, looking through the outstretched hands and fingers.

Dancer's pose

4. PRACTICE: No excuses—only choices

"Knowing is not enough; we must apply. Willing is not enough; we must do."
—Johann Wolfgang van Goethe

"Do everything possible on your part to live in peace with everybody."
—Romans 12:18

Intention: If you intend to live life to its fullest, make no excuses, only choices. Choose life, choose love, choose peace, and choose to believe. Believe that goodness is within you and all around you. In every day there are infinite opportunities to choose goodness—not only in what is good for me but choosing for the highest good, the good of all. Personally, I have tried, struggled, and strived to try and know or understand what is good and to do good things. I often forget that from my human eyes I cannot possibly see what is for the highest good. From my line of vision, I can't even see over the trees. If I truly want to choose for the highest good and not what is good for me alone, then I must learn to rely on what is unseen for guidance and direction. I must rely on God as I choose. Free will is a gift I must choose to exercise, mindful of the giver.

On the mat: When you find yourself on the mat—congratulations! You have taken the first step. If you are choosing not to practice now, that is not necessarily a problem. Both situations are opportunities. There is no reason not to love this day in either case. Choose to bring love to this day no matter what. In the next moment, the next day, you get to choose again. Practice by making the choices in thought, word, and action that are life-giving. Choose in ways that help you remember your true nature. You have within you a vital, balanced, strong, enduring, flexible, focused, and happy spirit.

Off the mat: Whatever challenges you may be facing, choose life and love by choosing to see the good in all things and all people. If you are facing a difficult decision, take a deep breath in, and as you exhale, hold in mind the intention of letting go and feel the body relax. Make your decision based on what will bring love and life to all involved. If you are trying to do what is good for others, remember that this is not about depriving yourself. Choose to believe in an abundant universe. You can choose to give and remain in a state of mind-body that is fulfilled by remembering the infinite source of all energy and love within.

Exercise 4: Standing crunch

Standing crunch/extension

1. Mountain pose.
2. Breathe in and extend the arms overhead to full length, aligned to your shoulders. Reach high enough to feel the pull in your abdominal muscles and lower back muscles at your core.
3. Feel both feet on the floor, push off the right foot, lift the left knee, and as you exhale, pull the elbows down toward the lifted knee. Maintain alignment to center. Do not twist the upper body.
4. Breathe in as you place the left foot down with arms extended, shift your weight to the left foot, and draw the right knee up as you simultaneously pull the elbows down toward the lifted knee.
5. Alternate the knee lifts as you feel the pumping motion engaging the muscles of the core. Feel the strength and stability of the core muscles as you push off alternating feet.
6. Exhale with every crunch. Get into a rhythm, and feel the flow as you pump the arms and legs using the core muscles.
7. Repeat x 8 repetitions.

Standing crunch/flexion

5. PRACTICE: Go the distance

"Love . . . bears all things, believes all things, hopes all things, endures all things . . . Love never fails."

—1 Corinthians 13:8

"Nothing happens to anybody which he is not formed to bear."

—Marcus Aurelius

Intention: To build endurance, you must go the distance. Endurance is of the heart, and as you build endurance, you build a strong heart. As the mind-body works in aerobic exercise, the heart muscle is strengthened by the increased demand on the heart to supply blood to working muscles and the brain. This increased demand strengthens the heart muscle, and the chambers of the heart literally expand. An open heart is a strong heart and can hold more blood. With every beat of the heart, more blood and therefore more oxygen is delivered to every cell of the body. Well-oxygenated tissues are healthy and strong. The brain performs more efficiently and effectively. You may notice greater mental clarity, improved ability to focus your attention, and increased creativity.

When the heart is open, the mind-body is full of energy and a sense of well-being. When the heart is able to pump more blood with each beat, the resting heart rate will decrease, which means fewer beats per minute. A lower resting heart rate is highly correlated with a long life. We are able to endure.

On the mat: In our practice on the mat, we can achieve a degree of aerobic capacity by letting our movements flow, one into the next. In this way, we purposefully stress the heart to deliver blood to working muscles by enduring as we go the distance without stopping. Ideally, our work should include aerobic exercise where the heart rate is elevated for an extended period of time. The American Heart Association recommends thirty minutes a day for adults. Walking is a great way to get started. Other aerobic exercises include biking, swimming, hiking, running, treadmills, stepper machines, rowing, and aerobic dance. Make a commitment to yourself now, in this moment, to make regular aerobic exercise a part of your life. The way to be able to work out every day is to learn to love it. Go the distance and feel the joy of an open heart.

Off the mat: Go the distance and keep love in your heart no matter what. An open heart brings goodness in many forms—patience, forgiveness, compassion, understanding, resiliency, and perseverance, to name a few. Open your heart today.

Exercise 5: Open heart

Open heart/center

Open heart/twist

1. Mountain pose.
2. Grounded in both feet, extend the arms from the space of open heart. Be mindful that the arms are at the level of the chest and not the shoulders.
3. Breathe in as you twist the upper body left, feeling the pull at the base of the spine.
4. The arms stay aligned to the level of the chest as you pull the shoulders back open into the heart center. Bend the right arm, bringing the hand to touch the heart center on the sternum. The left arm is fully extended behind you.
5. Turn the head and follow the left hand with your eyes.
6. Come back to center, and in a flowing, uninterrupted motion, twist right as you exhale.
7. Repeat four times.
8. Come back to center with the arms extended in front of you, aligned to the chest.
9. Repeat four times, breathing in as you twist right first and then left.
10. Slow your movements. Be patient. Deepen and lengthen the breath and the twist.
11. Twists are both invigorating and cleansing. We feel energized by the activation of the muscles at the base of the spine. The cleansing effect is felt with the movement of the breath deep into the belly with the resistance created by the compression of the muscles at the core.

6. PRACTICE: Move like you believe

From *Star Wars*: Luke: "I can't believe it."

Yoda: "That is why you fail."

"Go thy way; and as thou hast believeth so be it done unto thee."

—Matthew 8:13

"Do more than belong: participate. Do more than care: help. Do more than believe: practice. Do more than be fair: be kind. Do more than forgive: forget. Do more than dream: work."

—William Arthur Ward

Intention: Every conscious action is preceded by a thought and then the first step. Move like you believe. Believe in yourself. Believe in the greatness of life and the incomparable value of every human person. Believe in your inherent goodness and the goodness of others and all that is. Believe that life is an amazing gift to be cherished and enjoyed to its fullest. Believe with God, all things are possible.

On the mat: Practice the exercises, being mindful that any exercise is purposeful stress. We stress the body with various exercises to build qualities in mind-body that promote optimal well-being. The exercises are most life-giving if you believe in their goodness and perform the work in good spirits—with joy and enthusiasm. If you find that you are getting little return on your workout, examine your beliefs. A change in thoughts can change the outcome. Move like you believe.

Off the mat: Remember with every first step you have the opportunity to believe that within you is a vital source of energy that can move and inspire you. Believe that you are on solid ground, centered, stable, and balanced. Believe that you are strong and disciplined. Believe that you can go the distance and move with a sense of ease and grace. Believe that you can stay focused and move confidently in the direction of your goals and dreams. Take the first step now and move like you believe.

Exercise 6: Woodcutter

Woodcutter/forward bend

Woodcutter/ lateral stretch

1. Straddle the legs the width of your mat (the feet about twelve to eighteen inches apart).

2. Extend the arms from the space of open heart, and interlace the fingers with the index fingers pointing forward, the thumbs crossed. Make your two hands like one aligned to center.

3. Breathe in as you reach through center and draw the arms up and overhead. Extend the arms behind you as you reach into a backbend. Feel your feet grounded, and engage the abdominals for stability and strength. Follow the hands with your eyes, and lengthen the body from your feet to your fingertips.

4. Exhale as you bend at the waist and draw the upper body into a forward bend, reaching the joined hands through the legs. Keep the legs, back, and arms long, and pull gently to the point of resistance that you feel in the lower back and legs.

5. In forward bend, focus your eyes on the floor as you pull the arms through the legs at center. If you lower the head and look back through the legs, you are likely to feel dizzy when you come up.

6. Repeat four times.

7. From a forward bend, breathe in as you come up and arch the upper body right into the lateral stretch. Exhale as you move into a forward bend and then arch left. Alternate the stretch from right to left and repeat four times.

8. Keep the chin level, and look forward in the lateral stretch. Maintain alignment through the hips and shoulders. No twisting.

9. Let yourself experience the full range of motion. Honor the resistance you feel in the lower back, hips, and hamstrings. Work within the boundaries that challenge you but never to the point of extreme discomfort or pain.

7. PRACTICE: *Look no farther*

"Each man has his special gift from God, one of one kind, another of another."
—1 Corinthians

"How wonderful it is that nobody need wait a single moment before starting to improve the world."
—Anne Frank

"Let nothing disturb you. Let nothing frighten you. All things are changing; God alone is changeless. Patience attains the good. One who has God lacks nothing. God alone fills all our needs."
—Saint Theresa of Avila

Intention: We do not have to reach to the ends of the world to make a difference. Look no farther. The goodness and love we are meant to both give and receive are within our reach. Our human arms are the length they are for a reason. They are to help us remember that the good we seek to give and receive is close enough to touch. Focus your attention on the goodness and love within your reach. Trust in God to do the rest.

On the mat: Your time on the mat is practice. Look no further. Be present. Work with what you have in that moment, and begin to realize that the things we seek are within our reach. As you hold in the poses, experience the strength and stability the pose calls forth.

Off the mat: In every moment, goodness and love are within you and all around you. Begin to see the opportunities in every day to improve the world by reaching out to touch those who are near, with love, in its many forms and ways. This does not mean that we cannot reach out to those at a distance. The opening is always within our reach.

Exercise 7: Forward warrior

Forward warrior

1. Mountain pose.
2. Breathe in as you lift the left knee. Exhale as you step forward on the left leg into position. Stack the joints so the knee is directly over the ankle. Align the feet to the hips so that you have a solid foundation of support. Toes and heels are also aligned.
3. Shoulders are aligned over the hips, and your weight is equally distributed right to left and front to back.
4. Extend the arms overhead, aligned to the shoulders. Keep the shoulders down as you reach the arms overhead so you feel the pull into your abdominal muscles and lower back. This connection to the core is what keeps you steady. Feel your feet and your sense of center. Engage the abdominals for stability, and lengthen the spine as you lift into the heart center. Keep your chin level and focus forward.
5. Hold for thirty to forty seconds.
6. Repeat on the other side.

Side warrior

1. Mountain pose.
2. Straddle the legs about three feet apart. Align the heels. Pivot on the heels, and turn the left foot inward to an angle of forty-five degrees. The right foot is turned out to an angle of ninety degrees with the heels and toes aligned.
3. Maintain alignment of the hips and shoulders facing forward.
4. Breathe in as you lift and extend the arms to shoulder height.
5. Exhale as you bend the right knee, and position the right knee over the right foot. Gently draw the knee back over the ankle and feel the stretch to the inner thigh.
6. Feel the root into both feet, keeping the heels down, and notice the length on your spine with the lift into the heart center. The shoulders are directly over the hips.
7. Warrior embodies strength and stability. Hold for thirty to forty seconds. Keep your attention on the tension that you feel in the working muscles. Breathe easy.
8. Repeat on the other side.

8. PRACTICE: Begin now

"Give us today our daily bread."

—Matthew 6:11

"The journey of a thousand miles begins with one step. But where does one begin? The answer is simple: Begin where you are."

—Lao Tsu

"If one advances confidently in the direction of their dreams, and endeavors to lead a life which they have imagined, they will meet with a success unexpected in common hours."

—Henry David Thoreau

Intention: Whatever your goals may be, whatever dreams you hold in your heart—begin now to make them your reality. Set goals for yourself on and off the mat. Goals give you direction and purpose. It is much easier to move forward with confidence and strength when you know where you are going. If you feel stuck or inert, you may have plenty of energy but lack direction, and so you fail to move.

Set goals and begin to make them happen. Let go of the past and thoughts that limit you from realizing your dreams. Let go of worry over the future and begin now to hold in mind and heart the goodness you desire to know and experience. Work here now. Your dreams are coming true in each moment you remain fully present to the positive possibilities within you. Live in the present moment, and choose the thoughts, words, and actions that move you in the direction of your goals. However close or far away your goals may feel—begin now to move toward them.

On the mat: If you want the confidence, strength, and endurance to move forward, begin now to feel it within you. Bring yourself to the work. As you move in the exercises, stay fully present and become conscious of the life-giving energy within. Feel the flow of the breath, your strength and power. This is the way to help you *remember* all that is within. Move to awaken and remember that you have within everything you need to reach your goals.

Off the mat: Remember that each day is a gift. Be thankful for all that you have been given, and commit yourself to using your gifts to the best of your ability to give to others. Begin now this day. Let it be a good day. Remember that all your experiences and knowledge have brought you here to this point to act. Your potential is within; begin to realize it now.

"What then is your duty? What the day demands."

—Johann Wolfgang van Goethe

Set SMART goals and a plan of action:

SMART goals:

Specific: Write your goals, and include as much detail as possible. This detail gives the mind-body the direction it needs to move forward. Keep your written goals in mind by posting them where you can see them every day.

Example: Beginning today, I am losing ten pounds in ten weeks versus *I want to lose some weight.*

Measurable: Set goals in which you can measure your success. This keeps you in touch with your goals and gives you something to move forward to that is tangible.

Example: I am planning on earning $3,000 this summer versus *I would like a summer job.*

Attainable: Set yourself up to succeed by setting goals that are realistic. If you believe that you can attain the goal, you will be motivated to action. If you think it's out of your reach, it's unlikely that you will be able to sustain the effort to reach your goal.

Example: I am beginning a daily exercise program today. I will begin with ten minutes per day and work up to thirty minutes per day within three months or less versus *I want to run a marathon.*

Relational: You will have a better chance of reaching your goals if the realization of the goal has meaning that extends beyond yourself. The realization that reaching your goals can bring good to others is a powerful motivating factor.

Example: Losing ten pounds in ten weeks is a great example for my family and friends. I am going to learn how to do it versus *I want to lose weight.*

Time sensitive: Keep a time frame in mind. This keeps you on track and helps you stay focused. If you lose momentum or get stuck, a commitment that is time related can help you refocus and get back on track. Don't be discouraged if you need to reset the time frame. Be willing to adapt to your circumstances so you can continue to move forward.

Example: I will work for three hours per day to finish the project by the first week in September versus *I am going to work hard.*

Take a moment now and set a goal. Write it down. In order to give you the best chance to take the first step, determine now what plan of action is needed. Write three steps that you can *take today* to move you in the direction of your goals.

Example:

Goal: I am beginning a daily exercise program today starting with a ten-minute warm-up.

Action plan:

1. *Set up a space with everything I need to begin the work.*
2. *Invite others to work with me who share similar goals so we can support each other.*
3. *Determine the time of day for the work and write it in your calendar.*

Begin now. Set a goal today, and take the first step toward its attainment.

Exercise 8: Warm-up energy series

Exercises one through seven done in succession are the awakening and warm-up series. This series can be done every day prior to your practice and before your cardio workout. Warming up is essential for optimal performance. The warm-up awakens every system of the body. It increases the flow of blood and life energy throughout the body. The warm-up has many benefits:

- Enhances performance
- Optimizes results
- Reduces the risk of injury
- Promotes flexibility
- Increases endurance
- Increases energy level
- Focuses attention

As you practice the warm-up series, let one exercise flow into the next using the flow of your breath to guide your movements. You can link the exercises with the deep-breathing exercise (exercise 2). The warm-up series is summarized below:

1. Mountain pose
2. Deep-breathing exercise/postural pose
3. Knee-up/dancer's pose
4. Standing crunch
5. Open heart
6. Woodcutter
7. Warrior
8. Repeat deep-breathing exercise

CORE AND STRENGTH TRAINING

9. PRACTICE: Celebrate

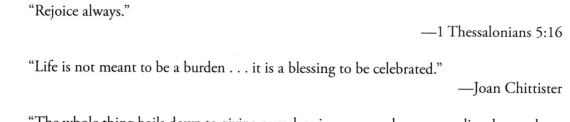

"Rejoice always."

—1 Thessalonians 5:16

"Life is not meant to be a burden . . . it is a blessing to be celebrated."

—Joan Chittister

"The whole thing boils down to giving ourselves in prayer a chance to realize that we have what we seek. We don't have to rush after it. It was there all the time, and if we give it time, it will make itself known to us."

—Thomas Merton

"The big question is whether you are going to be able to say a hearty yes to your adventure."

—Joseph Campbell

Intention: Celebrate is from the Latin *celebrare*, which means famous or well-known. To celebrate life then is to come to know ourselves and others well. When we are well-known to ourselves and each other, when we realize the truth of our being, we are a celebration of life. The joy we speak of is not always found in the circumstances of our lives but ever present within and experienced in loving relationships. Celebrate life by affirming in every thought, word, and action love for God, self, and others.

On the mat: Our work in the exercises can be a form of prayer, a moving meditation. The purpose of this movement is not to make us better or stronger or fix a wrong. The true purpose is to bring ourselves wholly to the present moment to know (in mind) and to feel (in body) the Good Within—God within. Through our work, we begin to realize that what we seek, we already have within. With practice and patience, it will make itself *known* to us. Believing in this truth makes it possible to find joy in the work. Let it be a celebration of life, the life that is yours. As you begin to experience this truth, you will know vitality, balance, strength, endurance, flexibility, focused attention, and coordination. Fulfillment is yours to celebrate.

Off the mat: In whatever circumstance you find yourself, the practice is the same. Be fully present and ask yourself, "What does love look like in this circumstance?" Open yourself to both give and receive this love. It is always there. Remember to see it, taste it, smell it, hear it, and feel it.

Exercise 9: Lightning bolt/step and touch

Lightning bolt/center

Lightning bolt/step and touch

1. Align the feet to center. Bend the knees and lower the hips, keeping the back long, with the shoulders above the hips. Draw your weight back into the heels.
2. Engage the abdominals, breathe in, and lengthen the spine, gently lifting into the space of open heart.
3. Feel the connection to your core muscles—the abdominals, lower back, and gluteus maximus (buttocks).
4. Bring the weights to touch at center at the level of your hips. Draw the elbows in close to the body.
5. Step right and draw the left foot toward the right, and touch the left foot at the toes to the floor.
6. Step left and draw the right foot across and touch the right foot to the floor.
7. Repeat the step and touch right to left eight times.
8. Repeat in sets of eight up to four sets.
9. Get into a rhythm, and feel the shift of weight as you move from side to side. Notice the push off the floor and the touch of the toes with each step.
10. Feel the flow of the breath. Exhale with each push off the floor with the foot.
11. Be mindful of your ABCs: alignment, breath, and control of the body through the full range of motion.

10. PRACTICE: Remember

"Be not afraid, only believe."

—Mark 5:36

"God enters by a private door into every individual."

—Ralph Waldo Emerson

"With God all things are possible."

—Matthew 8:26

Intention: We are human. We forget and make mistakes. We have to exercise the mind-body to help us remember our true nature and experience optimal well-being. We must not be discouraged by having to repeat the same lessons again and again but feel encouraged, even enthused about the *positive possibilities* ahead. The exercises repeated again and again help us to touch every cell in the living mind-body, awakening its potential. We are made of one hundred trillion cells. Every single cell within you is already filled with light and love. Begin to experience this goodness in your life, here and now. ***Believe*** *and move like you believe.* You do not have to understand everything; no evidence or proof is needed. The exercises are to help us remember, recognize, and realize our true nature—the infinite Good Within. In isolation, the exercises potentially lead nowhere. In faith, we open the mind-body to be transformed. You have the potential to experience optimal well-being in mind-body, not because you do the exercises *but because you believe.*

On the mat: Come to the exercises with an open mind and open heart. Believe in your goodness rather than your wrongness or weakness. When a wrongness or weakness surfaces, see it as an opportunity to bring a positive possibility into that space. Be willing to adapt the poses to your level of ability and desired intensity. All the work is good.

Off the mat: Our days can be repetitive at times, similar to our exercises. Be encouraged. Find ways to see the goodness in the simple things in life. Remember all that you have been given in the amazing gift of mind-body. Remember the gift of the earth and the universe we live in. Use these gifts to the fullest. Believe in your goodness, the goodness of all others and of all that is. Stay in touch. Feel connected to family and friends. It is through this touch, this connection, that we remember.

Exercise 10: Warrior lunge with bicep curl/overhead press

Warrior lunge/bicep curl

Warrior lunge/overhead press

1. Mountain pose.
2. Hold the weights in your hands with the palms up and the arms extended in front of you, aligned to your hips. The hips and shoulders are aligned over center. Keep the elbows rooted at your core by touching the elbows to your sides. Be sure your wrists are level, not bent by being flexed or extended.
3. Remember ABC:
   Alignment
   Breathe
   Control
4. Step forward on the right leg into lunge position as you bend at the elbows and curl the weights toward your shoulders. Alignment of the right knee over the ankle is most important to protect the knee joint from strain and to get the most effective use of the leg muscles. The knee should never be ahead of the ankle or foot in lunge position.
5. Feel grounded by distributing your weight equally on both feet. Keep the shoulders over the hips. Toes and heels are aligned on both feet. The front heel stays down, the back heel is lifted off the floor and the ball of your foot is your connection to the floor.
6. Engage the core, breathe in and lift into your heart center, exhale as you push the weights overhead directly over your shoulders. Keep the elbows in and aligned to the shoulders.
7. Focus your attention and bring the weight back to your shoulders. Control the weights through the full range of motion.
8. Step the right foot back to center as you uncurl the weights, bringing them back to starting position, aligned to your hips.
9. Repeat on the left side. Repeat in sets of eight, alternating the right and left legs.
10. You can also repeat four times to the right and four times to the left.
11. Modify the exercise by standing with both feet aligned to center and complete the curl and overhead press from standing position.

11. PRACTICE: Be happy

"He who lives in harmony with himself lives in harmony with the universe."

—Marcus Aurelius

"Peace cannot be kept by force. It can only be achieved by understanding."

—Albert Einstein

"It is the chaos inside of us that is the beginning of a relationship with God. It is here that the stuff of our unrest, our ambition, our narcissism, our confusion lurks. And so, it is here that we must begin to understand . . . it is here that we will find and name the real fears, the deepest hopes, and the fullest feelings of life."

—Joan Chittister

"Trust in the Lord with all your heart, on your own intelligence rely not; in all your ways be mindful of him, and he will make straight your paths."

—Proverbs 3:5

Intention: A string of events came together one weekend to remind me of a very important lesson in life—be happy. Simple things like a walk in the woods, a child home for the day, a homily, a few hours of work in the garden, and a quiet evening with my husband all seem to be reminding me to be happy. Sometimes I am just too busy to be happy. My mind is filled with things to do, and my priorities are misplaced. I say no to happiness and choose instead, "I've got too many things to do, too many obstacles to overcome, and too many achievements to be reached." I am not willing to let go of the demanding schedules, high expectations, frustrations, and anxieties as I try to make my way to something I think is better than what is here now. Striving and all the demands that go with it are good as long as we remember the balance—be happy with what is, here and now, first. If we cannot be happy here and now, true happiness will be hard to find because no matter how much we achieve today, there will always be another day and more to attain. That is until our days here are over. Be happy now.

On the mat: The exercises can be demanding. The work requires your time and attention. Focus on all that is good within you and others. Whatever your level of ability and intensity is in each moment—be happy with what is. Begin here, in being happy. When our priorities are straight and striving follows happiness, rather than chasing it, we will make great progress.

Off the mat: Look at the words that are the antonyms (opposites) of happy—sad, miserable, depressed, dejected. These feelings arise in all of us at times—not because we choose them but because we are called to face them with awareness that leads to understanding. We can choose how to respond to these feelings by literally staying in touch. Be willing to feel the sadness and see it as an opportunity to find within you a place of happiness. It may be a memory, but it is there, within you. The willingness to embrace even sadness can lead to understanding.

Exercise 11: Back lunge/twist

Back lunge/twist

1. Mountain pose.
2. Hold the weights touching at center at the level of the belly.
3. Engage the abdominals, lift the left knee, and step the left leg back into lunge position. Align the joints from top to bottom: shoulders, elbows, hips, knees, feet, and toes. Notice that the feet are aligned to the hips so you have a wide base of support.
4. Feel the weight of your body grounded and centered. Maintain a stable root in the feet and hips, keeping the abdominals engaged but not holding or tight.
5. Twist the upper body left, keeping the spine long and the shoulders back. Return to center.
6. Lift the left knee and return the left foot to center position on the floor.
7. Repeat on the right side. Alternate the twists with the right and left legs. Repeat in sets of eight.
8. Modify by working on the right side eight times and then the left eight times.
9. Use this word sequence to help you remember this six-step exercise: "Knee-up, back lunge, twist, back to center, knee-up, and place the foot down."

Isolate leg press/twist

Back lunge/leg press

1. Mountain pose.
2. Knee-up with back lunge on the right side.
3. While maintaining forward warrior position, isolate the leg press by bending the back leg and drawing the knee downward and then upward in a steady, slow pumping motion. Keep the front heel down and the knee stacked over the ankle.
4. Repeat the leg press eight times. Exhale with every press.
5. Come back to center position with the weights touching in front of you.
6. Isolate the twist by turning to the right and coming back to center. Turn to the left and back to center, alternating the twisting motion from right to left or left to right. The motion is smooth and steady.
7. Repeat both exercises on the other side.
8. Add variety by twisting eight times to the right and then eight toward the left.

12. PRACTICE: Nothing wrong in sadness

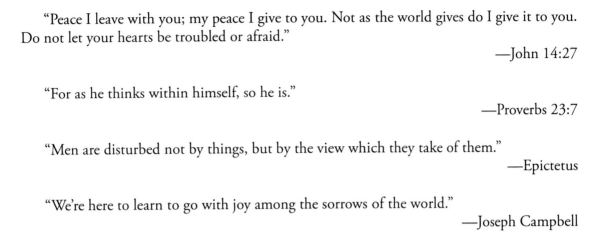

"Peace I leave with you; my peace I give to you. Not as the world gives do I give it to you. Do not let your hearts be troubled or afraid."

—John 14:27

"For as he thinks within himself, so he is."

—Proverbs 23:7

"Men are disturbed not by things, but by the view which they take of them."

—Epictetus

"We're here to learn to go with joy among the sorrows of the world."

—Joseph Campbell

Intention: There is nothing wrong with feeling sad. Sadness—and any other emotion—is a natural and needed part of being human. When you seem troubled or down, others may ask, "What's wrong?" When we learn to see more clearly the truth, we can believe in our hearts, "Nothing is wrong. I feel sad, and my response to this sad feeling will give my life direction." When sadness is what we feel in the moment, we should be willing to feel it without a sense of being wrong. We cannot always be up. This would defy the laws of physics. The feeling of sadness has no power over you, except that which you give it—by believing you *are* sad rather than "I *feel* sad." Do not make sadness a part of you. See it for what it is. You are not sad. You are the one called to respond to the feeling of sadness that is moving through you. Learn to respond to that feeling with an awareness of all that is Good Within.

On the mat: When negative emotions or thoughts arise in your consciousness, practice being the observer. Simply take notice of the feelings of impatience, frustration, disappointment, anger, jealousy, pride, or other negative emotions. Be willing to stay with the feeling without judgment. Notice the flow of the breath in the body. Now choose how you want to respond to that feeling. Choose to move in ways that help you remember your true nature. Feel grounded, centered, and strong. Open the heart and feel the flow of the breath moving within you. Focus on what you want in life and then take the first step.

Off the mat: Every day will present numerous opportunities to access your emotions as a source of life-giving energy. When we can stay fully present to the feeling and recognize that we are not the feeling but the one called to respond, we will harness the power in our emotions, both positive and negative. Happy and sad are considered opposites, but they are not separate feelings. They are one feeling, at opposite ends of a single continuum. We cannot know happiness without having been touched by sadness. Imagine that this continuum is not linear but circular and not two-dimensional but three-dimensional. When you feel sad, recognize that when you are able to embrace and understand the feeling, it can lead you back to happiness that is within.

Exercise 12: Upright row/back lunge

Upright row/start

Upright row/back lunge

1. Mountain pose.
2. Hold the weights touching at center with the arms fully extended. The weights can rest on the front side of the body at the level of the hips.
3. Breathe in, and as you exhale, bend the elbows and lift the weights to chest height. As the elbows bend, extend them upward and outward. The weights remain touching and aligned at center.
4. In a flowing motion, step the left leg back into a lunge as the arms are being lifted to the chest. Bring the left leg back to starting position at center as you return the weights to starting position with the arms extended in front of you.
5. Alternate the right and left legs into lunge with every upright row eight times. Repeat four times to the right and four times to the left.
6. Keep your attention focused, and exhale with every lift. Feel a flow and rhythm to your movement that is aligned to the flow of the breath.
7. Counting the repetitions out loud is one way to develop a rhythm and flow. Your voice flows on the exhale.

13. PRACTICE: On your own

"Believe in yourself. You gain strength, courage and confidence by every experience in which you stop to look fear in the face . . . You must do that which you think you cannot do."

—Eleanor Roosevelt

"The teacher, if indeed wise, does not bid you to enter the house of their wisdom, but leads you to the threshold of your own mind."

—Kahlil Gibran

"God has given each of you special abilities, be sure to use them to help each other, passing on to others God's many kinds of blessings."

—1 Peter 4:10

"For the one who is least among all of you is the one who is the greatest."

—Luke 9: 48

Intention: In the days and weeks ahead, take time to practice on your own. Practicing on your own builds discipline, inner strength, and self-control. Work with the external cues you have learned to guide your movements. Begin to strengthen your sense of internal cues also. We all take cues from the outer world when we look at the clock to know when to eat or follow a recipe to make dinner. We listen to the experts and read articles that move us to action. All this is good. We also want to be able to receive cues from within by listening to the inner wisdom of our own mind-body. Draw forth this inner power by calling on it daily. Eat when you feel hungry. Create your own recipe.

On the mat: Stay present to the external cues and begin to direct your attention inward. Stay in touch with the body. Listen and observe. Allow your inner cues to guide and support you in the exercises. Sensations that arise in the body, even discomfort and pain, are not bad. They are information. Pay attention. Practice being on your own, and trust in the Good Within for guidance.

Off the mat: Notice what cues provide direction for your daily movements. Do you rely solely on external cues? Take time to let you attention move inward by getting in touch with the body and the feelings within. Maybe you have a gut feeling about an upcoming decision. Is there a passion waiting to be fulfilled in you? Observe, reflect, and ask yourself, "What other internal cues move me?" Begin to discover a whole new world, an inner source of energy that you can call on for guidance, strength, and wisdom. Ironically, as you practice on your own, you will discover that you are never alone. You have within you a source of energy and love much bigger than the small self of the ego. This source is ever-present. Begin to call on it. Like a muscle, the more you call on it, the stronger it gets. Muscles, however strong, are still limited by physiology and physics. The inner source is infinite.

Exercise 13: Lightning bolt/double squat

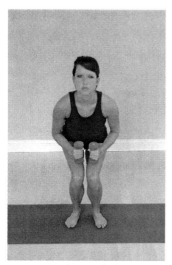

Lightning bolt

Lightning bolt/squat

1. Mountain pose.
2. Bend the knees and draw the hips downward. Engage the abdominals for strength and stability. Keep the back long and the shoulders above the hips. The heart center is open and lifted.
3. The squat movement is up and down and right to left over center. Exhale with each squat or leg press. Breathe in as you lift the body upward, exhale as you step right, and press both legs by bending at the knees and drawing the hips downward.
4. Inhale and move the right leg back to center. Exhale as you squat to the left side.
5. Alternate the movement from right to left eight times. Repeat up to three sets of eight.
6. Stay connected to your core by keeping awareness of the abdominals and lower back. Draw power from your core.
7. Press the weight of the body equally over both feet and legs. Keep the heels grounded, and feel your body aligned over center.
8. Keep the back long and the upper body lifted. Shoulders are open and stay above the level of the hips.
9. Remember to breathe as you exhale with each squat. This will help you get a rhythm going and bring needed oxygen to the working muscles, tissues, and organs.

14. PRACTICE: More is not always better.

"As for you, do not seek what you are to eat and what you are to drink, and do not worry anymore. All the nations of the world seek for these things, and your Father knows that you need them. Instead, seek his kingdom, and these other things will be given you besides."

—Luke 9:29

"There are different kinds of spiritual gifts but the same Spirit; there are different forms of service but the same Lord; there are different workings but the same God who produces all of them in everyone."

—1 Corinthians 12:4

"So much has been given to me; I have no time to ponder over that which has been denied."

—Helen Keller

"I have lived long enough to learn how much there is I can really do without . . . He is nearest to God who needs the fewest things."

—Socrates

Intention: As we give thanks for all that has been given, it can be helpful to remember that more is not always better. With that thought, the simplest of practice for today:

There is no way to happiness . . . happiness is the way.

Be the way.

Be happy.

On the mat: Be thankful and stay focused on all that you are able to do. Let it be enough.

Off the mat: The practice is the same. Remember, more is not always better.

Exercise 14: Lightning bolt/triceps extension

Lightning bolt/triceps
extension

Lateral view

1. Lightning bolt is a power position that brings up heat within the body as you draw on the large muscles at your core (abdominals, lower back, and gluteus). Root the body in the core muscles by drawing your weight into your heels with the hips drawn down; shoulders are above the level of the hips.

2. Begin with the arms extended at your side aligned to the shoulders.

3. The movement in this exercise is in four distinct motions. 1. Bend at the elbows and lift the weights to the chest, keeping the elbows close to the body. 2. Extend the forearm to the level of the shoulder but no higher. 3. Draw the forearm back to center at the level of the chest. 4. Bend the knees, and press the hips toward the floor.

4. Remember the sequence with the words: "lift and extend, back to center, and press."

5. Repeat eight times up to three sets of eight.

6. Remember ABC—alignment, breathe, and control.

15. PRACTICE: Be thankful

"Gratitude can transform common days into Thanksgiving, turn routine jobs into joy, and change ordinary opportunities into blessings."

—William Ward

"When one door closes, another opens; but we often look so long and so regrettably upon the closed door that we do not see the one which has opened for us."

—Alexander Graham Bell

"This day I call heaven and earth as witnesses against you. That I have set before you life and death. Blessings and curses. Now choose life."

—Deuteronomy 30:19

"Rejoice always, pray constantly, and give thanks for everything."

—1 Thessalonians 5:16

Intention: Today is the perfect time to practice thankfulness. Being thankful can bring many gifts, mostly the gift of abundance. Abundance is the feeling of being satisfied and the thought that all is well. Life is not perfect. Life is not always fair and just. Be thankful for the mind-body and your awareness of the inner strength that allows you to endure life's imperfections. By choosing life and love, we get through.

On the mat: Thankfulness feels like an inner smile. We are thankful we are on the mat. We are thankful for the mind and body, for the legs we stand on or a place to sit, for the arms that lift and support, and for the muscles that stabilize and move us. We are thankful for a mind-body more intricate, beautiful, and amazing than we might ever realize. Be thankful for the smallest of things, like the feeling of one moment held in beautiful balance.

Off the mat: Gratitude is a deep appreciation for all that is. There is so much good in this world. Open your mind, your heart, and your eyes, and begin to see this goodness. Be thankful. The intention alone will bring greater abundance into your life. What you focus on expands. Begin to see all that is good and be thankful.

Exercise 15: Leg press from straddle position/chest press

Leg press/chest press

Leg press/4-count

1. Straddle the legs with the toes on both feet turned slightly outward aligned to center. The weights are held at center at chest height. Level the wrists by drawing the first set of knuckles of your *hand* to touch. The wrist joint should *not* be flexed or extended but level.

2. Breathe in, and as you exhale, bend the knees and draw the knees outward over the ankles as you press the hips downward with your weight being drawn into your heels. At the same time as you are pressing the legs, pull the elbows back at the level of the chest and feel the opening into the heart center.

3. The motion is smooth and controlled. Do not strain or jerk the weight back. Keep the elbows lifted and aligned to the chest.

4. Feel the body aligned to center. Press evenly into the heels, and draw the knees wide to feel the pull to the inner thigh. Exhale with every press.

5. Deepen the work by going to a four-count press. Keeping your weight aligned to center: 1. Press the weight to touch the floor at center by pulling the hips down. Keep the shoulders above the level of the hips. 2. Lift the upper body, and bring the weights to the shoulders. 3. Press the weight overhead aligned to the shoulders. 4. Return the weight to the shoulders.

6. Remember the sequence with these words: "floor, shoulders, overhead, and back to the shoulders."

7. Repeat steps one through four for eight repetitions.

16. PRACTICE: Only love

"Let love be rooted in you, and from that root nothing but good can grow."

—Saint Augustine of Hippo

"Love is patient, love is kind. It is not jealous, love is not pompous, it is not inflated, it is not rude, it does not seek its own interests, it is not quick-tempered, it does not brood over injury, it does not rejoice over wrong-doing but rejoices with the truth. It bears all things, believes all things, hopes all things, endures all things. Love never fails."

—1 Corinthians 13:4-8

Intention: When the demands are high and the stress is bearing down on you, remember what is truly needed—only love. It is tempting to want or need things to go our way. It is easy to be disappointed, even frustrated or angry, when things don't go the way we want or expect. We may think or feel we cannot love in a day that brings disappointment, failure, or loss. These thoughts are simply not true. It is in these moments we are called to respond from the state of mind-body that is only love. This is what is most needed on these tough days. Suffering does not transform a burden into a blessing. Only love transforms. Choose love in one of its many forms and feel transformed.

On the mat: Practice open heart posture each morning this week. Open your heart with a good cardio workout. As you move, keep in mind the thoughts that root you in love and feel the lift of energy that will allow you to endure. It is not easy to keep going when the work feels like a burden. Let an open heart be the cure.

Off the mat: Change your mind about one thing or one person this week, and let that change be for love.

Exercise 16: Lateral raise/knee-up

1. Mountain pose.
2. Weights are held at your sides with the arms extended.
3. Bend the elbows and draw the elbows behind the level of the shoulders, bringing the weights aligned to center at the level of the hips.
4. Breathe in, and as you exhale, lift the weights to a level just below the shoulders. Keep the elbows bent and behind you.
5. Inhale and bring the weights back to center, your arms at your side.
6. Notice the lift originating at the core. Feel the muscles of the back contracting as the chest expands away from center.

Lateral raise/knee-up

7. Repeat eight times.
8. Add variety and challenge by adding the knee-up lift.
9. Lift the leg into knee-up position at the same time as you are lifting the arms into lateral raise.
10. You can alternate the leg lifts eight times or perform eight times to the right and eight times to the left. Exhale with every lift.
11. Take a breather if you feel the need. Rest for a minute or so, slow the pace, or decrease the intensity. Try just the opposite. Push a little harder.
12. When we are able to adapt, it allows us to sustain our efforts for the long run. Adaptability promotes endurance and resilience.
13. Remember the balance of work/rest. Feel the work as you lift the weights and the muscles contract. Notice the rest as the muscles relax and the arms come back to center.

17. PRACTICE: As we look out

"Be on your guard, stand firm in the faith, be courageous, be strong. Your every act should be done with love."

—1 Corinthians 16:13

"The universe is my way. Love is my law. Peace is my shelter. Experience is my school. Obstacle is my lesson. Difficulty is my stimulant. Pain is my warning. Work is my blessing. Balance is my attitude. Perfection is my destiny."

—Guillermo Tobentino

Intention: One weekend some time ago, my husband and I were hiking in the woods near our home west of Boston. As we hiked, we came to a vista, and we looked west to see the setting sun. The yellow light shone brightly on the colored hills. I thought of all those who had stood there before us, looking west. They must have seen the same beauty and envisioned a bright tomorrow when they gathered their families and possessions and headed west. They must have known from their past experiences that they would face challenges, but they had already come so far. They never would have set out unless they imagined that what lay ahead of them would be good for themselves and their families.

At the end of the day, when the sun is setting, remember how far you have come and be thankful. As you look out, see the goodness and light in the positive possibilities that lay ahead. You will be readied to take the next step—a new day—a new beginning.

On the mat: As you continue in the exercises, imagine the positive possibilities as you look ahead. You have come far, and you have much to look forward to as you build yourself stronger in mind-body.

Off the mat: As we look out, we have a choice. We can focus on the positive possibilities and step forward in the direction of our goals, or we can let the challenges frighten and immobilize us. Look out today and see a bright future.

Exercise 17: Squat/full-body extension (no weights)

Squat/starting position

1. Lightning bolt position
2. Breathe in, and as you exhale, bend the knees and lower the hips into a squat position. Pull your weight into your heels and draw the hips toward the floor. Do not take the hips lower than the level of the knees.
3. Breathe in as you lift and lengthen the body, drawing the right leg up behind you. Keep the leg extended straight, and feel the origin of the lift in the lower back and gluteus maximus.
4. Maintain alignment of the legs to the hips and hips to shoulders. Keep the right knee and the right foot pointed downward toward the floor. Right and left hips stay level, not tilted or twisted.
5. Notice the opposing muscle groups working together. Feel the contraction of the lower back and gluteus as the abdominals lengthen with the extension. The abdominals contract and the back muscles lengthen with the squat.
6. Develop a rhythm and flow to the movements. Inhale with the extensions and exhale with the squats. Alternate the lifts between the right and left legs for two sets of eight.

Full-body extension

18. PRACTICE: As we look in

"Nothing can bring you peace but yourself."

—Ralph Waldo Emerson

"Who looks outside, dreams; who looks inside, awakes."

—Carl Jung

"It is not up in the sky . . . Nor is it across the sea . . . No, it is something very near to you, already in your mouths and in your hearts, you have only to carry it out."

—Deuteronomy 30:12-14

"If you remain in me and my words remain in you, ask for whatever you want and it will be done for you."

—John 15:7

Intention: As we look in, let us see clearly our true being. What is seen on the surface is a small fraction of all that we are. If we only give weight to what is seen on the outside, we can fail to see the good within that is perceived in the space of open heart. Within you is an inner source of love that is infinite and able to work through you, even in your "smallness." Within you is a sense of balance and strength that readies you to be "response-able." When the heart is open, the life energy will begin to flow. As you look in, stay focused on that love and you will awaken to find your dreams coming true.

On the mat: As we look in, we remind ourselves to be thankful for the outer world, which provides context, meaning, and balance to our experience. In the exercises, keep your eyes open. You need that information from the outer world to know your place and to sense where you belong in relationship to other things and beings. With your eyes open and conscious of your surroundings, begin to draw your attention to look inward. Feel the flow of the breath, and notice the sensations within as you practice.

Off the mat: Take time each day to focus your attention inward. Consider beginning a practice of meditation. Guidelines to begin a practice follow the exercises for today. Meditation is a way to initiate a personal, intimate relationship with God. Like any relationship, it takes time, effort, and giving of yourself. Unlike any other relationship, God gives back a most perfect and beautiful love that will comfort, nourish, and sustain you always.

Exercise 18: Knee-up/back lunge (no weights)

Knee-up

Back lunge/side view

1. Mountain pose.

2. Breathe in, and as you exhale, lift the left knee as you draw the hands under the left leg to touch at center. Engage the abdominals for strength and stability. Maintain control of the left leg through the full range of motion.

3. Inhale and reach the left leg back into lunge position, at the same time reaching the arms overhead in a swinging motion. Feel grounded in both feet with your weight equally distributed over center right to left, front to back, and top to bottom. The knee is directly over the ankle of the front (right) leg. Keep the right heel down. The back heel is off the floor, and the heel remains aligned to the toes.

4. Try to get full extension of the arms overhead, and keep the arms aligned over the shoulders and hips for greatest stability. Reaching the arms long overhead draws deeply from your core. Feel the connection to the belly and back.

5. The back is long, and the heart center is lifted.

6. Repeat eight times to the right and eight times to the left.

7. Vary the speed and depth of the repetitions and notice how the mind-body is challenged in different ways.

8. Visualize the exercise before you practice. Feel both feet on the floor and the body centered. Close your eyes and picture yourself moving through the exercise with balance, stability, and ease. As you visualize, imagine the body moving in the exercises. Picture as much detail as possible.

9. When you are ready, open your eyes, assume mountain pose, and begin the exercises.

MEDITATION: Guidelines for your practice

"True silence is the rest of the mind; it is to the spirit what sleep is to the body, nourishment and refreshment."

—William Penn

"Be still and know that I am God."

—Psalm 46:11

"Draw near to God and he will draw near to you."

—James 4:8

"For it is in this blessed stillness He may speak to us living words of life and healing and freedom . . . Only this kind of prayer frees the conscience from the condemning voices within us. Only this kind of prayer prepares the soul to receive God's strengthening grace—strength, I say, both to overcome sin and perform the will of the Father."

—Julian of Norwich

Research in the last decade has proven that practicing meditation has numerous benefits. The inner silence is rest for the mind and body and can be a respite from stress, tension, and anxiety. Meditation can comfort, nourish, guide, and sustain us. The benefits from meditation that are supported by research include:

- Deep rest/sleep
- Reduced stress
- Decreased heart rate, breathing rate, oxygen consumption, muscle tension, blood pressure, and presence of stress hormones in the blood
- Mental clarity and boost to creativity
- Emotional ease
- Coherence of brain wave activity
- Increased energy
- Increased immune function and slowing of the aging process
- Improved learning and increased self-esteem
- Achievement of ideal weight
- Improved performance and productivity

Pursuing any or all of the benefits listed above can be a motivating force to help us begin a meditation practice. Once we begin, however, the benefits become secondary; they are the effects of our meditation practice, not our reason for meditating. We must bring to our practice a sense of *purpose,* a reason to meditate beyond the physical benefits, if we are to sustain our practice and reap the many benefits that are both seen and unseen. We may meditate to connect with an inner source of knowing that some call intuition, to receive guidance or inspiration, or to experience a sense of peace and contentment. Some believe we meditate to connect to a higher power or infinite intelligence. Scientists have named this higher power the universal field of intelligence, the implicate order, and the info-realm. Many call this higher power God. If prayer is talking to God, meditation is an essential part of prayer, and that is listening. Meditation is a form of communication. We commune in a conscious union of human being and divine light and love. God knows each of us intimately. He wants us to know Him. Meditation is a space to spend time with God and listen. Get to know God, and you will know love. Love will be your purpose and your sustenance.

The benefits of meditation are experienced in mind-body as we both understand and feel God's goodness and love. We willingly give our time and attention to God and listen with the intention of following. We ask to be guided so we are able to align our will to the most beautiful and perfect will of God. In meditation we let go of our desire to think, reason, and plan. We sit quietly, we wait and listen. We do not try to push away thoughts or empty the mind of thought. An empty mind is neither possible nor desirable. Meditation trains the mind to focus with attention and will. When thoughts or feelings arise in our awareness, we simply notice and gently call our attention back to the space of listening. We discipline the mind-body and open ourselves to perceive God's presence within.

When I first began a practice of meditation, and even to this day twenty years later, there are times when I sit and the mind-body is filled with thought and sensation. I feel anxious and I worry. I am restless, and in this state of discomfort I think, "This is not good" and I am tempted to get up from my space of listening. When I think, "This is not good," I am also feeling, "This is not God." And I am right. It is not God. It is me alone who is afraid. I am afraid because I have forgotten that God is with me always. I think of a distant God in heaven. I do not remember the feel of God's loving touch or recognize Him here with me now. And for me to be face-to-face with God in heaven seems to mean death, which I fear most of all. I try to remember that God placed the fear of death in me because He wants me to live, to stay, here on earth for a time. When I am afraid, God wants me to call on Him. God wants me to live, to know, and to feel love. He knows it will take time to learn the lessons of love. He knows that like a child, I will make many mistakes as I learn and grow. God, as father and mother, is always loving, patient, and forgiving. God is with us always. If I am able to believe, I can begin to let go of my fear of death and live more fully in the truth. God is ever-present. There is nothing to fear. It is me who is not present to God within because my mind is elsewhere.

In meditation, we discipline the mind to be present wholly within the body, to be present to God within. When the mind seems to be unruly and out of control, do not be tempted to judge or condemn. We are the child. Stay present and accept the remedy to ignorance and fear, which is understanding and love. Train and discipline the mind to be fully present in the body so we can exercise our inherent freedom to choose. Choose to abide in God's loving presence, aligning your will to God's, making it as one. As we learn that we have the power to choose our thoughts, words, and actions, we gain a measure of self-control in our lives and feel more confident and self-assured. Do not ask to control others or every circumstance of your life. Trust in God, and let God work through each person for His purpose, which is love. *Be able to choose your responses: choose life and love.*

We can experience the touch of God's Holy Spirit in meditation through our awareness on the physical level of the movement of the breath within us. We allow the mind to be fully present in the body, and we focus our attention on the life force, the breath, the Spirit within. The breath is literally our inspiration. The body becomes the space or the opening for the mind to reside. The mind is fully present and at ease in the body with a willingness to receive what is in each moment. With every in-breath we feel the lift of the vital life energy and with every out-breath we let go of unneeded tension and tightness. When the mind is fully present in the body, every breath in has the power to lift and energize us, and every breath out will ground and relax us, thus restoring equilibrium.

As you practice, follow the flow of the breath as it moves in the body. The touch of the breath becomes our point of awareness. When we feel the breath, it literally keeps us in touch with the body so we are able to consciously reside in the dwelling place of Spirit that moves within us. As you come to the meditation, remember that you can relax because there is nothing you have to achieve. You do not have to reach for anything. You only have to be present to feel the flow of the breath within.

The purpose of our meditation is not to lie down or sit down and do nothing. Our purpose in sitting to do nothing is in rising, getting up from the meditation, and doing everything with an awareness of the touch of God's Holy Spirit within.

"Meditation, then, is bringing the mind home."

—Sogjal Rinpoche

"Neither height nor depth nor anything else in all creation will be able to separate us from the Love of God."

—Romans 8:39

There are many different methods utilized to prepare for meditation. You can begin your practice with these simple suggestions.

1. Sit in a chair with your back straight but not stiff. Place your feet flat on the floor, your hands in your lap. You can also lie flat on your back on a mat or padded surface. If you feel strained in the lower back, elevate your knees slightly with a bolster placed evenly under the knees. Wear loose clothing that does not restrict your breathing.
2. Close your eyes. Center yourself by becoming aware of the midline of the body through the spine, and allow the right and left sides of the body to align over center.

3. Relax, taking several deep breaths, inhaling and exhaling through your nose if possible.

4. Bring your awareness to the breath at the nostrils as it passes in and out. You may also sense the breath as it flows over the back of the throat, at the heart center, with the rise and fall of the chest or with the rise and fall of the belly. Let the breath flow naturally. You do not have to try to control your breathing in any way. Keep your attention on the sensation of the breath. If your mind wanders and thoughts, sounds, or sensations arise in your awareness, this is to be expected. Allow the thoughts and sensations. When you notice, with that same awareness, begin to let go of the thoughts and sensations and bring your attention back to the breath.

5. Every time you come back to the breath, you deepen and strengthen your awareness of the life energy within. Every time you let go of the thoughts, sounds, and sensations, you release unneeded tension and tightness. In this way, every in-breath has the power to lift and energize you, and each out-breath is the opening to let go of what is no longer needed. Simply note the thoughts or sensations without judgment or criticism. Gently return your attention to the sensation of the breath. This technique of repeatedly returning your attention to the breath is not "trying" to meditate. It is the meditation. The power is in your intention, not in your "doing." Without the distractions and resistance, there is no practice.

6. Begin your practice with as little as five minutes a day. You can increase the time to twenty minutes twice a day as you feel able.

7. Develop a daily practice, once in the morning upon rising and in the evening before dinner or at bedtime. Practice at the same time and place each day as much as you are able. When beginning a practice, choose a location that is quiet and free from distractions. The mind-body will adapt more readily to the practice when you make a commitment and establish a structure for your time and attention.

8. Practice when your stomach is empty. Before meals is best or two to three hours after a meal.

9. Read an inspirational passage from a book prior to your practice to strengthen your intention. This type of meditation is often referred to as contemplation. Let your thoughts remain with the words of the passage, asking yourself questions to deepen your understanding. The Bible is a good place to start.

10. You can choose a word or phrase, a *mantra,* to repeat silently to yourself as you begin the meditation. You can use the title from your daily exercise, create your own, or draw from inspirational books. Here are a few suggestions:

    ❖ God is love.   John 4:11
    ❖ God is light.   1 John 1:5
    ❖ Rejoice always.   1 Thessalonians 5:16
    ❖ Follow me.   Matthew 9:9
    ❖ The Lord is my shepherd. Psalm 23

- ❖ Be patient.   Ephesians 4:2
- ❖ Live in peace.   Romans 12:18
- ❖ I am with you always.   Matthew 28:20
- ❖ You are with me.   Psalm 23
- ❖ Peace I leave with you.   John 8:32
- ❖ I am in you.   John 17:21
- ❖ Give thanks.   Psalm 107:1
- ❖ Be not afraid.   Jeremiah 1:7
- ❖ You are my strength.   Psalm 46:1
- ❖ I will give you rest.   Matthew 11:28
- ❖ Be brave, be strong.   Corinthians 16:13
- ❖ Believe.   Mark 5:36

11. During the course of the day, you can call on the mantra in times of difficulty or when negative thinking arises. Bring the mantra to mind, and it will help you focus and stay present.

19. **PRACTICE: Be the one**

"We learn to do something by doing it. There is no other way."

—John Holt

"Knowing is not enough; we must apply. Willing is not enough; we must do."

—Johann Wolfgang van Goethe

"So strengthen your drooping heads and your weak knees. Make straight paths for your feet, that what is lame may not be dislocated but healed."

—Hebrews 12:12

"Learning is movement from moment to moment."

—J. Krishnamurti

Intention: Movement, like water, is the key to life. Movement is the medium for all of our experiences and keeps the mind and body alert and attentive. It promotes a flow of information between us and our environment that is essential if we are to become optimal learners. Movement is stimulating. It activates brain cells and improves receptor networks, revitalizing brain function. The breath is the movement of the life force within us. The experience of breathing fully as we move can have a dramatic impact on our learning and well-being. Deep breathing that occurs during exercise plays a key role in expanding the capillary network and producing feelings of high energy and well-being. Oxygen-rich blood is delivered to tissues and organs, promoting optimal function. Deep breathing is one of the simplest, most powerful ways to activate energy reserves, enabling us to experience life more fully and vigorously.

On the mat: Be the one. Step up, accept the challenge, and begin to move in ways that promote life. Bring yourself fully to the practice. Give more of yourself. Challenge yourself to try new moves and take note of your responses. As you give the practice your time and attention, your work will lift and inspire you. You will feel and see the results.

Off the mat: Be the one to bring movement to thoughts and ideas by taking action today. Let your movements be focused and purposeful. Set short and long-term goals to give yourself direction. Move in mind and body. Try new exercises and activities, different foods, or new places and see things from a new perspective. Move and feel the flow of life energy within you. Laugh and have fun.

Exercise 19: Knee lift/leg extension

Tabletop position/knee lift

1. Tabletop position: Kneeling on the floor, position the upper body so that the hands are aligned under the shoulders and in the lower body the knees are aligned under the hips. Align yourself to center from right to left, front to back, and top to bottom. Right to left, you are centered over the midline through the spine. Front to back, you notice equal weight distributed on the hands and knees. Feel the touch of the feet behind you. Top to bottom alignment results in a neutral spine—the back is not curved upward or downward but in neutral position (like a tabletop).

2. Tabletop position is the basis for the core exercises to follow.

3. Lift the right knee to hip height, maintaining alignment of the right knee to the left knee on the mat. The right foot stays aligned to the knee also as you lift, lifting the entire leg, not only the knee.

4. Exhale with every knee lift. You can count aloud to develop a rhythm and flow to your movements.

5. The core muscles of the abdomen, lower back, and gluteus provide the strength and stability for this exercise. The core stays steady and is the origin of the movement.

6. Notice the muscles contracting with the lift and relaxing as you bring the knee down. Feel the flow from contraction to relaxation as you do the repetitions.

7. Keep in mind that the movement is the balance of work and rest, contraction and relaxation.

8. Repeat eight times on the right and then left side. Repeat up to three sets of eight.

Add leg extension

Knee lift/leg extension

1. Tabletop position.
2. Begin with the knee lift on the left side. Extend the lower leg away from the knee with the toes pointing forward. Maintain alignment of the leg to the hip. Keep the shoulders and hips squared to the mat, and keep the core steady.
3. Draw the lower leg back, and bring the knee down to starting position.
4. The sequence is four counts and can be remembered as lift, extend, bring the knee in and down, or more simply, up, out, in, and down (contraction, contraction, contraction, and relaxation).
5. Keep the core steady and the motion smooth, without jerking. Exhale with exertion.
6. Extensions are more difficult as the muscle is working harder. Three parts work and one part rest.
7. Repeat eight times on the left/right up to three sets of eight.

20. PRACTICE: Explore the unseen

"And do not seek what you should eat or what you should drink, nor have an anxious mind. For all these things the nations of the world seek after, and your Father knows that you need these things. But seek the Kingdom of God, and all these things shall be added to you."

—Luke 12:29

"We are not human beings having a spiritual experience but spiritual beings having a human experience." (Maybe we are both.)

—Wayne Dyer

"Fear and worry as to whether or not we have sufficient understanding or wisdom to discharge our responsibilities are dispelled when we know that it is not our wisdom or our understanding, but God's wisdom, understanding, justice and benevolence that governs all of us."

—Joel Goldsmith

Intention: There is a part of you that is unseen—a part of you that does not need food, water, or shelter, a part of you that has no lack or limitation. This part of you is not of the material world but experienced within. This inner presence has been given many names—spirit, soul, inner wisdom, divine intuition, Holy Spirit, and others. Although it is unseen, we can feel this presence within when we are willing to give time and attention to an inner life. The material world is not to be denied, but neither can we live in equilibrium if we fail to explore the unseen.

On the mat: Move with greater awareness of the life energy within you. This energy can be felt within as the movement of the breath. When you exercise, you breathe more deeply and vigorously. Paying attention to the flow of the breath can lift and energize you. You can feel the life energy in the heat that arises in the body during exercise or the sweat that trickles down your back. Notice the muscles contracting and relaxing as you feel the flow in your movements. Stay present, and explore the unseen.

Off the mat: Remind yourself of the balance needed for optimal well-being. Excess energy and attention on the self of the material world and all its needs can lead to a feeling of heaviness. Too much weight on the self leaves you feeling burdened unnecessarily. You would not deny yourself food and water. Remember to feed and nourish your awareness of spirit as well.

Exercise 20: Leg press

Leg press/start

Leg press/extension

1. Tabletop position.
2. Lift the left leg to the level of the left hip. Hips and shoulders remain aligned and squared to the floor. The left foot is flexed and positioned over the left knee.
3. Press the left heel toward the ceiling in a smooth pumping action. Exhale with every press.
4. Feel the gluteus muscle contract with the press and relax as you bring the knee back to the level of the hip. Be mindful that the leg press, as in any exercise, is not all work. It is half work and half rest. When the leg is being pressed, the muscles are contracting and working. When the leg is lowered, the muscles relax and rest. If you notice this flow from contraction to relaxation, you will be able to move with this flow and go the distance. If you perceive the exercise as all work, it will seem more difficult and you will be more likely to tire easily.
5. Keep the core steady and feel the work at the lower back and gluteus. The abdominals can be engaged to offer stability at the core. Do not over-tighten the core muscles, as this will restrict both your breathing and the natural flow of the movement.
6. Focus at a point on your mat at center to maintain alignment in the head, neck, and shoulders.
7. Repeat eight times on the left/right up to three sets of eight.

21. PRACTICE: Get back in the swing

"For we need to remind ourselves of this very basic and very modest fact that we are essentially rhythmic creatures, and that life needs this rhythm and balance if it is to be consistently good and not drain from us the precious possibility of being or becoming our whole selves."

—Esther de Waal

"The Lord is with me, I am not afraid."

—Psalm 118:6

Intention: I still love to swing. I mean the kind of swing in the playground. Swinging is a good feeling that can awaken a sense of inner rhythm. In the movement and flow, we recognize the balance of effort and relaxation. We expend effort to get the swing moving and sustain the lift and then experience relaxation as we fall back to gravity. Once we get going and take advantage of the momentum, it hardly feels like work even though there are equal amounts of work and rest. When there is work to be done, get back in the swing, knowing that the movement between work and rest establishes a rhythm that can bring joy and a sense of ease to all you do.

On the mat: Continue to make time for your daily exercise. Be mindful that you allow a space for rest and relaxation also. The freedom to move from work to rest is what establishes a rhythm and flow to life. Notice in every exercise the movement of the breath. Each inhalation has the power to lift and energize, and every exhalation is the opening to let go of unneeded tension or tightness and relax. Feel the muscles contracting. Also notice the softening and relaxing. A sit-up is not all work. It is half work, half rest, contraction and relaxation. If you see it as all work, it will be much more difficult to endure.

Off the mat: All work and no rest can be maddening. Think about the beautiful harmonies in music. The beauty of the sound comes with the silence or rest between the notes. If there was constant sound, it would be irritating noise rather than beautiful music. Get back in the swing of things. A rocking chair is another option to feel rhythm. Remember the feeling of the swing. Better yet, take a walk, find a playground, and get back in the swing. The work will not feel so hard, and any fears of not getting it all done will fade away as you find in balance, increased energy, productivity, and creativity.

Exercise 21: Iliopsoas extension/flexion

Iliopsoas extension/swing

1. Table top position. Bring elbows to the mat directly under the shoulders.
2. In a swinging motion, extend the right leg back and upward. Maintain the alignment of the hips to the shoulders and keep the knee and foot pointed downward to the floor.
3. As you lift and extend the right leg, keep the leg long and engaged. Feel the lower back and gluteus contract as you lift and extend the leg up and behind you.
4. The core muscles are your root and stability. Keep the back stationary as you extend the leg.
5. Bring the leg back down to the level of the hips, and in a continuous motion, contract the abdominals and draw the right knee in toward the chest as you relax the upper body, round the back, and lower the head.
6. Repeat this swinging motion on the right side eight times. Inhale as you extend and exhale as you draw the knee in toward the chest. Let the motion be smooth, and control the movement through the full range of motion.
7. Repeat eight times on the other side.

Iliopsoas extension: Four-count variation

Iliopsoas extension/4 count

1. Tabletop position. Come down to your elbows, and position them under your shoulders.
2. We are going to take the same exercise and separate the movement into four parts.
3. Extend the right leg to hip level.
4. Lift the right leg up and behind you, keeping the leg engaged and long.
5. Bring the right leg back to hip level.
6. Pull the right knee toward the chest.
7. Remember the four counts with the words: "extend, lift, down, and in."
8. Keep your weight equally distributed right to left and front to back. Notice the pull along the front side of the body with the extensions as the muscles of the abdomen lengthen. Note the corresponding contraction of the muscles at the back side of the body.
9. Keep your attention focused, and maintain four distinct movements. Keep some weight back into the legs and hips to prevent undue strain on the upper body.

22. PRACTICE: Be good to you

"Things which matter most must never be at the mercy of things which matter least."
—Johann Wolfgang van Goethe

"A man cannot be comfortable without his own approval."

—Mark Twain

"We are the temple of the Living God."

—2 Corinthians

"Glorify God in your body."

—1 Corinthians

Intention: Some time away from your busy routine each day to exercise is a way to be good to you. Taking care of your mind-body is not selfish or foolish. It is just the opposite. It is life-giving and prudent. It enables you to give the most of yourself as you share all you are with others. Our ability to give of ourselves is what makes life most beautiful and fulfilling.

On the mat: Your daily exercises become the means for you to experience the seven gifts—vitality, balance, strength, endurance, flexibility, focused attention, and coordination—as you remember your true nature. In your practice, bring the mind consciously into union with the body by choosing the thoughts that awaken and build these and other positive qualities within you. Remember what is most important.

Off the mat: The ways we choose to move in life reflect how we think and feel about ourselves. Begin to move like you know and feel God's presence within. Give yourself a chance to experience in each and every day the gifts of God's goodness. When you come to know and feel the Good Within you, you will begin to see it in others and in all things. Make a list of all the activities you enjoy. Give yourself the time to partake in the activities that awaken the life energy within you. Keep your list in sight, and be willing to be good to you.

Exercise 22: Pelvic lift

Pelvic lift/contraction

Pelvic lift/relaxation

1. Lie on your back and center the body over the midline. Draw the feet in so you can touch your fingertips to your heels. This touch maintains a connection between the upper and lower body and will help you stay aligned to center throughout the exercise. If you cannot touch your heels, reach the fingertips evenly toward the heels.

2. Breath in, and as you exhale, press both feet to the floor as you lift the hips upward. Keep the heels pressed to the mat; contract the muscles of the gluteus, abdomen, and the pelvic floor as you lift. The upper body is relaxed, allowing the weight of the lift to be rooted in both feet and both shoulders, balanced over center.

3. Keep the back long and lift the hips as high as possible while maintaining alignment and control. Feel the work, but do not strain.

4. Inhale, release the muscles, and lower the hips to a position just off the floor. Notice the flow of movement from contraction to relaxation as you repeat the lift and then the release. Exhale with every lift.

5. Repeat eight times up to three sets of eight.

23. PRACTICE: Be good to others

"It is one of the most beautiful compensations of this life that no man can sincerely try to help another without helping himself."

—Ralph Waldo Emerson

"For the whole law is fulfilled in one statement, namely, you shall love your neighbor as yourself."

—Galatians 5:14

"Do unto others whatever you would have them do to you."

—Matthew 7:12

"Blessed are the merciful, for they will be shown mercy."

—Matthew 5:7

Intention: Being good to others follows naturally from being good to self. When you recognize and know the feeling of goodness within, you can more easily extend that goodness to others. Honor all that is good within yourself and others. This goodness is sometimes described as light. The light and love within us does not always shine through in ways that we expect or desire. It is not always seen on the surface, but it is always there—ever-present. See the good and then be good to others.

On the mat: Honor all those who practice with you. This includes those who have gone before you, those who stand beside you, and those who will follow you. It includes those who are both able and unable. It includes those who are known and unknown. It includes all.

Off the mat: Consider today how you might give of yourself by being good to others. Involve yourself in a team, group, or community with the intention of becoming a part of the force for good in the world. Make a contribution, and make a difference in this world. Church is a good place to start. Become a vital part of the infinite good that is God.

Exercise 23: Sit-ups

Sit-ups/center

1. Lie on your back centered over the midline. Bring the knees up and align the feet to center on the mat.

2. Engage the abdominal muscles by drawing the belly button toward the spine. Feel the press of the lower back to the floor.

3. Keep the lower back grounded, touching the floor throughout the lifts. The touch of the lower back to the floor is your root and foundation for the sit-ups. The core remains steady. Eyes are focused on the ceiling to maintain alignment through the head, neck, and shoulders.

4. Lift the shoulders slightly off the mat, and feel your lower back pressed against the floor.

5. Exhale as you lift the upper body toward the ceiling (your focus point) in a smooth motion. Notice the contraction of the abdominal muscles that provide the strength for this lift.

6. Do not worry about how high you can lift the upper body off the floor. First things first; focus your attention on the contraction of the abdominals and the press of your lower back to the mat. As you strengthen and deepen the contraction of the core muscles, the height will follow.

7. Exhale with every lift to synchronize the contraction of the core muscles that are the cause of both the lift and the exhalation. Working the muscles so they contract simultaneously will give you greater power.

8. Repeat eight times for up to three sets. You can vary the speed of the lifts. When you add speed, maintain alignment and control. Smooth and steady lifts will give the best results and prevent injury.

Oblique sit-ups

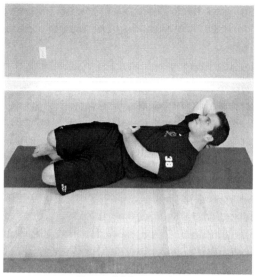
Sit-ups/oblique right

1. Lie on your back centered over the midline. Bring the knees up and the heels and toes to touch at center on the floor.
2. Maintain alignment of the hips and shoulders as you drop both knees left. Stack the knees and stack the feet one on top of the other.
3. Keep the right hip open to the ceiling, and feel the tension or pull on the right oblique muscle at the level of the belly on the right side, just above the hip bone.
4. Bring the left hand across the body, and place the hand on the right oblique muscle. Contract the abdominal muscles and feel the muscle tighten under your hand. The hand is literally the contact point, keeping you in touch with the strength at your core. This is the root of the lift and the origin of the movement. Lift with this muscle, and feel the muscle contract under your hand with every lift.
5. Exhale with every lift. Eyes remain focused on the ceiling. Maintain the alignment of the hips to the shoulders, taking the shoulders straight up toward the ceiling.
6. There is NO twisting motion.
7. Repeat eight times for up to 3 sets.
8. Repeat on the other side.

24. PRACTICE: Need less

"When you realize there is nothing lacking, the whole world belongs to you."

—Lao Tzu

"God is able to provide you with every blessing in abundance."

—Saint Paul

"The whole thing boils down to giving ourselves in prayer a chance to realize that we have what we seek. We don't have to rush after it. It was there all the time, and if we give it time, it will make itself known to us."

—Thomas Merton

Intention: When you begin to recognize yourself as part of a larger whole, when you realize your true nature and your oneness with the infinite source of all love and goodness, you will need less. We need less from the outer world because the inner world has been discovered, and we remember what it feels like to lead a balanced life.

On the mat: Need less and accept things just as they are in the present moment. Come to the practice with an open mind and open heart. Try not to demand that external circumstances be aligned to your desires in order to find joy and fulfillment in the exercises. There will be days when you will feel challenged by the working conditions. Need less from the outer world and you will be more able to find the inner strength to respond to the challenge with greater ease.

Off the mat: Observe and reflect on what you perceive to be your needs and desires. What do you need? Do you need others to behave in certain ways to feel centered yourself? Do you have cravings and wants that cause you to act in ways that you sometimes regret? These feelings are not to be denied or ignored but understood. A healthy ego is an essential part of who we are as human beings. We are looking for ways to experience the balance between our human needs and desires and the perfect will of God. Make room in your life for God and you may find that you need less.

Exercise 24: Leg pump

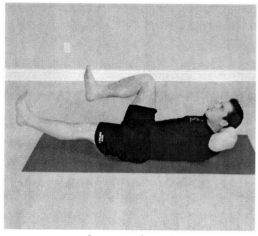

Leg pump/center

1. Lie on your back aligned to center. Lift the feet off the floor and stack the knees over the hips. The ankles are positioned in alignment to the knees with the lower leg parallel to the floor.

2. Engage the abdominal muscles and feel the lower back pressed to the floor. Lift the upper body slightly off the floor.

3. Flex the feet by drawing the toes toward the body. Extend one leg at a time with a driving motion through the heel. Alternate the leg extensions in a pumping motion similar to riding a bicycle. Leave a slight bend in the knee as you extend the leg.

4. Keep the eyes focused on the ceiling to maintain alignment of the head, neck, and shoulders. Pain or tightness in the upper body is a signal that the upper body is tense. The upper body stays aligned to center, engaged but not rigid or tense. The focus of the work is at the abdominal and lower back muscles at the core. Bring the shoulders to rest on the floor if you notice tension in the neck or shoulders.

5. The core stays steady, grounded, and centered. Feel the touch of the lower back to the floor throughout the exercise. The pumping motion is smooth and controlled.

6. Exhale with every pump to keep the breath flowing to maintain adequate oxygenation of the working muscles.

7. Repeat eight times up to three sets of eight.

Leg pump/oblique

Leg pump/oblique

1. The oblique muscles on either side of the abdomen are stabilizers for the core and can be strengthened by repeating the above exercise and adding movement of the upper body.

2. In addition to pumping the legs as above, draw the opposite elbow toward the knee, alternating right to left in unison with the leg pump. Keep the lower back pressed to the floor by engaging the abdominal muscles. Keep the eyes focused on the ceiling to maintain alignment of the head, neck, and shoulders.

3. Add variety and challenge by increasing or decreasing the speed, intensity, and number of repetitions. Be sure when you add speed you maintain control and alignment.

4. Repeat eight times up to three sets of eight. Take a breather as needed. Tension in the lower back can indicate fatigue in the abdominals. Take a break and let the muscles recover before repeating another set.

25. PRACTICE: Let it be enough

"We cannot be what we are not. We can only become the whole of what we are, and learn to accept it and learn to enjoy being it."

—Joan Chittister

"Peace I leave with you; my peace I give to you. Not as the world gives do I give it to you. Do not let your hearts be troubled or afraid."

—John 14:27

"But he said to me, 'My grace is sufficient for you, for power is made perfect in weakness.'"

—2 Corinthians 12:9

Intention: In the work we do, we often try to better ourselves in some way—bigger, better, stronger. We may look for evidence or proof of our improvements. This is all good. There are times, however, when the demonstration is lacking and we perceive failure. When the mind-body does not always demonstrate as you would like, in these times, let it be enough. In this moment, let it be as it is. Want nothing more than what is.

On the mat: When we experience a pose that we cannot hold or control, we may feel disappointment, frustration, and even anger. We cannot always control the body as we would like, but we can learn to choose our response. When you want or expect strength and you experience weakness, let it be enough. Choose to respond by accepting what is and embody peace. This puts us in touch with our inner strength, which is not always visible to the eye.

Off the mat: Remember how able you are in many ways. When you feel unable at times or do not get everything done, remember to let it be enough. John Wooden, the most successful college basketball coach in history, told his players, *"Do not let what you cannot do interfere with what you can do."*

Exercise 25: Sun salutation

Sun salutation is an awakening series of eleven postures done in sequence with the flow of the breath. This series touches every muscle and bone in the body to awaken the life energy.

Up dog

1. Mountain pose in prayer position
2. Breathe in as you begin to extend the arms upward into backbend. Feel your feet on the floor as your root, move through center, and engage the abdominals for stability and strength. Open the heart center as you reach the arms back behind you. Follow the movement of the hands with the eyes.
3. Exhale to forward bend. Keep the legs straight; honor the resistance you feel in the lower back and back of the legs. Work to a level that you feel the pull but never to the point of strain or pain.
4. Breathe in to lunge by drawing the right leg back and root the right foot on the mat with the right leg fully extended. The ball of the right foot is grounded; the heel is off the mat. The left knee is over the ankle. The back is long, the core is engaged, and the heart center is lifted and open.
5. Exhale to plank position by releasing the left foot and bringing it into alignment with the right foot. Level the body, parallel to the floor. The hands are directly under the shoulders.
6. Continue the exhale to lower plank as you lower the body to the floor and release your weight to the mat. Soften the feet behind you.
7. Breathe in to up dog, lifting the upper body, lengthening the spine, and lifting into the heart center. The chin stays level, and the hips will come off the mat.

Down dog

8. Exhale to down dog by bringing your feet to the mat, jumping in several inches, and drawing the legs long, pulling the heels toward the mat. Stay rooted in both hands; draw the upper body toward the legs, looking at your knees.

9. Breathe in and draw the left foot forward back into lunge position.

10. Exhale to forward bend with the feet aligned to center.

11. Breathe in to backbend.

12. Exhale as you return to prayer position.

13. Repeat on the other side.

14. Modify this series for an easier variation by following this sequence: backbend, forward bend, half lunge right leg, return to standing position, half lunge left leg, return to standing position, backbend to forward bend, return to prayer position.

26. PRACTICE: Meet the challenge

"Believe in yourself. You gain strength, courage and confidence by every experience in which to stop to look fear in the face . . . you must do that which you think you cannot do."

—Eleanor Roosevelt

"Out of clutter, find simplicity. In discord, find harmony. In the middle of difficulty, lies opportunity."

—Albert Einstein

"We are afflicted in every way, but not constrained; perplexed, but not driven to despair; persecuted, but not abandoned; struck down, but not destroyed, always carrying about in our body the dying of Jesus, so that the life of Jesus may be manifested in our mortal flesh."

—2 Corinthians 4:8

Intention: We all face challenges daily, big and small. The challenges we face are not meant to tear us down and destroy us but to build us up, to revitalize and restore us. Meet the challenge. It is for you, not against you. Face fear to know courage. Embrace your weakness to gain strength. Encounter change, even chaos to find a new order.

On the mat: Meet each challenge in the present moment. Breathe in, and as you breathe out, begin with, "I am willing and able." This mindset allows you to take the first step to move yourself in ways that allow you to meet the challenge. As you move forward, you gain the knowledge, skills, and experience to overcome the challenges before you.

Off the mat: Take a good look at the challenge before you. Ask yourself, "How do I want to respond?" Set a plan of action, and write it down in easy-to-implement action steps. Move now; take the first step to overcoming this challenge. Remember, "I am willing and able."

Exercise 26: Side warrior/lateral angle/exalted warrior

Lateral angle

Exalted warrior

1. Straddle the legs, aligned to center. The heels are aligned to each other.
2. Turn the right foot in by forty-five degrees; turn the left foot out at ninety degrees.
3. Breathe in as you draw the arms to shoulder height.
4. Exhale, bend the left knee, and stack the knee over the ankle, aligned top to bottom and front to back.
5. Look through the left hand for your focus point. Notice the flow of the breath. Feel strong, stable, and focused. **Remember to hold the yoga postures for thirty to forty seconds. (Side warrior.)**
6. Breathe in and bring the left hand to touch the left thigh. Do not lean on the left leg. Let your core do the work to support the upper body.
7. Exhale and draw the right arm overhead, reaching as you create a straight line from the outer foot to your fingertips. Keep the right shoulder open and aligned to the hips. Hold for thirty seconds. (**Lateral angle.**)
8. Breathe in, and as you exhale, come back to side warrior position.
9. Release the right arm, and let the right hand come to touch the space behind the right knee. Draw your attention to this back leg.
10. Turn the hips and shoulders aligned now to the left leg. Breathe in and reach the left arm up and overhead.
11. Exhale as you pull into the backbend, reaching the left arm up and behind you, the palm facing the ceiling. The heart center is lifted toward the ceiling, and your weight is shifted primarily to the back leg. Both legs are extended straight. Feel both your feet for your grounding points.
12. Contract the abdominals for stability and strength.
13. Open the heart center in the beautiful backbend. **Hold for thirty to forty seconds. (Exalted warrior.)**
14. Repeat on the other side.

27. PRACTICE: Observe and reflect

"The Word of God who is God wills in all things and at all times to work the mystery of His embodiment."

—Maximus the Confessor

"God's gaze is fixed on us, our thoughts and actions lie totally open to his view, we are always seen, everywhere in God's sight."

—Saint Benedict

Intention: Take a moment to observe and reflect on the training in mind-body on a personal level. You might ask yourself, "In what ways, seen and unseen, has the work of Mind-Body Training had an impact on my life?" Some of the effects may seem small. Others may feel more significant or maybe you have not really noticed at all. Write down your observations and reflect on your responses.

On the mat: As you exercise today, observe and reflect on your practice. Consider the time and attention you devote to the work and reflect on what you are receiving in return. With this information, consider if you want to make any changes. Am I doing what I want to do? Am I being who I want to be? Remember that all the work you do is for the good, great or small. Let it be good. Let it be what is needed to move you forward. The mind-body can reveal many truths when we take the time to notice.

Off the mat: Examine your daily habits and look at where you choose to put your time and attention. Reflect on the results of these choices. Let your observations and reflections shed light on all the positive possibilities within you and all around you. Think about how you would like to move forward from this point. Honor all that you have done; be present to the possibilities that exist in each moment. Remember that you have a bright future with much potential.

Exercise 27: Tree pose

In tree pose we purposefully challenge or stress the mind-body by creating an imbalance as we support our weight on one leg. The key is to allow the mind-body to move in ways that restore equilibrium and balance rather than trying to hold the body still in the pose. Balance is a fluid state, and there will always be movement. Allow this movement rather than resisting it and you will come to feel center.

Prayer position

Tree pose

1. Mountain pose.
2. Shift your weight to your left foot and leg. Let the left foot stay soft rather than creating tension by trying to grip the floor with your foot. Lift the right heel, and feel the shift of weight to the left leg.
3. Engage the abdominals, lift into the heart center, and focus your attention. When you feel ready, lift the right leg and plant the right foot on the left leg. You can work at whatever level suits you, placing the foot on the ankle, the shin, or on the inside and toward the front of the upper thigh. Avoid the knee.
4. Turn the right knee outward.
5. Feel your left foot relaxed as your root, notice alignment to center, engage the abdominals, and bring the hands to prayer position. Lift into the heart center and find your focus point at center.
6. Going further, reach the arms overhead fully extended, palms drawn together at center. The arms should be touched against the head just behind the ears. Reach high enough to feel the draw from your belly and back, establishing depth into your core for stability and strength. If you feel discomfort or pain in the neck or shoulders, check your alignment and make any necessary adjustments. If the discomfort persists, bring the hands to prayer position and hold here.
7. Repeat on the other side.
8. Remember, balance is experienced as a state of mind-body. When the body is in motion seemingly unbalanced, you have the power to give meaning to that movement. You can choose to see the movement as an essential part of the action needed to restore balance. Focus your attention on all that is good within—feel your feet grounded, notice your sense of center, engage the core for strength, open the heart, and feel the flow of the breath. What is seen on the surface is a small fraction of all that is. Keep your eyes open. You need the information from the world around you. Remember, within you is the power to give meaning to your experience. Balance is achieved in realizing your position in relationship to self and environment. It helps you know where you stand and to feel that you belong.

28. PRACTICE: Write

"The act of writing is a step beyond thinking, stimulating a movement within you that draws forth awareness and inner strength."

—Julia Cameron

"Your thoughts are the words on the pages of the book that is your life."

—Anonymous

Intention: Each time we sit to write, we are training the mind-body to work together to bring our thoughts and ideas into being. Our thoughts "matter" as they become the written word on the paper. Writing is a form of self-expression. We literally put ourselves out there when we write. We begin a flow of energy from within to the outer world, a movement that some call grace or inspiration. Research at the Mind-Body Medical Institute in Boston, Massachusetts, has shown that individuals who practice journaling experience a marked improvement in psychological and physical well-being. Writing also improves your communication skills.

On the mat: Your thoughts become etched in mind-body through movement and experience. Your thoughts give meaning to the experience. Be mindful of your thoughts as you practice on the mat. What do you have to say about yourself and others? Are your thoughts aligned with the highest good you can imagine? Remember that although your thoughts can reflect your state of mind-body, you are not your thoughts. You are the thinker.

"Writing is a physical as well as psychological act. Many of our most marvelous writers have been great walkers. There is something about the rhythm of the walk. There is a musicality in motion that spills onto the page."

—Julia Cameron

Off the mat: Let go of the thoughts that prevent you from expressing yourself and *write*. Try a few of these suggestions to get your thoughts flowing and have fun writing.

- Write a letter to a friend or family member. Stay in touch.
- Write short notes to your children and put it on their pillows or in their lunch boxes.
- Write the words peace, love, or joy in the snow.
- Begin a journal. Write every day if you can. No rules—allow your thoughts to flow.
- Write down a to-do list. Check things off as you get them done.
- Write down your goals, both short and long-term. Keep them where you can see them.

Exercise 28: Triangle/half moon pose

Triangle

Half moon pose

1. Straddle position with the feet aligned.
2. Turn the right foot in forty-five degrees; turn the left foot out ninety degrees.
3. Breathe in, and lift the arms extended to shoulder height.
4. Exhale as you extend the upper body out over the left leg until you feel the pull at the inner thigh. Turn the palms to face forward.
5. Maintain alignment of the arms to the shoulders and bring the left hand toward the floor with the arm resting inside the left leg in front of the knee. The upper body is drawn down parallel to the floor, aligned to the hips. The legs, back, and arms stay long. Reach the crown of the head out over the extended leg. Touch the fingertips to the floor, if possible, but do not put weight into the fingertips or hand. If you cannot reach the floor, let the hand touch on the leg at the level that you feel resistance but not discomfort or pain. Reach the right arm to the ceiling, keeping the heart center open. Turn the head and focus on a point through your fingertips on the ceiling. Hold for thirty seconds. (**Triangle.**)
6. Bend the left knee and stack the knee over the ankle. Bring the left hand to the mat about twelve inches away from and behind the foot at a forty-five-degree angle to the foot.
7. Lengthen the left leg as you lift and extend the right leg from the hip. The right arm is reaching to the ceiling. The right leg remains fully extended, aligned to the hip, parallel to the floor.
8. Turn your gaze upward and find a focus point on the ceiling as you look through the fingertips.
9. If this feels awkward, you can look straight forward or to a point on the floor. Hold for thirty seconds. (**Half moon.**)
10. Repeat triangle and half moon posture on the other side.

29. PRACTICE: Allow a space

"Be still and know that I am God."

—Psalm 46:10

"Only those who have experienced the solitude and silence of the wilderness can know what benefit and divine joy they bring."

—Saint Bruno

"Unless I am silent I shall not hear God, and until I hear him I shall not come to know him. Silence asks me to watch and wait and listen, to be like Mary in readiness to receive the Word. If I have any respect for God I shall try to find a time, however short, for silence."

—Saint Benedict

Intention: As I was preparing to write today I found myself searching for something to say. It occurred to me that it's not necessary or desirable to fill every moment with "some thing." It can be pleasing and rewarding to allow a space for "no thing." Allow a space without thoughts, words, and actions. Breathe and be fully present. Appreciate all that the moment holds in the peace and quiet of stillness, of nothing. Listen, observe, and recognize that a good part of who we are is not seen, is not measurable, is not a thing, but exists within us in the empty space. Allow a space and you may find in that space—peace.

On the mat: Let the body be the space, and invite the mind to come wholly into the space of the body for your practice. Allow a space free of unnecessary clutter and distractions. Practice in a space without music, television, books, and props. Give your full attention to the work.

Off the mat: Allow a space in your day for nothing. Go without things for some length of time. Sit in quiet prayer or meditation. This time of allowing a space is not idle or wasted time. On the contrary, it will lift and energize you. It will bring balance and strength. It will teach endurance and put you at ease. Allow a space and let God into your life.

Exercise 29: Standing forward bend (Tabletop back)

Forward bend (Tabletop back)

Forward bend

1. Straddle position with the feet aligned to center.

2. Breathe in and draw the arms overhead. Exhale as you fold at the hips, drawing the upper body forward. Feel the push of your feet to the floor.

3. Keep the legs long. The knees are drawn back, the back is long. and the arms are fully extended.

4. Bring the shoulders in alignment to the hips with the back parallel to the floor. The head is lifted with your focus forward. **(Tabletop back.)**

5. Breathe in, lengthen the spine, and lead with the heart center as you deepen into the forward bend, drawing the upper body toward the mat. Let the hands come to the floor if you are able to reach. If the tension is too great at the back of the legs or lower back, let the hands rest on the legs at whatever level you feel able.

6. Honor the resistance you feel at the lower back, hips, and down the length of the back of your legs by working in the pose at a level where you can feel the pull but not to the point of discomfort or pain.

7. Keep your attention in the space of the body where you feel the tension. The space of resistance is also the space of opening and release. Work with the tension to feel its gentle release with each exhale.

8. Let yourself ease into the pose, feeling the release of unneeded tension rather than allowing the tension to build as you hold in the posture.

9. Breathe easy. Without straining to deepen physically into the posture, notice the feeling of being more at ease just where you are. Let go of tension where it is not needed with every exhalation. Let the face soften and the fingers and toes relax, and feel the weight of your body. If you begin in the posture with a certain level of tension and thirty seconds later, in the same posture, you feel less tension and greater ease, you have gained flexibility. Congratulations!

30. PRACTICE: The power of one

"If a man is called to be a street sweeper, he should sweep streets as Michelangelo painted, or Beethoven composed music, or Shakespeare wrote poetry. He should sweep streets so well that all the hosts of heaven and earth will pause to say, here lived a great street sweeper who did his job well."

—Martin Luther King Jr.

"So that they may all be one, as you, Father, are in me and I am in you."

—John 17:21

"I sought the Lord, who answered me, delivered me from all my fears. Look to God that you may be radiant with joy and your faces may not blush for shame."

—Psalm 34:5

Intention: Our last session we practiced allowing a space for nothing. Spending time in this space of peace and quiet can be enjoyable and fruitful. We realize, however, that we live in a world filled with many things and we want to be able to enjoy this world and see all the good that it has to offer. At times it can feel like there is so much out there to manage that we cannot keep up with it all. When you are feeling overwhelmed by the many things, practice the power of one. Choose one thing and focus your attention and energy. All things are connected. Completing one thing impacts the whole and allows you to move forward one step at a time.

On the mat: The power of one begins in the space of "no thing." Let go of the long list of things to do, and bring your attention to the flow of the breath in the body. Let the mind come wholly into the space of the body and be present. Bring your awareness now to one thing. Choose a focus point aligned to your center, and stay with this one point alone. If you are distracted, come back. Bringing your focus to one thing is very powerful. This power is so strong that it tends to pull everything else into place.

Off the mat: The power of one is simply giving your full attention to one thing at a time. Trying to do two, three, or four things at once splinters the attention and can leave you feeling torn. When you are cooking dinner or doing the dishes, give the task your full attention. Be willing to let go of everything else. Everything has its time and place. Listen to the child in your presence.

Exercise 30: Cross bar

Cross bar (flexion)

Cross bar (extension)

1. Center yourself in kneeling position on the mat.
2. Extend the right leg, aligned to the hip with the bottom of the heel on the floor. The toes are pointed up aligned to the heel. Be mindful *not* to rest on the back of the heel to prevent undue stress on the Achilles tendon.
3. Breathe in as you raise the arms to shoulder height. Exhale, and bend at the trunk sideways over the leg in this powerful side stretch. Bring the right hand to rest on the right shin. Lift the left arm up and extend it overhead in line with the ears.
4. The body is curved in a beautiful, long arc. Turn the head to look through the extended arm.
5. Feel the flow of the breath deep into the belly as you deepen into the pose by letting the hand slide down the shin.
6. If the breathing feels restricted, lift out of the pose slightly until you notice the sensation of breathing easy. **(Cross bar posture/flexion.)**
7. Breathe in, engage the abdominals, and lift the trunk back to center position. In a flowing motion, bring the left arm to the mat directly under the shoulder. Reach the right arm over the head, extending the arm long and lengthening the body. **(Cross bar/extension.)**
8. Come back to center.
9. Repeat on the other side.

31. PRACTICE: Goodness in unexpected places

"Let everything that has breath give praise to the Lord."

—Psalm 150:6

"Do not forget all the gifts of God, who pardons all your sins, heals all your ills, delivers your life from the pit, surrounds you with love and compassion, fills your days with good things; your youth is renewed like the eagle's."

—Psalm 103:2

Intention: A friend handed me a sheet of paper and said, "I think you'll like this." I put it in my bag, and it was several days before I remembered that she had given it to me. When I pulled it out to read the message, it reminded me of two good friends of our family we sometimes fail to appreciate and understand fully. They have taught us a lot about unconditional love. Our two good friends are Chessa and Cody, our golden retrievers. Here are a few words about the animals that are man's best friend. They can help us remember to see goodness in unexpected places.

- Allow the experience of fresh air and the wind in your face to be pure ecstasy.
- When loved ones come home, always run to greet them.
- Practice obedience.
- Take naps and stretch before rising.
- Run, romp, and play daily.
- Enjoy every meal with enthusiasm.
- Be loyal and trustworthy.
- Never pretend to be something you are not.
- If what you want is buried, dig until you find it.
- When someone is having a bad day, be silent, sit close by, and nuzzle him or her gently.
- Thrive on attention, and let people touch you.
- Wait patiently.
- Keep your eyes on the prize.
- On hot days, drink lots of water and sit under a shady tree. Don't complain.
- When you are happy, dance around and wag your entire body.
- No matter how often you're scolded, don't buy into the guilt thing and pout—run right back and make friends.
- Stay close and bond with your pack.
- Delight in the simple joy of a long walk.
- Coming home is the best.
- Don't be afraid. You're not alone. You've got a friend.

On the mat: Appreciate the smallest things like being able to stand on two feet. Find pleasure and satisfaction in the poses that can be most challenging for you. Enjoy your practice. Let it lift and energize you. Find goodness in unexpected places.

Off the mat: See the good in all things. Having a dog for a pet is one way to practice. They are always present, and they want to be with you. They want to please you, and it makes them happy to know that they are your friend. Be kind and good to them. Learn about man's best friend. They are a touch of love. Learn about all God's creatures. To know more fully is to understand the truth and goodness of every being.

Exercise 31: Boat/extension

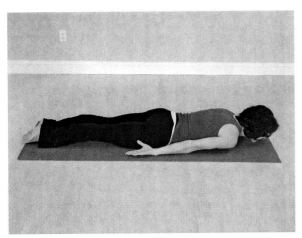

Boat /starting position

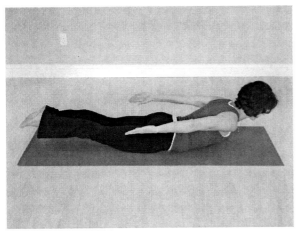

Boat/extension

1. Lie in prone position and center the body on the mat.

2. Bring your chin to the mat and rest your arms at your side with the palms up.

3. Draw the heels and toes to touch, engage the abdominal and gluteus muscles.

4. Breathe in as you simultaneously lift the upper and lower body off the floor, lengthening the body from the crown of your head to your toes.

5. As you hold, feel the muscles at the lower back and buttocks support the body in this powerful backbend, which strengthens the core and opens the heart.

6. Notice the strength and stability of the lower back by feeling the hips as your grounding point.

7. Focus forward at center, level the chin to a point where you feel no strain in the neck or shoulders.

8. Deepen into the pose by extending both arms out in front of you about six to twelve inches off the mat.

9. Bring the arms back to your sides if you feel any strain in the lower back.

10. Breathe in, feel the lift and length of the body, and exhale as you release your weight back to the mat.

32. PRACTICE: The dwelling place

"As we look not to what is seen but to what is unseen; for what is seen is transitory, but what is unseen is eternal."

2 Corinthians 4:18

"And now here is my secret, a very simple secret; it is only with the heart that one can see rightly, what is essential is invisible to the eye."

—Antoine de Saint-Exupery

"But we hold this treasure in earthen vessels that the surpassing power may be of God and not from us."

—2 Corinthians 4:7

"Only that day dawns to which we are awake."

—Henry David Thoreau

Intention: Remember that there is no amount of effort in mind or body that you can exert to bring you closer to God, for you are already there in God's presence, always. Our effort is to awaken to this presence by disciplining the mind to stay wholly present in the body. The body is the dwelling place, and God is there as both the space and substance of our being. God is a light within that is unseen to the eyes. We are called not to dwell *on* the body but to *dwell in* the body.

On the mat: Exercise is purposeful stress. As you move, dwell in the space within. Call on the body in ways that awaken the vital energy within you to complete the task at hand. Feel the heart rate increase as you sustain the movement. Know and feel that the heart is opening, and become more aware of your ability to endure. By dwelling in the body, we become more conscious of the gifts God has given. If we dwell **on** the body, we may be paying attention to how difficult the work feels, how much time we're spending, how hot or cold or thirsty we feel. We may be thinking of all that we have to do in the future. This is not necessarily putting your attention in the wrong place. It is an opportunity to discipline the mind to notice the difference and reside in the dwelling place of the body.

Off the mat: When you are under pressure or feeling stressed, you have your best chance to respond effectively when the mind is fully present in the body. Feel the breath moving within. Stay present by residing in the dwelling place of the body. You will be most able.

Exercise 32: Cat/cow

1. Tabletop position. The hands are directly under the shoulders and the knees under the hips. The back is in neutral position. The body is centered right to left, front to back, and top to bottom.

2. Exhale as you draw the belly button toward the spine, arching the back upward, and lower the head.

3. Breathe in, and draw the hips downward as you lift the shoulders and head, pulling the belly away from the spine.

4. Deepen and lengthen both the exhalation and the inhalation. Feel the depth of the breath as you draw deeper into the core muscles of the abdomen and lower back.

5. Repeat three times.

Cat

Cow

33. PRACTICE: Feel lifted

"Nothing great was ever achieved without enthusiasm."

—Ralph Waldo Emerson

"Only goodness and love pursue me all the days of my life; I will dwell in the house of the Lord for years to come."

—Psalm 23:6

Intention: Life has its ups and downs. This is part of the natural cycle and is to be expected. On occasion, when you feel down or out, let the feeling run its natural course. Let it ground you and remind you of your humanness. Dwell comfortably in the body, and soon you will feel lifted again. As sure as day follows night, if we allow ourselves to flow with life's natural cycles, we will feel lifted. We also have free will and the power to choose to live in ways that promote natural highs. When we feel low, there is an opportunity to make choices that awaken the life energy within and allow us to feel lifted. To meet life with this enthusiasm allows us to be productive and creative in our endeavors. The word *enthusiasm* is from the Latin word *enthousiazein,* which means to "be inspired by God." Be inspired, feel lifted, and do good works.

On the mat: Feel lifted in your practice by staying in touch with the breath. Let every breath remind you of the inner source of life energy that has the power to lift, energize, and inspire.

Off the mat: When you need a lift or natural high, try one of these suggestions:
1. Lighten the load. If you feel burdened and weighed down, it makes sense to lighten the load. Prioritize and let go of a few things that do not matter as much.
2. Keep moving. Movement is the key to life. Stay active in mind-body. Do not let what you cannot do interfere with what you can do.
3. Laugh. Laughter is the best medicine. Even a smile can increase levels of serotonin in the blood, promoting a natural high.
4. Practice deep-breathing exercises. Feel lifted and grounded. This is the balance of the breath.
5. Avoid alcohol. It is a depressant.
6. Choose wholesome, natural foods that are high in life energy.
7. Drink plenty of water and refresh a wilting body.
8. Come to your senses. Smell, touch, taste, hear, and see in ways that lift your spirits—favorite foods, music, photos, warm sunshine, and cool water.
9. Spend time in nature.

10. Find a furry friend to keep you company. Animals and pets can be there for us as an unconditional source of love. If you don't have a pet, look in nature, spend time with a friend's pet for the day. or look at pictures of animals online or in a book.
11. Write your thoughts and feelings in a journal.
12. Talk with someone.
13. Write a letter to a friend or family member.
14. Pray or meditate.
15. Remember—you are never alone.

Exercise 33: Child/up dog

Child

Up dog

1. Tabletop position.
2. Breathe in, and as you exhale, lower your hips toward the heels. Allow your hips to rest on the heels if possible. Let the top side of your feet lie on the floor, soft and relaxed.
3. Lengthen the spine, and allow the arms to extend out in front of you. Bring your forehead to the mat. If you cannot rest the forehead on the mat comfortably, rest on your elbows, aligned to your shoulders.
4. With the forehead on the mat and the upper body relaxed, release the arms and let them rest by your sides with the hands beside the feet, palms up. Breathe easily. *Child pose* is meant to be relaxing and restorative.
5. Breathe in as you lift the hips and draw the body forward, aligned to center. Lengthen your arms with the hands directly below the shoulders and shift your weight forward, letting the upper body be supported by the arms.
6. Exhale as you let the hips relax and move toward the mat. Lengthen the spine, and lift into the heart center. The hands are directly under the shoulders. (**Up dog.**)
7. For variety, rather than holding the two positions, move from child pose to up dog with the flow of the breath. Exhale to child and breathe in as you flow into up dog.
8. Repeat three times.

34. PRACTICE: The gift of vitality in the bones and blood

"Twas grace that taught my heart to fear, and grace my fears relieved; how precious did that grace appear the hour I first believed."

—John Newton, "Amazing Grace"

"Go into the whole world and proclaim the gospel to every creature."

—Mark 16:15

"He took away our infirmities and bore our diseases."

—Matthew 8:17

Intention: The seven remaining exercises will each focus on one aspect of the amazing gift of mind-body. Remember in your practice that the self can only be truly known in relationship, not in isolation. Consider the gift of self, and come to know the self more fully. In this way, you can know fulfillment in both giving and receiving this precious gift.

We begin with the root and foundation of the body in the bones and blood. The bones are the foundation in which the entire body rests. The blood is the river of life. The red blood cells that carry life-giving oxygen to all your tissues and organs are derived from the bone marrow deep within the bones.

Incredibly, a living bone is as strong as a steel rod but five times lighter. Bones provide the framework for the moving body, protect soft organs such as the brain, heart, and lungs, and supply red blood cells to carry oxygen. The blood not only delivers oxygen to tissues and organs, but it also carries away toxins, supplies nutrients, distributes heat to maintain body temperature, plays an important role in the immune system, and transports hormones that regulate and maintain all bodily functions.

There are 200 million red blood cells in a drop of blood and over 25 million, million (25,000,000,000,000) in your circulatory system. Red blood cells live only about one hundred days. About 100 million cells are made every minute of your life in the bone marrow. Blood travels to all parts of your mind-body through a network of blood vessels. The total length of this river within is about one hundred thousand miles. If were laid end to end, it could go around the world four times.

Amazing! How much of this do you have to control? The answer is none. The mind-body is truly a miracle. However, you do have the choice to do your part to take care of the mind-body that has been given to you. In mind, stay rooted. Be grounded in the present moment. This present moment awareness becomes the foundation for all growth.

On the mat: Recognize that the source of all life is within. The vital energy that supports, nourishes, and sustains us is the very substance of our being. Stay fully present, and feel the flow of the breath. Let every breath remind you of the inner source of vitality.

Off the mat: Learn more about the mind-body through both study and experience. Take a course in anatomy and physiology. Watch the Olympics and observe what the human body is capable of achieving. Look around you and observe the many miracles in everyday life.

Exercise 34: Pigeon series

Pigeon

Quadriceps stretch

1. Plank position.
2. Engage the abdominals, and draw the left knee forward toward the chest and hold in place, off the mat. Release the left foot to the mat, beneath the right thigh. Lower the hips to the mat, centered over the midline.
3. Breathe in and lengthen the spine. As you exhale, walk the hands out on the mat, lowering the upper body over center. Bring the head to rest on the mat and hold for ten to twenty seconds.
4. Engage the abdominals, and place the hands on either side of the body, aligned to the chest. Push off the floor and lift the upper body, bringing the shoulders back over the hips. Feel the work at the lower back to maintain the lift and alignment.
5. Breathe in and lift the arms to shoulder height. Feel the opening through the hips and heart center. Notice that the right and left hips stay aligned front to back and right to left. Hold for thirty to forty seconds. Release the arms to your sides. **(Pigeon.)**
6. Bend the right leg at the knee and reach back to take the right foot into your right hand. Gently draw the right foot toward the hip. Feel the stretch in the quadriceps muscle on the front side of the upper leg. Breathe. Notice the muscles softening with each exhale.
7. Breathe in and pull the right foot toward the hip. Exhale as you release the right foot.
8. Draw the left leg back and return to plank position.
9. Walk the hands back toward the feet and pull into down dog. Feel the length of the legs, back, and arms.
10. Walk the hands out again as you draw the body back into plank position.
11. Repeat pigeon and the quadriceps stretch on the other side.

35. PRACTICE: The gift of balance in the reproductive and excretory systems

"Then God said, 'Let us make man in our image, after our likeness' . . . God created man in his image and likeness; in the divine image he created them, male and female, he created them."

—Genesis 1:26

"Your children are not your children. They are the sons and daughters of Life's longing for itself. They come through you but not from you. And although they are with you yet they belong not to you."

—Kahlil Gibran

"As truly as God is our Father, so truly is God our Mother."

—Julian of Norwich

Intention: Through the reproductive system, we can experience the union of father and mother, male and female, to bring new love to life. God has designed a beautiful world in which opposites come together in a productive and creative union. From the moment of conception, forty-six chromosomes (twenty-three from the male and twenty-three from the female) with thirty thousand genes combine to determine all your physical characteristics. Even more amazingly, intelligence and personality were already in place within your genetic code. You were essentially and uniquely you; from a single cell to a tiny human being in forty weeks. Your heart started beating at eighteen days old when you were only 0.1 inches long. Your brain was functioning at forty days when you were .75 inches long. You could hear sounds in your mother's womb that an adult cannot hear. Your brain was more active during fetal development than any other time in your life.

In the excretory system, the kidneys and the lower intestine work to maintain the balance between the inner and outer worlds. The excretory system filters and excretes what is no longer needed while absorbing the nutrients and substances that maintain life. There is a balance between what is good for us to hold onto and what we need to let go. What we retain as goodness becomes fully integrated into our being. We let go of what is no longer needed. To hold onto what is no longer needed becomes toxic.

On the mat: Balance is achieved when you recognize and feel within you the union of two opposites. Find these opposites within you: right/left, front/back, top/bottom, tension/relaxation, up/down, strength/weakness, open/closed, long/short, movement/stillness, inner/outer. You may experience many others. The point is, you cannot know one without the other. In the balance postures, it is essential that you keep the eyes open to take in the information that allows you to see and feel your place in space and time. The body's center of gravity is through the space of the pelvis.

Off the mat: The experience of balance in mind-body is relational. In essence, it is being able to discern, "Where do I belong in this world?" Belonging implies the self in relationship to others and to the environment. Leading a balanced life requires that we are aware of the dual nature of our earthly existence and we feel able to make the choices that move us toward equilibrium. Consider how to balance work/rest, day/night, full/empty, giving/receiving, high/low, rich/poor, black/white, young/old, and male/female. There are many more to consider.

Exercise 35: Reclining pigeon/compression

Reclining pigeon/compression

Reclining pigeon

1. Lie on your back and bring the knees up with your heels and toes touching, centered on the mat.

2. Breathe in and draw the right knee in toward the upper body, aligned to the hip and shoulder. Use your hands positioned below the knee to compress the leg to the core. Breathe in deeply and feel your belly press up against the leg. As you exhale, notice the belly falling away from the leg.

3. Release the right leg and extend the leg straight, with the foot over the hip at a ninety-degree angle. Feel the length of the leg and the stretch of the muscles along the back side, the hamstrings.

4. Bend the right knee and feel the muscles in the leg relax. Place the right foot on the left thigh just below the knee. Turn the right knee outward away from the midline.

5. Engage the abdominals and press the lower back to the mat. Keep your shoulders and head relaxed on the mat and the chin level. Draw the left knee toward you and feel the resistance in the right hip.

6. Keep your attention in the space of resistance in the right hip. Gently work the edge where you feel the tension but can breathe easy. Notice the release of tension with each exhalation, and feel the muscles soften as the hip opens.

7. Deepen into the posture by adding resistance as you reach under and on either side of the leg, using the arms to draw the left knee in further. Maintain alignment to center; keep the hips and shoulders on the mat and the chin level.

8. Breathe in, pull the knee toward you, and as you exhale, feel the release and let go of the leg. Let the right foot touch the floor.

9. Repeat on the other side.

10. Remember the space of resistance is also the space of release. Keep your attention in the body in the space where you feel the resistance. You will be present to feel its release.

36. PRACTICE: The gift of strength in the digestive and endocrine systems

"Be brave and steadfast; have no fear or dread of them, for it is the Lord, your God, who marches with you; he will never fail you or forsake you."

—Deuteronomy 31:6

"For all our insight, obstinate habits do not disappear until replaced by other habits . . . no amount of confession and no amount of explaining can make the crooked plant grow straight; it must be trained upon the trellis by the gardener's art . . ."

—Carl Jung

"A man's stomach shall be satisfied from the fruit of his mouth, and from the produce of his lips shall he be filled."

—Proverbs 18:20

Intention: Strength in body is self-control and discipline in mind. We are strong when we are able to choose the thoughts, words, and actions that bring goodness to life. Through our digestive and endocrine systems, the food we choose to eat becomes us. On average a person eats fifty tons of food and drinks thirteen thousand gallons of liquid during a lifetime. If you eat more than the body needs, the excess gets stored as fat. Your body needs carbohydrates, fats, and proteins to function optimally. Vitamins and minerals are also essential.

Your digestive system is a tube about thirty-three feet long and is open at both ends. It digests, assimilates, and integrates the food you eat to sustain, nourish, heal, and provide energy for bodily functions and growth. Without a thought on your part, an apple becomes the cells in your heart, replaces worn-out red blood cells, provides the energy for cell growth, and keeps you moving.

The digestive system does more than digest food. We know that the brain-like tissue is found throughout the body. The same nerve cells that exist and process information in the brain also exist in our digestive system. A gut feeling is intelligence at the cellular level. Trust your gut instinct. It is more than a feeling.

The endocrine system is the self-regulating system of the mind-body. The hormones secreted by the endocrine glands control all bodily functions. Not only do these hormones regulate all internal processes, but they also help us adjust and adapt to the external environment. With increased awareness and understanding of the internal mechanisms of self-control, human beings can learn to work with the mind-body to accomplish amazing acts of self-control. A guru in India can meditate under an ice cold waterfall and maintain his internal body temperature at 98.6 degrees. A specially trained navy seal can remain under water without oxygen for extended periods of time. Patients with heart disease can learn to voluntarily reduce their blood pressure. Monks in Tibet are able to ingest poisonous substances and experience no harmful effects.

What does all this mean for you and me? It means that what we think and perceive with the mind is directly linked to our experiences and the feelings we have in the body. In other words, our thoughts and emotions affect our health and well-being. How we perceive ourselves and the world we live in plays a significant role in our health and happiness. If we think negative thoughts and feel stressed over extended periods of time, our bodies may manifest this stress as disease ("dis-ease"). The disease is not necessarily bad and can lead us to healing when we come to realize the truth of our being, when we know ourselves and others more fully. The disease is something for us to understand about ourselves and each other, rather than fear. Come to know yourself and others more fully.

"Nothing in life is to be feared. It is only to be understood."

—Madame Curie

On the mat: When you need to be strong, look to your core. Physical strength is located in the core muscles of the abdomen, lower back, and gluteus maximus. To activate and experience this strength, you must first feel grounded and centered. From that foundation, engage the muscles of the core to help you remember that you are strong. Let your movements originate from your core strength and stability. Avoid over-tightening of the muscles, as this will restrict breathing and limit mobility.

Off the mat: Exercise the mind and discipline the will by making choices that are aligned to the most loving, gracious and perfect will of God. In every thought, word, and action choose love.

"And so I understand that any man or woman who voluntarily chooses God in his lifetime for love, he may be sure that his is endlessly loved . . . That we are as certain in our hope to have the bliss of heaven whilst we are here as we shall be certain of it when we are there . . . and always, the more delight and joy that we accept from this certainty, with reverence and humility, the more pleasing it is to God."

—Julian of Norwich

Exercise 36: Seated twist

Seated twist/start

Seated twist

1. Sit in staff pose with both legs extended out in front of you. The back is long, the shoulders are over the hips, and the hips stay rooted on the mat. The body is aligned to center. Press your hands into the mat at the level of the hips, and feel the back lengthen. Draw the toes of both feet toward you. Feel the legs lengthen. In the twisting poses, it is important to get the back long, decompressing the spine so the vertebrae are free to move in the twist. Decompress and lengthen the spine before every twist. (Staff pose)

2. Bring the right foot over the left leg, and place it on the floor in line with the knee.

3. Bring the right hand behind the right hip and turn the fingers away from the hip with the hand placed flat on the mat close to the hip. Face forward, and feel your body centered over the midline.

4. Extend the left arm and place the elbow on the outside of the right knee.

5. Breathe in, lengthen the spine, and twist the upper body from the base of the spine, opening through the heart center and looking over your right shoulder.

6. Feel the resistance at the lower back and core. Breathe deeply into the belly in this invigorating and cleansing twist. **Remember to hold the poses for thirty to forty seconds.**

7. Breathe in, lengthen the spine, and exhale as you feel the muscles release. Let the upper body return to center position.

8. Repeat on the other side.

37. PRACTICE: The gift of endurance in the cardiovascular system

"Love is patient, love is kind . . . it does not rejoice over wrongdoing but rejoices with the truth. It bears all things, believes all things, hopes all things, endures all things. Love never fails."

—1 Corinthians 13:4

"All, everything that I understand, I understand only because I love."

—Leo Tolstoy

"He did not say you will not be troubled, you will not be belabored, you will not be disquieted; but he said: you will not be overcome. God wants us to pay attention to these words and always to be strong in faithful trust, in well-being and in woe, for he loves us and delights in us, and so he wishes us to love him and delight in him and trust greatly in him, and all will be well."

—Julian of Norwich

Intention: Our most precious gift is the heart. Your heart began to beat when you were eighteen days old in your mother's womb and you measured little more than a quarter inch in length. On average your heart will beat 2 ½ billion times and pump more than 352 million pints of blood in a lifetime.

During exercise, the heart rate increases to meet the increasing oxygen demand of working muscles, tissues, and organs. Normally, all the body's blood is pumped through the heart in one minute. During exercise or when stressed, the blood passes through the heart five times in every minute. Some muscles get twenty times the amount of blood during exercise than they normally receive while you are resting. Other parts of the body, like the digestive system, shut down to allow more oxygen-rich blood to be diverted to working muscles.

With exercise, the heart muscle is strengthened. As the heart becomes stronger, it literally opens. The chambers of the heart expand, creating a larger, more open space for blood to be received into, and with every pump of the heart muscle, more oxygen-rich blood is delivered to tissues and organs, including the brain. Heart disease occurs when the heart and blood vessels narrow or close. The arteries that feed the heart become clogged, thus obstructing the flow of life-giving blood to the heart. Without blood and the oxygen it carries, the heart muscle begins to die. The result is a heart attack.

Endurance is a gift of the heart. Endurance is the ability to go on, to persevere. No matter what circumstances we find ourselves in, we endure when we are able to love, to be patient, to feel compassion, and to forgive ourselves and others. We are able to endure when we remember that we are grounded and rest in an inner source of goodness and love that allows us to accept all that comes to us in faith and trust. As we learn to embrace life, we will find the strength, the will, and the discipline to choose love.

On the mat: Keep the heart center open. Let the breath fill and lift you. To practice endurance, we must move without ceasing. Aerobic exercise is the best way to open your heart on the physical level. The American Heart Association recommends thirty minutes a day for adults and sixty minutes for children. Walking is a great way to get started. Other aerobic exercises include running, bicycling, swimming, rowing, and aerobic dance. Get started. Remember the benefits of aerobic exercise are many and include:

- Increased energy and sense of well-being
- Decreased tension and anxiety
- Improved immune function
- Increased cardio-respiratory capacity and ability to do work
- Decreased body fat
- Increased muscle tone and strength
- Reduced heart rate and blood pressure
- Improved brain function

Off the mat: Try to reside in the space of open heart and feel the love of God's presence. When you are challenged, when you feel afraid, when you experience pain or sorrow, without God, without consciousness of His goodness and love within you, you are not fully present to your true nature and therefore you act, not as yourself, but as someone who is alone. You are not aware that God is with you in your heart and soul. And so we do foolish things, and even worse, we hurt ourselves and others because we do not feel God's presence within ourselves nor see it in others.

God's Word, which is love, must be held close in our heart and repeated daily in thought, word, and action.

"Accept it and believe it and hold firmly to it and comfort yourself with it and trust in it, and you will not be overcome."

—Julian of Norwich

Exercise 37: Seated forward bend

Seated forward bend (bent leg)

1. Staff pose.

2. Bend the right knee, and bring the sole of the right foot to rest, touching the inner thigh. The left leg remains extended on the mat, with the body aligned to center.

3. Extend the arms in mountain pose, and as you breathe in, lift the arms up and overhead. Exhale as you fold the upper body over the left leg The back is kept long, drawing from the root at the base of the spine. The heart center is lifted as you draw the upper body into forward bend.

4. Honor the resistance you feel at the lower back and down the length of the leg, feeling the gentle lengthening of the hamstring muscles.

5. Deepen into the stretch on two levels—mind and body. In body, you may notice the upper body moving closer to the leg. Gently work the edge of resistance as you feel the tension easing with each exhalation. Keep the leg straight and the knee down. Release any tension that is not needed in the face, hands, arms, feet, toes, and belly.

6. In mind, you do not have to move the body to deepen. Simply notice the feeling of being more at ease just where you are.

7. If you begin the posture with a sense of tightness and in time, in that same position, you feel a greater sense of ease; you have become more flexible. Good work!

Note: If you have knee discomfort with the knee bent in forward bend, use the variation in which both legs remain extended in front of you. You can repeat the bend twice over center. Do not try to pull to the right or left if both legs are extended.

Seated forward bend (variation)

38. PRACTICE: The gift of flexibility in the muscle and respiratory systems

"Let everything that has breath praise you."

—Psalm 150:6

"And hope does not disappoint because God's love has been poured out into our hearts through the Holy Spirit that has been given to us."

—Romans 5:5

"The exercise of an extraordinary gift is the supremest pleasure in life."

—Mark Twain

"Health is aliveness, spontaneity, gracefulness and rhythm."

—Alexander Bowen MD

Intention: As we continue to learn more about ourselves both in mind and body, we begin to realize that to know oneself is to know the other. If we see only our differences, we may forget that we are essentially the same. We might believe we are separate and lose sight of the truth that we are indeed one. The gift of self is one for the other and for the good of all.

The muscles and respiratory system carry the gift of life in our movement as the breath moves in us. You can live for a few days without food or water, but without air to breathe, you will die in a few minutes. The oxygen in air sustains life. The lungs, working with the heart, have the amazing capacity to pull oxygen out of the air and into your blood. The blood then carries the oxygen to all parts of the body where it works with the nutrients, vitamins, and minerals to produce the energy that sustains all life processes, including growth. Carbon dioxide and water are the waste products of this energy production, and they are carried by the blood back to the lungs and breathed out with each exhalation.

A pair of lungs weighs about 2.2 pounds. Lungs do not have muscles. We breathe using the muscles at our core, including the intercostals (between the ribs) and the diaphragm. When the breathing muscles contract, the diaphragm moves down and the ribs move up and out so that the size of the chest cavity expands and the air rushes into the lungs. When the muscles relax, the chest cavity is compressed and the air is forced out. Breathing is a beautiful balance between contraction and relaxation.

In a day we breathe 2,200 gallons of air into the lungs. About ninety-four gallons of oxygen are removed and seventy-four gallons of carbon dioxide are exhaled. For a person working strenuously, these figures are doubled, and during vigorous exercise ten times the amount of air is breathed each minute.

The brain uses the same amount of oxygen whether we are thinking hard or just resting. Our muscles may need one hundred times more oxygen when exercising than when resting. The muscles that control breathing are involuntary and under control of the autonomic nervous system. The skeletal muscles are under our control. There are about 650 named muscles in the body. About six hundred of these are voluntary. When you walk you use at least two hundred different muscles.

On the mat: As you work, let the touch of the breath remind you that every in-breath has the power to lift and energize and each out-breath is an opening to let go of unneeded tension and tightness, allowing you to feel grounded and relaxed. Align your movements to the flow of the breath, and feel the beautiful balance in each breath. Each in-breath that you feel the lift of the breath in the body can help you remember the weightless, Spirit within. Every exhalation reminds you to let go and feel at ease with the weighted humanness of the body.

Off the mat: When you are faced with a challenge, take a deep breath in and remember that the Holy Spirit is with you. Trust greatly in the loving presence of God, and let go of worry and anxiety. Without God, it is easy to feel alone and afraid. With God, anything is possible. Don't worry. Be happy.

Exercise 38: Abdominal rock/half-shoulder stand

Abdominal rock

1. Begin in seated position with the knees up, feet aligned to center.
2. Grasp both legs above the ankles, and bring the feet just off the mat.
3. Engage the abdominals, round the back, tuck the chin, and pull the knees to the chest.
4. Breathe in as you rock backward over center, maintaining the tucked position. Exhale as you rock forward, returning to the starting position with the feet just off the mat. *Be sure the mat is clear behind you before you rock backward.*
5. Feel the back softening with the rocking motion as you release unneeded tension and tightness from the spine.
6. Repeat four times.
7. On the fifth rock backward, lift the hips off the mat and bring the legs over the head parallel to the floor. Maintain alignment and control. Notice the flow of the breath.
8. The arms can be extended on the mat aligned to the hips, or you can position the hands on either side of the spine at the level of the hips for support.
9. Maintain stability at the core, and straddle the legs outward, reaching the toes toward the floor behind you. Bring the legs back to center. Notice the flow of the breath. Maintain alignment and control. The core is rooted and stable. Repeat eight times.
10. Next, in a scissor motion, drop the right leg toward the mat behind you as you extend the left leg to the ceiling. Repeat eight times, alternating right to left. Keep the legs extended, and maintain alignment and control through the full range of motion.
11. Half-shoulder stand is an inverted position, which increases blood flow to the upper body and brain. *Avoid this pose if you are prone to high blood pressure, nasal problems, thyroid irregularities, or weak neck muscles and during menstruation.*
12. To modify, keep the hips on the floor and straddle the legs by bending at the knees and drawing the knees away from center and then back to center. The scissor motion is modified by keeping the hips down and bringing the knees into alignment over the hips. Keep the knees aligned to the hips, and extend the right lower leg to the ceiling. Alternate the right and left leg eight times.

Half-shoulder stand with
straddle

39. PRACTICE: The gift of focused attention in the central nervous system

"To my words be attentive, to my sayings incline your ear, let them not slip out of your sight, keep them within your heart; for they are life to those who find them, to man's whole being they are health."

—Proverbs 4:20

"Keep your tongue from evil, and your lips from speaking lies. Turn from evil and do good, seek peace and pursue it."

—Psalm 34:14

"The lamp of the body is the eye. If your eye is sound, your whole body will be filled with light. But if your eye is bad, your whole body will be in darkness, how great will the darkness be."

—Matthew 6:22

"Nothing happens unless first a dream."

—Carl Sandburg

Intention: All the systems of the body are brought together to function in harmony through the workings of the central nervous system (CNS). The CNS, which is comprised of the brain and spinal cord, reaches out to all parts of the body and is the command center. Massive networks of cable-like nerves relay messages between the body and the CNS. The CNS receives and delivers a constant stream of information about what is happening inside and outside the body from sensors. It also sends out instructions to muscles, organs, and glands.

We are born with 100 billion brain cells or neurons. It is not the number of neurons itself that determines our mental characteristics; it is how they are connected. Each cell reaches out to other cells to connect and form the neural network. It is in the mind-body that the knowing and feeling of "self" is generated. Exactly how this works is still largely a mystery. One researcher estimates that it would take some 32 million years to count the connections in the cerebral cortex alone.

Every time we learn, we reach out, so to speak, and build the neural network. What is even more amazing, as we have seen, is that our learning is not confined to the brain alone. Neurons exist in other parts of the body, and through our senses, we are able to literally stay in touch with our world, both within us and around us.

The potential in our being is best realized when all the systems are functioning as one. Just as the CNS brings all the bodily systems to work together, when we focus our attention we are most able to bring our whole self to the work.

On the mat: Choose a focus point that is at your center. Keeping the attention one-pointed requires discipline and strength. Notice when the attention wavers and gently call it back to your focus point. Keeping the attention focused will improve your stability and control in the exercises. In the balance postures, focus points that are lower to the ground and closer to you will give you a greater feeling of being grounded and stable than points higher and farther away. Try both and observe the mind-body in action.

Off the mat: Complete one task at a time, and give it your full attention. When you have many tasks to complete, make a list and set priorities. Put first things first. Do not let what is least important occupy the space and time of what is most important. If you feel uncertain about what is most important, pause, take a deep breath, and when you exhale, feel the body relax. Ask for guidance. Call yourself by name. "Joe, what is most important here and now?" Allow a space of still quiet and listen. The answer is within.

Exercise 39: Knee-down twist

Knee-down twist/knee-up

Knee-down twist

1. Center the body in supine position on the mat. Breathe in, and extend both arms overhead. Lengthen the body from your toes to your fingertips.

2. As you exhale, bring your arms in alignment to the shoulders, perpendicular to the body. Turn the palms toward the floor. Feel your body centered over the midline through the spine. Notice the upper body is relaxed and the shoulders are on the floor. Chin is level.

3. Breathe in, lift the leg, bending at the knee, and place the knee over the hip.

4. As you exhale, let the knee fall across the midline toward the mat.

5. Try not to push or pull into position but let gravity work for you. Feel the weight of the leg draw you deeper into this passive stretch. Notice the resistance in the right hip. Feel the muscle softening as the hip relaxes and opens with each exhale.

6. Breathe easy, and keep both shoulders on the mat. The heart center is open to the ceiling, and the eyes remain focused on the ceiling.

7. Breathe in, and bring the right knee back to center. Exhale as you release the right leg to the mat.

8. Repeat on the other side.

9. Notice the beauty of opposing forces working together in this stretch. The upper body is opening, and the lower body is closing. The resistance and the release are felt in the space of the hips where the two opposing forces meet or touch.

40. PRACTICE: The gift of coordination in the wholeness of self in the present moment

"The body is good: listen to what it tells you."

—Thomas Merton

"For everything, absolutely everything, above and below, visible and invisible . . . everything got started in him and finds its purpose in him."

—Colossians 1:16

"The eye cannot say to the hand, 'I do not need you,' any more than the hand can say to the feet, 'I do not need you.' And even those members of the body which seem less important are in fact indispensable."

—1 Corinthians 12:21

"The privilege of a lifetime is being who you are."

—Joseph Campbell

Intention: The mind-body is truly an amazing gift. We cannot fully comprehend all that is possible. What we know is the smallest fraction of all that comes together to create life. Knowledge alone is insufficient to understand the truth of our being. There is only one way to the truth, and that is through the body. We must come to our senses. Literally, the senses open the mind-body to experience the world around us and the world within us. The senses (hearing, sight, taste, touch, and smell) allow us to take in the world around us and through the mind give meaning to all that we receive. The senses are the opening and the means by which we can unite and balance the outer world with the inner world.

Hearing: We hear when sound waves are transmitted through the eardrum to the inner ear and then to the brain, we hear. The eardrum moves only 40 billionths of an inch for us to perceive sound. The inner ear also controls our sense of balance. Babies can hear their mother's heartbeat and other sounds while in the womb. From our time in the womb and throughout our life we associate sounds with experiences and give them meaning.

Sight: The pupil at the center of the eye opens in the dark to let in more light. The pupils can open wide not only at the sight of something beautiful but also when we see something that frightens us. In the dark, the eye becomes seventy-five thousand times more sensitive to light. The eyes do not "see." The eyes are the opening. They take in information, which is carried to the brain by the optic nerve. The brain interprets the information, and we "see." Blinking and tearing keep the eyes clean and moist. In a year you will have blinked about 8 million times, and blinking will have kept your eyes closed for over 170 hours. You produce about a cupful of tears in a year that prevent bacterial infections. Tears also excrete toxins from the body. Crying can be cleansing and helps the body to release tension.

Taste: There are four basic sensations of taste: sweet, sour, bitter, and salty. All flavors are a combination of these four. You have about three thousand taste buds in your mouth. You can detect a bitter taste in a dilution of one part in two million. We are not as sensitive to sweetness and can detect sweet in one part in two hundred.

Touch: The sense of touch includes all the sensations we feel with our skin: touch, pressure, pain, heat, and cold. Our skin is the interface between the outer world and the inner world. It is permeable, allowing substances to pass in and out of the body. Our skin is the largest organ of excretion and weighs about 6½ pounds. In twenty-four hours, a billion skin scales will fall from your body, carrying several hundred million bacteria.

In an experiment with touch, patients suffering severe pain were given tablets that contained only sugar and no pain-relieving medication. The patients were told that they were getting medicine, and one-third of them no longer experienced any pain, just as if they had been given the medication.

Smell: The olfactory organ inside your nose is responsible for your sense of smell. The molecules of the substances you smell enter the nose and have to dissolve in the mucus before they can be detected by tiny, hairlike projections called cilia. The olfactory nerve carries this information to the brain to be interpreted. We are able to smell the difference between more than ten thousand different odors. Babies seem to have an especially sensitive sense of smell and at six days old can smell the difference between milk from their mother and any other milk.

On the mat: Come to your senses and be fully present to the world around you and the world within you. Perceive God in all things. This awareness will improve your performance in the exercises. The work will lift and energize you. You will notice the energy and your ability to use it with focused attention throughout your day.

Off the mat: Faith changes everything. What you believe decides it all. Know God through the Word and sense God within you. Let the mind-body be the instrument of knowing and being in God. Come to your senses in faith. All that you perceive will lead you to God, who is love, when you believe. The neural network that is formed within you when you have faith is made to perceive God. We are made for God, and therefore we are made for love and happiness. Come to your senses and believe.

Exercise 40: Iliopsoas stretch, compression, and release

Iliopsoas stretch

Iliopsoas compression

1. Center yourself on the mat in supine position.

2. Bring the hands to prayer position at the heart center. Draw both knees up and place the feet on the floor with the heels and toes touching at center.

3. Breathe in as you simultaneously extend the arms overhead, keeping the palms touching, and lengthen the left leg. Both the arms and the leg are fully extended and approximately six inches off the mat. Point the toes.

4. Extend through the length of the body and feel the pull into the core muscles at the abdomen, groin, and lower back. Maintain alignment to center.

5. As you exhale, simultaneously draw the left leg in, and using your abdominal muscles, compress the left knee to the abdomen as you bring your hands back to prayer position at the heart center.

6. Continue the exhale as you release the left leg and let the left foot come to the mat. Your feet aligned to center in the starting position.

7. Repeat on the other side.

8. Repeat three times, alternating your left leg and right leg.

9. Move with the flow of the breath. Inhale as you lengthen and stretch. Exhale with the compression and release.

10. The iliopsoas is a very important core muscle that lies deep beneath the abdominal muscles. In this exercise, we get a deep stretch into the core, followed by compression and release. This exercise releases unneeded tension and tightness from the iliopsoas muscle.

The Road Less Traveled

"Somewhere ages and ages hence:
I shall be telling this with a sigh,
Two roads diverged in a wood, and I—
I took the one less traveled by,
And that has made all the difference."

—Robert Frost

Our Daily Practice

"Give us today our daily bread."

—Matthew 6:11

"Encourage yourselves daily while it is still "today", so that none of you may grow hardened by the deceit of sin."

—Hebrews 3:13

"The real purpose of teachers, books and teachings is to lead us back to the Kingdom of God within ourselves."

—Joel Goldsmith

Our daily practice is nourishment and sustenance for mind and body. Consider your practice as the food that provides the energy for life and growth. Take care to accept with gratitude the many blessings in each day. Remember that just as the food we consume is a gift from the earth, our mother God, to nourish our human being, so is His Word a gift to nourish, sustain, move, and inspire His divine presence within us. Our daily practice prepares and opens us to receive the Word and to respond to it in thought, word, and action.

When we receive nourishment in the gift of food, the food becomes fully integrated into our being through the digestive process. We do not have to concern ourselves with how to digest and assimilate the food, for the mind-body in its inherent wisdom takes in the apple and transforms it into the cells of our heart, lungs, and brain. The mind-body also knows how to let go of what is no longer needed.

And so, as we take in the Word, we do so knowing that God, through Christ, the Word made flesh, will bring all things to Himself in love and goodness. We can let go of the need to understand, analyze, and control the workings and beautiful mystery and wonder of God.

Require no evidence or proof. Work to prepare yourself to come to the table and be open to receive God's love in its many forms.

"Fear not, believe only, and she shall be made whole."

—Luke 7:50

Come to the table in mind and body to be nourished in the gift of life. Be mindful that you can choose to open yourself to receive this gift of love. In practice, try conscious eating:

- Be nourished in a settled atmosphere.
- Sit down and take time to receive the gifts that nourish.
- Share meals with family and friends. Break bread together—commune.
- Listen to your body. Eat when you *feel* hunger but not otherwise.
- Balance full with empty. Know what it *feels* like to be hungry. We cannot always be full. Do not starve yourself either by skipping meals.
- Take smaller portions and leave one-third of your stomach empty to aid in proper digestion.
- Drink plenty of water—eight glasses a day or more if you are exercising.
- Eat at a moderate pace, and chew your food well. Chewing your food twenty to thirty times is a good measure.
- Pay attention to all the goodness: taste, smell, texture, and sight. Let it satisfy you.
- Avoid distractions like television, reading, walking, and driving while you eat. When you do not pay attention, the mind does not perceive the goodness being received. You will feel hungry again in no time.
- Say a prayer of thanks: "In the name of the Father and the Son and the Holy Spirit, bless us, O Lord, and these, thy gifts which we are about to receive through Christ our Lord, amen. Bless this food, bless these people, bless this house, bless this world, and bless this universe." Add any special intentions or blessings for the day.
- Practice *aparigraba—greedlessness. Take only what you need.*

Be willing to work hard and rest easy. Take responsibility for your thoughts, words, and actions, knowing that God is the very substance and space of your being. Make a commitment to God, to yourself and to others to practice love in all its forms. Make no excuses and do not give away your freedom to choose by blaming others. Be able to go with the flow, adapt and be resilient. Alone, you are small and have many failings. Remember this truth and remain humble. With God, the one source of love and life, all things are possible. You can do this. Keep up the good work.

"To whom much is given, much is required."

—Luke 12:48

The work may seem difficult at first, but in time, you will move with greater ease. Your efforts will be the opening for you to feel energized and lifted. This is a great investment of your time, with far-reaching returns. You can spend as little as thirty to sixty minutes a day and experience a greater sense of well-being and ease in all your movements.

Begin your daily practice by choosing a routine from Appendix A. The routines are ordered from least to most rigorous. Choose a routine that suits your ability and desired intensity. More is not always better. If you are unsure of where to begin, start with the least rigorous and progress as you feel able.

Each day read one message that outlines the focus for your practice. As you perform the exercise routine for the day, keep in mind the thoughts that bring meaning to your practice. Use the suggestions provided for your practice both on and off the mat. You may have your own ideas. Write down your observations, thoughts, and reflections in a journal. Stay with the message for a week or longer to expand and deepen your awareness. Some messages you may decide to work with for one day and move on. You cannot go wrong. Work at a pace that suits you day to day. Be flexible.

When you feel you have mastered one routine, try another. As you become familiar with the exercises, you may decide to create your own routine. Continue to learn and stay open to new ideas and exercises that keep you energized, uplifted, and inspired.

Consider these suggestions to incorporate the seven ways to bring the Good Within to your daily practice:

1. **Cardio-respiratory training:** Walk or perform other aerobic exercise thirty to forty minutes every day. Balance the workload over the week. Work hard on two days. Practice in moderation for three of the days and take it easy for two days, not necessarily in that order. Trying to push hard every day or take it easy every day can lead to imbalance.

2. **Core and strength training:** Practice the core exercises two days a week for fifteen to twenty minutes. Balance your work by choosing exercises that strengthen the core on both sides of the body, on the front side, the abdominals, and on the back side, the lower back and gluteus maximus. Do as many of the core exercises as you are able. Modify as needed to suit your ability and desired intensity.

3. **Flexibility training:** Practice at least two days a week for fifteen to twenty minutes. Use sun salutations for a full body stretch. You can move from posture to posture with the flow of the breath or hold each posture for thirty to forty seconds. Try both approaches for both flow and depth in the exercises. As you feel able, perform the full set of yoga postures once or twice per week.

4. **Adequate rest/prayer/meditation:** Adequate rest is essential for a healthy mind and body. Eight hours sleep per night is a general guideline to follow. You should feel rested and ready to go when you awake. If you feel tired, you may not be getting adequate rest or the stress load may be too high. The body is resting, but the mind is overloaded. If

you are eating late at night, the work of digesting your food through the night may be keeping you from getting a good night's rest. Pay attention, and address this imbalance. Stop eating at least two hours before bedtime. Prayer and meditation can also help to restore the balance. Pray and/or meditate every day, morning, and night, if possible. Learn how to pray. There are five types of prayer to consider. *Adoration* is a prayer of worship in which we praise God for His greatness and acknowledge our dependence on Him in all things. In prayers of *contrition,* we acknowledge our sins and ask God for forgiveness and mercy. Prayers of *love* express our love of God, self, others, and all that is. A prayer of *petition* is asking God for things we need for ourselves and others. In prayers of *thanksgiving,* we thank God for all that has been given.

5. **Life-giving nutrition:** Take a simple and easy approach to nutrition. Choose foods that nourish, lift, and sustain you. The foods with the highest life energy are the foods closest to their natural state, like fresh fruit, vegetables, whole grains, raw nuts and seeds, and fresh meat and fish. Highly processed foods are low in life energy and can be mostly empty calories. When we consume these foods, the body does not feel nourished but empty, and so it craves more food. This can lead to overeating and weight gain. Adequate hydration is also important in establishing an optimal state of wellness. Drink eight glasses of water a day or more if you are exercising.

6. **Family/community/church:** Relationships are the key to our happiness. We must be willing to give our time and attention to fostering love with others. Family is first. A strong family is a root for a happy life. Moving beyond the family, we connect with others who live near us. Church draws us together in God. Come back to church. Invite your family and friends to come with you.

7. **Written goals and a plan of action:** Consider keeping a journal. Write down your goals, and include a plan of action. Goals can be as simple as a list of what needs to be accomplished for the day, week, month, or year. Set short and long-term goals. Be sure to identify the first step toward reaching that goal and take that step today.

41. PRACTICE: Do what you can

"Do what you can, with what you have, where you are."

—Theodore Roosevelt

"To each individual the manifestation of the Spirit is given for some benefit."

—1 Corinthians 12:7

Intention: Rather than concern yourself with what you cannot do, do what you can. Keep coming back to the work. Try not to judge or demand proof that you are able. Simply take it as it is and let it be good work. Let the movement work for you. Let it awaken in you an awareness of an inner source of vital energy that balances, strengthens, sustains, nourishes, and moves you toward all that is good in life.

On the mat: As you practice the exercises, let go of the thoughts that expect or demand a certain outcome and accept what is. Let go of "I can't do this" and remind yourself to do what you can. Let go of the thoughts that lead you to believe that what you can do is not as good as what others are doing. Be happy being you.

Off the mat: No one is asking you to change the world. Do what you can. If a change is needed, let it be in you.

42. PRACTICE: Strength for today

"Meet today's problems with today's strength. Don't start tackling tomorrow's problems until tomorrow. You do not have tomorrow's strength yet. You simply have enough for today."

—Max Lucado

"Do not worry about tomorrow; tomorrow will take care of itself."

—Matthew 6:34

Intention: Be present for each day and every moment. The strength you need is within you. It cannot be felt in the past if your mind is stuck there. It cannot be experienced in the future if you are constantly worried over it. The strength you need is for today. Today's challenges are opportunities to know your strength. The only way to know your strength is to exercise it. Use it today.

On the mat: Strength and stability are felt primarily at the core—the muscles of the abdomen, lower back, and glutes. We can become more aware of our strength by focusing on these muscles as the origin of our movements. Remember that in order to feel strength at the core, the mind-body must first feel rooted. Our foundation is the touch of the feet to the ground. In order to move, we must also be aware of our sense of center. This provides us with the balance and stability to move beyond ourselves and away from center. As you move in the exercises, feel your feet on the ground, center the body over the midline, and engage the abdominal muscles. This is the foundation for all movement.

Off the mat: Be strong for today. Here are a few ways to practice being strong in mind-body:

- Stay active. Exercise every day in ways that make you feel good.
- Choose variety in your activities, meals, and all that you do. Avoid the rut.
- Choose foods as close to their natural state as possible for high energy to sustain you.
- Think and practice moderation. Overdoing anything, even a good thing, can be highly stressful.
- Do not skip meals. Eat breakfast. If you are not hungry in the morning you probably ate too much the night before.
- Be decisive. Collect the information you need, consider your options, and make a decision.

43. PRACTICE: Listen

"Listening is a fundamental attitude called for in prayer. The one who truly prays is the one who listens."

—Enzo Bianchi

"Know this, my dear brothers, everyone should be quick to hear, slow to speak slow to wrath, for the wrath of a man does not accomplish the righteousness of God."

—James 1:19

Intention: Maybe there is a reason we cannot talk our first year of life. Maybe it's because we have so much to learn. To listen is to learn. If the mind is preoccupied with what it already knows or doesn't know, it becomes inattentive and closed to new information. To pay attention is an act of giving and opening oneself. One who is able to listen is relaxed, not anxious, patient, rather than in a hurry, and humble, not proud. The opposite of to listen is to ignore, neglect, and shun.

On the mat: Be attentive. Give the work your full attention. Open the mind and heart and be receptive to all that is coming into your awareness. Listen. You may hear something you have not heard before. You may hear the same words or sounds you have heard hundreds of times, and this day, they may take on a whole new meaning. Listen not only to the sounds and voices around you but to the still, small voice within. We all have much to learn.

Off the mat: This week, be the one who listens. Do not hurry. Slow down and open the mind and heart. Reside in the space of quietness. Let your voice be silent and listen. Try not to interrupt when others are speaking. When they speak, rather than planning what you are going to say, let those thoughts wait and simply listen.

44. PRACTICE: New beginning

"That's why many fail—because they don't get started—they don't go. They don't overcome inertia. They don't begin."

—W. Clement Stone

"The journey of a thousand miles begins with one step. But where does one begin? The answer is simple: You begin where you are."

—Lao Tzu

"Remember not the events of the past, the things of long ago consider not, see I am doing something new!"

—Isaiah 43:18

"Do not conform yourselves to this age but be transformed by the renewal of your mind, that you may discern what is the will of God, what is good and pleasing and perfect."

—Romans 12:2

Intention: Every day presents an opportunity to begin anew. In this day is the possibility to choose the thoughts, words, and actions that move each of us closer to all that is good. Whatever our goals, desires, hopes, and dreams may be, this moment can be a new beginning. The past is the basis from which we step forth. Take the first step. Take time to take care of yourself so you are most able to realize your dreams and fulfill your purpose. This is the perfect will of God—that we each know and feel love in its many forms within ourselves and in relationship with others.

On the mat: Every time you come to the mat to do the exercises, you open the mind and the heart to a new way of seeing yourself and others. As we move, we have the opportunity to discipline the mind to stay fully present in the body. The mind-body becomes the instrument of our knowing and feeling the seven gifts: vitality, balance, strength, endurance, flexibility, focused attention, and coordination. Give yourself the chance to know this goodness within.

Off the mat: Bring to mind one thing you want to accomplish today. Get started by taking the first step now. Let it be a new beginning.

45. PRACTICE: In place of fear

"God is love, and whoever remains in love remains in God and God in him. In this is love brought to perfection among us."

—1 John 4:16

"Believe in yourself. You gain strength, courage and confidence by every experience in which to stop to look fear in the face . . . you must do that which you think you cannot do."

—Eleanor Roosevelt

Intention: It is human to fear. In fact, fear can be life-giving. It can move us in ways that promote and foster our growth and development. When we perceive a danger, our sympathetic nervous system is activated and moves us to meet the challenge. Fear, however, can also immobilize, paralyze, and drain the life energy from us if we do not recognize that in every place of fear, there is also an opportunity to love. When you feel afraid, take a deep breath and remind yourself to choose love.

On the mat: In place of fear, choose love. Let go of the fear or worry that you're not doing enough and do what you can in love. Your efforts do not have to result in huge accomplishments or attainment of difficult postures. Any act, however small, when done with love promotes life. Move with love, and you will find beauty in your practice.

Off the mat: Take a closer look at the things you fear. See yourself in the situation and imagine how you can respond from love. You can be ready and able to manage this situation with greater ease when in place of fear you choose love. Here are a few examples:

- You have an important meeting with your boss. Are you fearful of the outcome? Do you perceive this person as a threat, or can you choose to see the good? More than likely what is good for you is also good for him or her. Honor the person rather than fearing him or her.
- What moves you to exercise? Do you love the life-giving energy it awakens in you and/or are you afraid what will happen if you don't exercise?
- What moves you to eat? Do you love to nourish yourself and share good food with family and friends, or are you afraid you won't get enough?
- What moves you to act? Is it love or fear? Maybe it is both. When you have a choice, choose love.

46. PRACTICE: Being happy

"Life is not meant to be a burden . . . it is a blessing to be celebrated."

—Joan Chittister

"The greatest discovery of my generation is that a human being can alter his life by altering his attitude."

—William James

"Let the plains be joyful and all that is in them. Then let all the tress of the forest rejoice . . ."

—Psalm 96:12

Intention: I came upon an interesting article by Daniel Gilbert, a Harvard psychologist, whose research focuses on how to be happy. He summarizes his findings in a short list of qualities that people who are happy seem to have in common:

1. *Make a commitment.* People who commit to relationships are much happier than those who don't . . . Commitment isn't just a sign of love; it's a cause of love.
2. *Pay attention to the little things.* To increase happiness, worry less about big sources of joy and find a steady stream of small sources.
3. *Hang in there.* Endurance in its many forms is a key to happiness.
4. *Go to church.* When we commune or come together in shared beliefs and practices we establish a foundation for happiness to grow.
5. *Give.* Not surprisingly, when we focus on all we have to give rather than what we need or want, we're happier.
6. *Invest in experiences rather than things.* Family trips together, a day of relaxation, a special occasion, a vacation, are all likely to bring more happiness than a new car, jewels or money.

On the mat: Being happy can enhance the work and its benefits. The suggestions above make sense when applied to our practice. Make a commitment and stay with it. Let each moment bring joy. Work together and focus on what you have to give. Let the experience energize and lift you.

Off the mat: Being happy is a state of mind-body that you can learn to choose. In each moment, choose happiness.

47. PRACTICE: Be the one

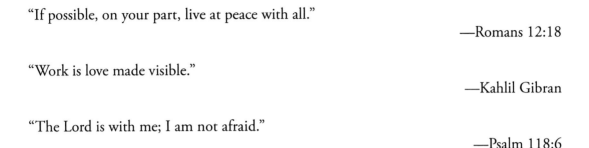

"If possible, on your part, live at peace with all."

—Romans 12:18

"Work is love made visible."

—Kahlil Gibran

"The Lord is with me; I am not afraid."

—Psalm 118:6

Intention: Movement is the key to life. When we move in mind and body, we learn and grow. Be the one to take the first step. Be the one to take action. Make a move. You will not always be right when you are willing to be the first. But you can never be wrong in trying. Think with the mind of a scientist. There are no "failed" experiments, only results. Observe your choices and the results and make your next move.

On the mat: Be the one who brings your full attention to the work. Challenge yourself to try new moves. With increased energy and attention, your practice will help you learn and grow. You will begin to see and feel the results.

Off the mat: Notice the movement of the breath in the body. Breathe easy. Let your movements be focused and purposeful. Set short and long-term goals to give yourself direction. It can be difficult for us to move forward if we don't know where we are going. Bring movement to something you have been thinking about for some time. Be the one to take action. Move the mind-body in ways that promote life.

48. PRACTICE: Let the breath lift you

"When you are inspired . . . dormant forces, faculties, and talents become alive, and you discover yourself to be a greater person by far than you ever dreamed yourself to be."

—Patanjali

"Now may the God of hope fill you with all joy and peace in believing, so that you will abound in hope by the power of the Holy Spirit."

—Romans 15:13

Intention: When you feel tired, heavy, or sluggish and unable to move in the ways you would like, consider letting the breath lift you. The breath embodies Spirit within, the weightless. When we feel weighted down, it is possible that we are indeed putting too much weight on the things of this world, including ourselves. We can get caught up in the ego and our perceived needs and wants. Let the breath lift you and offer you the balance that comes in mind-body when you let Spirit into your life.

On the mat: Begin with the deep-breathing exercises to increase your awareness of the movement of the breath deep into the belly. Take a deep breath in and feel the breath lift and fill you. When you exhale, let go. With each in-breath, the body will be lifted, the spine lengthens, and the chest expands. The out-breath is your chance to let go. Let go of unneeded tension and tightness and the thoughts that lead to that tension. Do not harbor regrets of the past or worries of the future. Let the breath lift you.

Off the mat: Balance your time and attention between the unseen, weightless Spirit within and the weighted matters of this world. Take time to focus your attention inward on the unseen Spirit that is weightless, pure energy, love, and light. It will lift you, inspire you, and lighten your load.

Be willing to let go of the thoughts that burden you and weigh you down, like, "I have to do everything myself. I can't stand this. This is too much to bear. I have so much to do and not enough time. This is really hard." These thoughts put all your attention and too much weight on the ego, and you literally feel the burden. You may carry it with you in the form of excess weight. To let go does not mean withdraw from the outer world. This would create an imbalance also. The key is held in every breath. See the beautiful balance in the gift of the body that is weighted in matter and filled with Spirit, and the mind that can perceive the two as one within you.

49. PRACTICE: Stay the course

"You may go; as you have believed, let it be done for you."

—Matthew 8:13

"The objective of our life is the kingdom of God, but we should carefully ask what we should aim for. If we do not look very carefully into this we will wear ourselves out in useless strivings. For those who travel without a marked road there is the toil of the journey and no arrival at a destination."

—St. John Cassian

Intention: As I sat in meditation this morning, my mind was wandering randomly. I was preoccupied with my long list of things to do. I took a few deep breaths and had the intention of beginning again. The same thing happened—more random thoughts. Nothing was coming that seemed of any value. When nothing comes, when nothing seems to be going our way, when there is a lack of guidance, direction, or support, what do we do? I asked that simple question, "What am I going to do?"

A surprising answer came to me: "*Stay the course.* You already know where you are going for now. Continue on. You know what you need to do in this moment. Take the next step. When guidance is needed, when a change of direction is at hand, it will come in good time. For now, stay the course."

On the mat: Our practice requires that we repeat the exercises again and again. Sometimes it may feel like we're going nowhere. When we sit in meditation or prayer, we may be tempted to think this "doing nothing" is not a good use of our time. Stay the course. Every effort will be rewarded. You may not always see or feel rewarded in that moment, but it will come.

Off the mat: Our ultimate goal is to know God and in drawing closer to Him, to experience His love and goodness in our lives. If we remain focused on this, our goal, every step will lead to Him. Keep God in mind as you set short nd long-terms goals for yourself. Plan your action steps as if God was with you, guiding you, loving you, and supporting you because He is. He is also counting on you.

"All the things of this world are gifts from God, presented to us so that we can know God more easily and make a return to love more readily. But if any of these gifts becomes the center of our lives, they displace God and so hinder our growth toward our goal . . ."

—St. Ignatius Loyola

50. PRACTICE: Take a breather

"God is there in these moments of rest and can give us in a single instant exactly what we need. Then the rest of the day can take its course, under the same effort and strain, perhaps, but in peace. And when night comes, and you look back over the day and see how fragmentary everything has been, and how much you planned that has gone undone, and all the reasons you have to be embarrassed and ashamed; just take everything exactly as it is, put it in God's hands and leave it with God. Then you will be able to rest in God—really rest—and start the next day as a new life."

—St. Theresa Benedicta of the Cross

"Come to me, all you who labor and are burdened, and I will give you rest."

—Matthew 11:28

Intention: Sustained effort does not necessarily mean there is no time for rest. Sustained effort requires purposeful rest. Work without rest will not bring the desired results of productivity and creativity. More than likely it will lead to dullness, boredom, and eventually a feeling of being drained or burned out. This state of mind-body is destructive to our well-being. Take a break. Take a rest. Take a deep breath and relax. It is very good for you.

On the mat: Take a breather. Listen to your mind-body. Honor the balance between work and rest. When you need a break, take one. Take a few deep breaths and feel the body soften and relax. When you feel ready, come back to the work. In the same way, when you need a day or a week off, take it. Give the same breaks to others. Things will work out much better.

Off the mat: We live in a very competitive world. It's understandable why we might feel that if we stop to take a breather we will fall behind. The answer is not to stop competing. Competition is a good thing. It can help us achieve more than we think is possible. The beauty in competition lies in three points of awareness:
1. When one person excels, it has the potential to lift us all. We do not have to compete *against* others. We compete with them.
2. When I see that you can do it, I begin to believe that I can do it too.
3. The joy of victory and the agony of defeat are experiences that bind us together. We all know both, and this allows us to share the highs and lows of other's experiences as well as our own.

51. PRACTICE: Begin with the end in mind: I am willing and able

"Do not be unbelieving, but believe . . . Have you come to believe because you have seen me? Blessed are those who have not seen and have believed."

—John 20:26-29

"God is near us at all times. God is available, a silence in the midst of chaos, a voice in the midst of confusion, a promise at the center of tumult."

—Joan Chittister

"Nothing happens unless first a dream."

—Carl Sandburg

Intention: Begin with the end in mind. Let the words, "I am willing and able" be your beginning. Do not underestimate what is possible when you believe. Take a moment and imagine yourself as you want to be. See yourself moving in ways that embody love in its many forms. When you say to yourself, "I can't even imagine being able to . . ." you won't be able to, and it is unlikely you will ever make it real.

On the mat: In the beginning, do not demand evidence or proof that you are able by comparing what you are doing to others. Rather, look within and know that you are able. No matter what you see on the outside, believe first that all you need is already present within. Nothing needs to be added or taken away. You only need to continue to come to the practice. As you prepare to meet the challenge of a particular task or exercise, take a moment and see yourself being able. Notice the feeling of being able. Let it happen just as you imagined.

Off the mat: You are capable of bringing good into the world. Keep in mind the gifts you have been given and the ways in which others need you to share these gifts. Begin with the end in mind:

1. **Breathe:** Remember, God is with you in the Holy Spirit. You need God.
2. **Believe:** You are able. God needs you.
3. **Engage:** Exercise your power to choose. Discipline the mind to stay present to God within you.
4. **Receive:** Open your mind and heart to receive all that life has to offer.
5. **Feel:** Stay in touch. Recognize the flow of God's grace, and let it move you to give freely of yourself.
6. **Think:** Focus your attention and energy on the good that you are able to bring to this world.
7. **Act:** Let it be.

52. PRACTICE: Your ABCs

"Whoever humbles himself like this child is the greatest in the kingdom of heaven. And whoever receives one child such as this in my name receives me."

—Matthew 18:4

"For everyone who exalts himself will be humbled, and the one who humbles himself will be exalted."

—Luke 18:14

"The privilege of a lifetime is being who you are."

—Joseph Campbell

Intention: There is goodness in childlike simplicity that is easily understood. I walked away from this sentence for days trying to think about what more to say. It occurred to me that I was reluctant to let it stand on its own—a single sentence. Be willing to let the simple have its place with honor.

On the mat: In both mind and body, keep your practice simple with this easy reminder: ABC.

A: Alignment: Center yourself in three dimensions—from right to left, front to back, and top to bottom. Stack the joints so they fall in line to each other in the horizontal, vertical, and diagonal planes.

B: Breathe: Breathe deep abdominal breaths throughout the work, not forced or exaggerated but an easy flow deep into the belly. Recognize the breath as the flow of life energy. Let it lift and ground you.

C: Control: Develop control through the full range of motion. Let your movements be purposefully directed while you maintain alignment and move with the flow of the breath. Discipline the mind to stay fully present to the work.

Off the mat: A simple reminder to keep perspective:
A: Alignment: Be present.
B: Breathe: Be thankful.
C: Control: Be yourself.
Live in the present moment. Be thankful for the gift of life. You do not have to impress or control others. Be yourself, and allow others the same privilege. A team of the most brilliant scientists could not design a body better than the one you already have. The body is the physical manifestation of a beautiful and perfect order. We do not have to create this order; we only have to experience it. In time, experience will bring understanding.

53. PRACTICE: Be a leader

"Whoever does not accept the kingdom of God like a little child will not enter it."

—Luke 18:17

"If there is anything that we wish to change in the child, we should first examine it and see whether it is not something that could better be changed in ourselves."

—Carl Jung

"The time and the quality of the time that their parents devote to them indicate to children the degree to which they are valued by their parents."

—M. Scott Peck, MD

Intention: Our children can teach us. Provide them with opportunities to learn, and be willing to pay attention to their responses. I had the opportunity to witness leadership in action when I went for a walk with two young children and two golden retrievers. We hiked in the woods with each child leading a dog on leash. It happened to be a frigid, windy day, but the children did not let that stop them. They dressed appropriately, hydrated before the walk, and discussed the plans for how long to walk given the weather conditions. They did a beautiful job leading the dogs, correcting them when necessary, and offering praise when appropriate to reinforce the behaviors they wanted from the dogs. The children moved forward confidently with the dogs at their sides. When we returned home, I asked them to reflect on their experience and to identify the qualities of a good leader. Here is what they said.

A leader is:

- **Strong**
- **Confident**
- **Brave**
- **Intelligent**
- **Tough**
- **A person who knows where he/she is going**
- **Prepared**
- **A person who stays on the trail and keeps track of the time**
- **Able to communicate with others**
- **A good decision maker**
- **Attentive and observant**
- **Willing to help others along the way**
- **Centered**

On the mat: Be a leader. Hold these qualities in mind, and embody them in your practice.

Off the mat: We each have opportunities daily to be a leader. Reflect on these qualities, and begin to notice them in yourself and others. Know when to lead and when to follow.

54. PRACTICE: Authentic praise

"The deepest principle of human nature is the craving to be appreciated."
—William James

"Be impeccable with your words. Speak with integrity. Say only what you mean. Avoid using the word to speak against yourself or to gossip about others. Use the power of your word in the direction of truth and love."
—Don Miguel Ruiz

"Anxiety in a man's heart depresses it, but a kindly word makes it glad."
—Proverbs 12:25

Intention: There is true power in authentic praise. When practiced mindfully, it can lift, inspire, and motivate. Authentic praise is rooted in the truth and given freely without expectation of a personal gain in return. If I offer authentic praise to a child for a good effort or an act of kindness, that praise can be a powerful motivator. However, if my praise is not grounded in the truth, if it is false, fake, or insincere, I can do more harm than good. If my praise is not directed solely to see and honor the goodness in the other but is intended for my own gain, then this praise is self-centered and shallow and has little power.

Stay rooted in the truth and your words will have great power.

On the mat: Listen to how you speak to yourself. Notice the words you choose and your tone. Choose the words and thoughts that support your learning and growth. Begin to see the goodness and offer authentic praise.

Off the mat: Be mindful of how you speak to others, especially children. Your words have the power to lift or depress, empower or disable, guide or distract. See the goodness in others. Authentic praise will flow easily from this truth. If someone is critical of you, honor the one who has criticized you and thank him or her sincerely for his or her point of view. You can say, "Thank you. I will take that into consideration." Say it and mean it. After careful consideration, abide in the truth as you choose how to respond. If the criticism has some truth in it, make an adjustment accordingly in thought, word and action. If the criticism is false, it has no bearing on you whatsoever and can do you no harm unless you are tempted to believe it. Let the one who has criticized bear this burden, for it is his or her responsibility.

55. PRACTICE: True humility

"I can of mine own self do nothing, the Father that dwelleth in me, he doeth the works."

—Joel Goldsmith

"You must not be proud."

—St. Benedict

"The real definition of pride is the desire to control; to control my day, my future, the other people in my life, to make sure the world is put together the way I want it. It is to deny the control to God, perhaps even to take it from him."

—Esther de Waal

Intention: When we talk about offering praise to self and others, it may raise the question about pride, arrogance, or inflated self-importance. It may be difficult for us to believe that we are filled with goodness and love, that we are strong, able to go the distance, and focused. It can also be a challenge to see this good in others. We may even feel uncomfortable extending praise to others and/or receiving this praise from others when they tell us we are "really good" at something. It can be hard for us to believe, "I am good. I am able. I am capable of great things."

We feel uncomfortable for a reason. We alone are capable of nothing. When we know and see the goodness within as God within, we experience true humility. All praise belongs to God. When we praise others, we are acknowledging that we see God's goodness in them. Being humble is a part of being human. The words *humble* and *human* have a similar origin—from the word *humus,* meaning from the ground. Being human is being of this earth. In our humanness we are small, finite, imperfect, and not always able. However, we are not alone in our humanness. God is with us always. This truth is pure potential within us to do great works.

On the mat: In all the standing exercises feel the touch of your feet on the earth. Remember you are grounded. You are here, now, for a reason. Be thankful for the gift of mind-body. Keep in mind your beginnings, in God who created you.

Off the mat: Wherever you stand, you occupy a place in space and time. The mind-body holds this place for you. True humility is being able to understand your place. Remind yourself, "I belong." Remember that we all belong. Begin to see that everyone has a place and purpose.

56. PRACTICE: Be a light

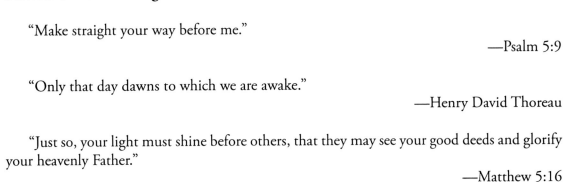

"Make straight your way before me."

—Psalm 5:9

"Only that day dawns to which we are awake."

—Henry David Thoreau

"Just so, your light must shine before others, that they may see your good deeds and glorify your heavenly Father."

—Matthew 5:16

"Everything that irritates us about others can lead us to an understanding of ourselves."

—Carl Jung

Intention: The sun is our source of light and provides the energy for all life on earth. The sun's energy is transformed to provide us with everything we know. It can lift, warm, and comfort us. There is also a source of *light* within. In moments when the sun is not shining brightly, let the light within be your source. Be the light for others. You have the power to choose the thoughts, words, and actions that can be a light for others and to brighten any day.

On the mat: Practice with enthusiasm and lightheartedness. Do not take matters too seriously or be tempted to feel burdened by your practice. Remember the light within and let that light shine for others to see by letting the things of this world remain transparent. See through the challenges and be a light for others.

Off the mat: See the light within others. Their light shines more brightly every time you take notice. Try to see through the judgments you make based solely on what is visible to the eye and see more deeply with the heart all that is good within them. Imagine if you saw someone sitting around the house doing nothing. It may look like laziness, but more than likely, that person wants to move, wants to succeed, but is uncertain about his or her direction and purpose. Be a light. Remind the person that he or she will have no trouble moving ahead once he or she decides where he or she is going and why. The mind-body's inactivity is not necessarily laziness but a natural means to conserve energy. There is no point in moving until you know where you are going.

57. PRACTICE: Honor the resistance

"Endure your trials as discipline, God treats you as his children."

—Hebrews 12:7

"The big question is whether you are going to be able to say a hearty yes to your adventure."

—Joseph Campbell

"No trial has come to you but what is human. God is faithful and will not let you be tried beyond your strength; but with the trial he will also provide a way out, so that you may be able to bear it."

—1 Corinthians 10:13

Intention: Right action will follow from right understanding. Contrary to popular belief, stress is not an affliction or disease. It is simply a force exerted on us—a powerful pressure that can be recognized and channeled productively. When we resist or misunderstand the value, the stress can undermine our ability to respond effectively. Resistance may manifest in time urgency, tension, tiredness, mistakes, irritability, distractions, hunger or thirst, depression, aggression, or hostility. When you feel these signs of resistance or distress, do not try to avoid the resistance. It is not present in your consciousness to put you down but to raise you up. It is there for you. Honor the resistance.

On the mat: Resistance is felt in a tight muscle, a pain, or discomfort as you practice, holding the breath, or feeling out of place. Resistance is the mind-body saying no. This no and the resistance it embodies is essential. It is the only way we can differentiate and learn to say yes. We must feel and honor the resistance. Come wholly into the body and abide in the space where you feel the tension. Work the edge of the tension gently, accepting it as part of the practice. Draw your attention to the breath, and with every exhalation, notice the mind-body letting go of unneeded tightness as you ease into the pose.

When you honor the resistance, you become more flexible in mind and body. When the mind accepts the tension as part of the work, you relax rather than resist and learn to feel more comfortable in the pose just where you are. By staying present, you realize that the space where you feel the tension is also the space of release. The body begins to relax, and as the muscles soften, there is potential for the muscle to lengthen, and you feel yourself deepening into the posture.

If you think resistance is a bad thing to avoid, imagine the muscles with no resistance or tension. The skeletal muscles that move us, the heart muscle that pumps blood to all organs and tissues, and the smooth muscles in our digestive tract would all become flaccid. You could not move, the heart would cease to beat, and your internal systems would come to a standstill. Balance is the key; a flow from tension to relaxation. Honor the resistance and you will experience greater flexibility and flow in your practice. You will be able to do more with less effort.

Off the mat: Recognize signs of resistance in your life. There is an important lesson to learn. It can only be learned by honoring and accepting. Become the observer. If you hear yourself saying, "I notice that I can never pay attention. I am constantly distracted. I feel overwhelmed. I am not able to make a decision," step back now and ask yourself, "Are these observations true?" The truth is you pay attention most of the time. It is how you pay attention that matters. If you see the world as a frightening place, then the mind-body is going to be on constant alert. This state of mind-body is characterized by diverting our attention from one thing to the next to perceive any danger. You are on the lookout. This is the mind-body's natural way to respond to the perceived threat. If you try to pay attention to more than one thing at a time, you are going to feel distracted. Begin to use every distraction as an opportunity to make a decision. Choose where to put your time and attention and let go of the thoughts that are no longer needed. Overcome the distractions one at a time rather than being overwhelmed by them. Every time you draw your attention back to your desired goal or focus, you strengthen and discipline the mind-body. Every time you let go of the distractions, you release unneeded tension and resistance. See the world as a place for you to learn and grow.

58. PRACTICE: In the darkness—see the light

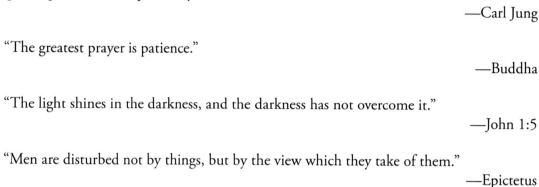

"Even a happy life cannot be without a measure of darkness, and the word happy would lose its meaning if it were not balanced by sadness. It is far better to take things as they come along with patience and equanimity."

—Carl Jung

"The greatest prayer is patience."

—Buddha

"The light shines in the darkness, and the darkness has not overcome it."

—John 1:5

"Men are disturbed not by things, but by the view which they take of them."

—Epictetus

Intention: When you find yourself in the midst of darkness, remember to see the light. The light is ever-present, like the stars in the sky. We can only see them in the darkness. When the days seem dark, let it be a time for going inward. Spend more time at home. Still the body, and allow the mind to let go of all the things you need to do and rest in the still, quiet space of "no-thing." Feel the movement of the breath within, and recognize it as the touch of Spirit. The light and love of God's Holy Spirit is within and flows through us without ceasing. We only have to begin to see and feel it.

On the mat: When it is difficult to find the energy to practice, do not give it a second thought. It makes little difference unless you make it into something by focusing on how low you feel. Take a few deep breaths. Notice the lift with each inhalation, and feel the body relax with the exhale. Your low point is an opportune time to move freely toward the high. Sit quietly for a moment, and notice your thoughts. Redirect your energy and attention. Say aloud, "I feel lifted." It will come. Be patient, and when you begin to notice your energy increasing, take action. Let the flow of the life energy within move you.

Off the mat: Darkness only feels bad when you want it to be light. Let it be dark. Don't be afraid. Open your eyes and see the light; see the beauty in the darkness. In the dark days of winter, enjoy the time for going inward. It can be a time of rest and renewal. Explore the rain, the snow, and the cold. They can be invigorating and refreshing. Dress appropriately, and get out there and see the good in all that is. Try not to limit yourself. See the light in the darkness. It only takes a moment.

59. PRACTICE: Set priorities

"A clean heart create for me, God; renew in me a steadfast spirit."

—Psalm 51:12

"We know that all things work together for good to those who love God, to those who are called according to His purpose."

—Romans 8:39

"The time and the quality of time that their parents devote to them indicate to children the degree to which they are valued by their parents."

—M. Scott Peck, MD

"If we all did the things we are really capable of doing we would literally astound ourselves."

—Thomas Edison

Intention: Do you often say or think, "I have too much to do and there is not enough time." It is easy to feel this way. We lead busy lives. Yet this is not the truth. The truth is, there is time. There is the same number of hours in each, and every day and every moment is an opportunity. Time does not change, but our perception of it can. To say you don't have time for whatever simply means that this "whatever" is not a priority for you. You have chosen to put other things first. Set priorities, and remember you are free to choose what is most important.

On the mat: The time you spend in your practice is not selfish. It is life-giving and allows you to be your best self. In time you will come to understand the truth about your being and your purpose. You are very capable and can bring much good into this world. Set priorities and make choices that promote life.

Off the mat: Let go of the idea that there is not enough time and embrace each moment, knowing you have time for those things you choose to set as priorities. We have been given this time here on earth. We are each chosen to be here now. It is up to us to choose how we are going to use this time.

60. PRACTICE: No matter what you do

"Doing what we can do in every situation, doing it well, and doing it with joy is not only good for us but it's good for those around us as well."

—Joan Chittister

"Give and gifts will be given to you . . . For the measure with which you measure will in return be measured out to you."

—Luke 6:38

Intention: No matter what you do, know that it touches others in some way. Everything you do is a matter of both giving and receiving in relationship with others. Consider the act of eating. It may seem that this action is about the self—satisfying a basic human need. You are receiving food that is to nourish and form your very being. Who is the giver? How did it come to you? It came from the earth, and the seed, water, farmer, trucker, grocer, and others who gave of themselves so you could eat. It came from God. Giving and receiving brings us together.

On the mat: Does your work have meaning for you alone, the practitioner? Most of us do not exercise so we can lift weights over our heads. Weightlifting is not our purpose. We lift to recognize and experience being grounded, centered, and strong. We lift to remember what we were made for. When we see it and feel it within, we can act from that space of knowing in all that we do. The strength is within you. You are made to know it. Use your time on the mat to realize the gifts of God's goodness within. More importantly, once you recognize these gifts within, you can more easily see them in others. It becomes a matter of giving and receiving these gifts in all we do.

Off the mat: You will not recognize something you do not know. Say you were to meet a distant relative for the first time. You must have some way of knowing this person or he or she could be standing in front of you and you would not recognize him or her. How do you come to know someone you have never seen? The answer is, "Know what to look for, watch, and wait patiently until you see him or her in your presence."

61. PRACTICE: Affirm goodness

"Trust them and they will be true to you, treat them greatly and they will show themselves great."

—Ralph Waldo Emerson

"One looks with appreciation to the brilliant teachers, but with gratitude to those who touched human feelings. The curriculum is so much necessary raw material, but warmth is the vital element for the growing plant and for the soul of the child."

—Carl Jung

"Take courage, it is I, do not be afraid."

—Matthew 14:27

"Give up your anger, abandon your wrath; do not be provoked; it brings only harm."

—Psalm 37:8

Intention: Thought leads to action. Begin to think in ways that affirm goodness, for goodness is our inherent and true nature when we realize our oneness in God. Affirm your goodness and the goodness of others and begin to see it manifest. Positive affirmations have the power to lift and move you. If you beat yourself or others down with negative judgments, expect to feel mighty low by the end of the day.

On the mat: Affirm the goodness within by reminding yourself in thoughts and words: "I am grounded. I am centered. I am strong. I am open to receive and give. I am at ease. I am focused and see clearly. I am able." Bring these thoughts and words to your practice and you will begin to experience the seven gifts—vitality, balance, strength, endurance, flexibility, focused attention, and coordination. All these are gifts of God's goodness given freely and without end.

Off the mat: Create your own affirmations. Think and speak in the present tense. If you have trouble deciding what to affirm, there is always one you can turn to for guidance. Turn to God. Let every affirmation be for love. Move beyond the self and consider affirmations that include others. We are one family, we respect each other, we know strength in numbers, we are patient and forgiving, we are moved by God's grace, we see the good in each other, and we work together for the good of all. The world needs each of us to do our part. Do not underestimate the good we can do.

62. PRACTICE: Keep coming back

"God is our refuge and our strength, an ever-present help in distress."

—Psalm 46:1

"'For all our insight, obstinate habits do not disappear until replaced by other habits . . . no amount of confession and no amount of explaining can make the crooked plant grow straight; it must be trained upon the trellis by the gardener's art . . .'"

—Carl Jung

"Ask and it will be given to you; seek and you will find; knock and the door will be opened to you."

—Matthew 7:7

Intention:
We all have things that we would like to accomplish.

We all set goals that we hope to reach.

We may have dreams that we imagine realizing one day.

Look at these statements. They are all thoughts of the future. If we want the thought to become a reality, we have to keep coming back to the present moment. We can only act now. Keep coming back to the present moment, and be willing to take the first step now. It is good to think ahead, set goals, and imagine, but we must keep coming back to act on these thoughts, goals, and dreams now.

On the mat: Keep coming back to the breath. In your practice, train the mind to stay present by gently drawing your attention back to the touch of the breath in the body. Stay in touch with the feelings of being grounded, centered, and strong. Keep the heart center open, and feel the flow of the breath as you move in the exercises. Keep coming back and you become more and more able.

Off the mat: Keep coming back to all that is good no matter how many times you might be distracted or lose focus. There are plenty of things in this world that can cause you to lose sight of the good. Take a deep breath and remember your freedom to choose. Choose to come back and act now. See more clearly all that is good in this world, and begin to realize your goals and your dreams.

63. PRACTICE: Let it work for you

"Not that I say this because of need, for I have learned, in whatever situation I find myself, to be content."

—Philippians 4:11

"Nothing happens to anybody which he is not formed to bear."

—Marcus Aurelius

Intention: Turn up the heat in your practice this week, and let it work for you. Heat can be perceived as a stress when we see the heat as undesirable. The truth is heat is energy and we can let that energy work for us rather than against us. The key is in preparation in mind and body. Come to the work prepared and confident. Know what to expect, and have a plan of action that will enable you to meet the challenge. Turn up the heat. Increase the intensity. Focus and give more energy and attention to all that is life-giving.

On the mat: Try this in the heat of the summer or turn up the heat in the room to seventy-four to seventy-seven degrees Fahrenheit. Be sure the room is adequately ventilated. Come to the work well-hydrated. Dress in layers so you can take off clothes as the heat builds. Be sure to hydrate well after your practice if you perspire. If you focus on the warmth and think it's too hot, it's too hard, it will overcome you. Stay focused on the work, and feel the touch of your feet to the floor. Feel centered and strong. Be open to the experience and notice the muscles soften and lengthen as you feel more at ease in the heat of the moment.

Off the mat: There will be times in life when the heat gets turned up. The work on the mat is practice and preparation. Find a way to let it work for you and you will enjoy these benefits:
- The heat will increase your flexibility and allow you to move in ways you once thought impossible.
- If well-hydrated, the body will perspire, and this can have a noticeable cleansing effect.
- A new experience always adds a degree of difficulty, and we learn to adapt and be resilient.
- Meeting the challenge and getting through can give you a sense of accomplishment. You will be more confident the next time the heat is turned up.
- The added energy of the heat paired with getting through can be exhilarating and fun.

64. PRACTICE: Realize your freedom

"And you will know the truth and the truth will set you free."

—John 8:32

"Those who have failed to work toward the truth have missed the purpose of living."

—Buddha

"Let us ask Mary to teach us how to become, like her: inwardly free, so that in openness to God we may find true freedom, true life, genuine and lasting joy."

—Pope Benedict xVI

Intention: It is truly a blessing to live in a state of freedom. True freedom is not granted by man but by God and has been given as a gift to every person equally. Many that claim to be free are indeed confined by their own thoughts and false beliefs. And there are those who are confined by the physical limitations of the body but are inwardly free. God granted us freedom so we may choose love. In an instant God could restore peace and love on earth. To do so, He would have to take away our freedom. He loves us too much. Remember how much God loves you. Remember that you are free. Choose love, give, and forgive and you will be truly free.

On the mat: Come to your practice freely. Your work is not intended to be a burden or an obligation, but an opening for you to experience God's love and goodness in yourself and others. Your work is what you make it. Realize your freedom and choose love.

Off the mat: When I take a day off from work and choose an activity I enjoy, I feel especially light and energized. I feel free. It occurs to me that I give meaning to these events I call work and play. I am the one who decides that a day off is freedom from work. I realize that I can choose freedom in each and every day. When I come to a day's work freely with enthusiasm and joy, my work is not burdensome or tiresome. I feel lifted and energized because I have realized my freedom to rest always in God.

"Jesus said, I no longer call your servants, because a servant does not know his master's business. Instead, I have called you friends, for everything that I have learned from my Father I have made known to you."

—John 15:15

65. PRACTICE: All your efforts

"The tyranny of self-absorption and the self-deception and the fear of failing in the goals I have set for myself . . . is not to relinquish free will but to choose freely to abide in the will of God."

Esther de Waal

"For everyone who asks, receives; and the one who seeks, finds; and to the one who knocks, the door will be opened."

—Matthew 7:8

"If you are not progressing as fast as you wish to, the remedy is this—to be still more careful to hold only harmonious thoughts. Do not dwell upon your mistakes or upon the slowness of your progress, but claim the Presence of God with you, all the more . . ."

—Emmet Fox

Intention: All your efforts are for the purpose of increasing within you the awareness of God in all things. Begin to recognize even in small measure the goodness and love within yourself and others. When we remember that we are indeed present to God's everlasting and infinite love, we will be more able to live each moment with vitality and enthusiasm.

On the mat: Remember:
I am grounded. I am here now. Feel your feet on the mat.
I am centered. Notice the union of right/left, front/back, top/bottom centered over the midline.
I am strong. Engage the abdominal muscles. Feel poised, not rigid.
I am open. Lengthen the spine, and lift into the space of open heart.
I am at ease. Feel the flow of the breath. Move with ease and grace.
I am focused. Keep your attention one-pointed.
I am willing and able. Let it all come together. Move in the direction of your dreams.

Off the mat: We need God. God is the one source of all life and love. God needs us to bring this life and love into the world. Aligning our will to the will of God means we must be strong enough to choose love in good times and in bad. We must endure with an open heart so we can both give and receive this love. When the heart is open, His love will flow through us and into the world. We can choose how to focus this energy and move in the direction of our dreams.

66. PRACTICE: Want nothing more

"I know indeed how to live in humble circumstances; I also know how to live with abundance."

—Philippians 4:12

"So much has been given to me; I have no time to ponder over that which has been denied."

—Helen Keller

Intention: What do you want? I want many things. I want peace, health, love, and strength. I want to be able to choose. My list could go on. Wanting is a good thing. It can be the emotion that moves us in a positive direction. However, too much wanting creates an imbalance that can lead to disappointment, frustration, unhappiness, anger, and other negative emotions. If we focus on what "I" want only, there is so much emotion directed inward that we can become self-absorbed and self-centered. The "I" wanting keeps all that energy locked up inside. We must look beyond ourselves to begin the flow of that energy into the world.

On the mat: Want nothing more than what is. Be content with things as they are. When forward bend feels tight, rather than wanting it to feel relaxed, want nothing more than what is. Honor the resistance and let your attention come to the flow of the breath in the body. Stay in the space where you feel the tightness. This is the same space where you will notice the release. Breathe in, accept what is, and as you exhale, feel the sensation of letting go. Let go of wanting things to be different and accept what is.

Off the mat: When it is hot and humid outside, rather than wanting cool and dry, want nothing more than what is. Step outside, and let hot and humid be endurable. When you are having a crazy day, want nothing more. Stay with it and bring calmness to crazy. When people are not acting like you want or expect, want nothing more. Keep an open mind and heart, receive them as they are and try to understand what they want.

We live in New England, and for some winter can seem way too long. Often by April there is much complaining going on about how spring will never arrive. I remember going out for a walk one morning in late April. As I stepped outside, I felt the cool air, but the sun was warm on my face. I paused for a moment, and I heard the birds singing. They were not squawking or complaining but singing. Remember to listen for the birds. They will remind you that spring is coming.

67. PRACTICE: The harvest is abundant

"The harvest is abundant but the laborers are few."

—Matthew 9:37

"Let it be done for you according to your faith."

—Matthew 9:29

"Great spirits have often encountered violent opposition from weak minds."

—Albert Einstein

Intention: A tightening in the body at the thought of going back to school or back to work is a normal response to ready oneself for the labor ahead. If we see the work ahead as bad, that tightening will not prepare us to move forward but immobilize us. The word *labor* can have a negative connotation. Look at a few of the synonyms: toil, drudgery, sweat, plod, strain, strive, and struggle. However, when you read over the antonyms or opposites, things don't look much better: idleness, inaction, shirks, and sloth. How do we find the good in labor? Believe in abundance, and labor in love. Those who are not willing to labor are not necessarily lazy or undisciplined. They are reluctant to work hard because they do not believe in the possibility of an abundant harvest. They believe in scarcity. They see their own lack—I'm not good enough. They see the lack of our world—there is not enough for all. If the laborers are few, it is because the believers are few.

On the mat: Believe in abundance. Believe that your efforts will reap benefits, whether those benefits are seen or unseen. Stay with your practice, and be willing to work hard. In one week's time (seven days of work), you can balance effort with rest in this way: work hard for two days, work at a moderate pace for three days, and go easy for two days. Do this in any order that suits you and the demands of the day. If you try to go hard every day, you will wear yourself out in no time. Overworking demonstrates a belief in scarcity, not abundance. Do what you can and labor in love.

Off the mat: Change your beliefs about what is possible when you are willing to labor in love. Why do you work? If you come to your work out of fear and a belief in scarcity—although fear can be a powerful motivator and get you moving—chronic fear eventually takes its toll and wears you down. Fear triggers the fight or flight response, and the body produces stress hormones to get us going, but it cannot sustain us over the long run. This continued state of high alert leads to toil, drudgery, and struggle.

In order to sustain your efforts and to build the endurance that allows you to go the distance, believe in abundance and labor in love. Be fully present to your work. Notice all that you bring to the effort. See what you are giving and also receiving in return. This is love manifesting itself, which opens the heart and allows us to endure. As we endure, we find in our labor a love of doing, of moving in ways that bring goodness into the world.

"Work is love made manifest."

—Kahlil Gibran

68. PRACTICE: No words

"Trust in the Lord with all your heart, on your own intelligence rely not."
—Proverbs 3:5

"A certain philosopher asked Saint Anthony: Father, how can you be so happy when you are deprived of the consolation of books? Anthony replied, My book, O philosopher, is the nature of created things, and anytime I want to read the words of God, the book is before me."
—Desert Fathers: C111

Intention: Our busy lives are filled with thoughts, and we think through language. Words fill our days. We process and give meaning to words in conversations, books, magazines, newspapers, television, radio, memos, emails, and more. We act according to our understanding. Thoughts, however, are not the only source of information. Put aside words briefly today. Let it be quiet, and get in touch with your feelings. Let the body be the opening or channel to receive information from within. It is not that the sounds, through words, are undesirable. Words are necessary. Sometimes, however, there are no words to accurately convey an experience. In this instance, try to stay in touch with the feel of things.

On the mat: Put the book aside for today. Listen to your body. Feel the touch of the breath. Notice the sensation of your feet on the floor. Engage the abdominal muscles, and feel the strength at your core. Lengthen your spine, and feel the heart center open. Receive this information in the space of an open mind. Remember to see and feel all that is good within.

Off the mat: When there are no words to describe what you are feeling, open your eyes to see in a new way. Open your ears to hear the soft, gentle voices of nature, a message on the wind. Open yourself to the soft touch of a loved child, parent, or friend. Open to a deep breath and the sweet smells of being outside on a cool morning at sunrise. Open to the subtle flavors and textures in all new experiences. Allow a space for no words. Turn off the television, and shut off the computer and the phone. Let it be quiet, and get back in touch with something living.

69. PRACTICE: You have a choice

"Try this on for size. Happiness isn't found on a clothing tag. We've looked. We find happiness in making healthy choices, getting outside and keeping fit—choices that make us feel better, inside and out. Often, living a healthier lifestyle begins with what we choose to eat . . . And that moves us to be more active . . . So now you have a choice—to spend your time counting calories . . . or to spend your calories doing things that count!"

—Brendan and Kelly Synnott (founders of Bear Naked granola)

"I remind you to stir into flame the gift of God . . . For God did not give us a Spirit of cowardice but rather of power and love and self-control."

—2 Timothy 1:6

Intention: You have a choice where to put your time and attention. If you spend your time and energy focused on counting calories and diligently watching your weight, that is what is likely to expand. Calories and weight expand because that is what you are focused on. What you focus on expands. Diets do not work in the long run. People who diet become overweight because there is too much attention on the weight. Consider changing your focus to think, feel, and do what really counts. Focus on what matters most, not what matters least.

On the mat: Pay attention and be thankful for all that you can do. Come to your practice just as you are and begin to see more clearly all that you are capable of being. No matter what you are doing, you have a choice to be grounded, centered, and strong. You have a choice to keep your heart open and move in ways that remind you of your true nature. See yourself in the exercises, and focus on all that is good within.

Off the mat: Right now, just as you are, you are doing many things that count for the good. Acknowledge the things you do for yourself, your family, and your friends no matter how great or small. If you feel able and you want to give more, find a way. See all the positive possibilities before you and begin to take action. You have a choice. You can make a difference and bring good into this world.

"In the end the sight of goodness undeterred has more power than all the forces on earth arrayed against it."

—Joan Chitister

"You must be the change you wish to see in the world."

—Mahatma Gandhi

70. PRACTICE: Look within

"God is our refuge and our strength, an ever-present help in distress."

—Psalm 46:1

"What lies behind us and what lies before us are small matters compared to what lies within us. And when we bring what lies within us into the world, miracles happen."

—Ralph Waldo Emerson

Intention: Work hard and good things happen. I think we work hard, believing we will reap what we sow. We believe in the harvest. This is the harvest of the outer world, the world of doing and getting the "things" that matter to us. This work is essential and good. We need things. We need food and shelter, and beyond the essentials, we need things that bring us pleasure, that let us experience a life of goodness and happiness. These things can connect us to each other.

Beyond the outer world, however, is an inner world that is unseen. Look within—the harvest is truly plentiful. The outer world's harvest is finite, unpredictable at times, and is not always as you expect or desire. The harvest of the inner world is infinite, eternal, unchanging, and more than you can imagine.

On the mat: Look within as you practice. See beyond the external. This work is more than exercise for mind and body. This work has the potential to be a useful tool to increase your awareness of God's presence in all you do. The particular exercises you practice do not matter nearly as much as what the exercise awakens within you. How much weight you can press over your head matters very little compared to your belief that you are strong. Look within, and let the exercises awaken that strength. No doubt, it is there.

Off the mat: As we look out into the world, there is so much to do. Look within and find yourself in the space on non-doing. Simply be present. Non-doing can take the form of prayer, meditation, rest, sleep, and quiet time alone or with others. In the space of non-doing, we experience the union of mind and body in the present moment. As you practice being fully present in non-doing, you can learn to bring this unified state of mind-body to all you do. Look within. The harvest is truly plentiful.

71. PRACTICE: Strength in numbers

"That they may all be one, as you, Father are in me and I in you."

—John 17:21

"All your strength is in union, all your danger is in discord."

—Henry Wadsworth Longfellow

Intention: We all want to be strong in mind and body. We want to be able to meet the challenges we face. We want to feel confident in our abilities and in control of our lives. We sometimes think we've got to do it all and that we are on our own. Remember in these times that there is strength in numbers. If you are having difficulty with any task great or small, recruit another pair of hands and work together.

On the mat: It can be difficult to get to the mat when you are alone. Remember there is strength in numbers. Connect with a few friends and come to the work together. Once you are on the mat, the energy of the group can be uplifting. The practice of working together builds strength that can surpass the work you can do alone. You do not necessarily have to think about how to work together. Simply being together can strengthen your practice.

Off the mat: My sister almost died in a car accident years ago. We all came to her side and witnessed her amazing strength and will to survive. We saw the many miracles that happened through all those who came together to save her life. Years later, she said to us, "I could not have done it without you." We were inspired and moved by her strength. She felt supported and loved by our presence. She reminded us that there is strength in numbers. Recognizing the strength in each other is what brings us together for the good of all.

Come together to get things done. Work together in your family, your community, your school, your place of employment, your church, and other groups large and small. There is strength in numbers.

72. PRACTICE: Expand your vision

"But I say to you, love your enemies, and pray for those who persecute you."
—Matthew 5:44

"Life is no straight and easy corridor along which we travel free and unhampered, but a maze of passages, through which we must seek our way, lost and confused, now and again checked in a blind alley. But always, if we have faith, a door will open for us, not perhaps one that we ourselves would ever have thought of, but one that will ultimately prove good for us."
—A. J. Cronin

Intention: We all develop beliefs about what is good and bad in life. We make judgments every day based on what we perceive to be the truth. Expand your vision, and begin to see the good in all things. There is perfect order to the universe. Everything has its place and purpose, and that includes each of us. Even those things, events, people, and circumstances we believe to be bad must exist as they are so we can begin to see the big picture. We may experience "bad" in times when our sense of "good" needs to be realigned. We have all learned what works by experiencing what does not. In other words, we cannot always move forward. We sometimes learn by moving back, moving to the right or left, up or down, and every which way.

On the mat: When you are struggling with a particular exercise, before you judge, expand your vision to see how the struggle can work for the good. We will not always feel strong. Weakness can be an ally too. Pay attention to where the problem seems to be. The answer, the adaptation or adjustment, is in the same space. It is there for you to see.

Off the mat: Our human vision is imperfect. We can be nearsighted and not see that the job we lose today creates a space for a new opportunity tomorrow. We can be farsighted and forget to spend time with our family because we have too much to accomplish. We can be shortsighted and think only about what is good for us. Bring to mind a difficult situation you are currently facing or have faced in the past that caused you distress. Take a moment to visualize yourself in the situation in as much detail as possible. Expand your vision now and look beyond your current perspective. Open your mind and imagine how this situation could work for the highest good—the good of all.

73. PRACTICE: Take notice

"Oh, that today you hear his voice: Do not harden your hearts . . ."

—Psalm 95:7

"To make an end is to make a beginning
To end is where we start from . . .
And the end of all our exploring
Will be to arrive where we started
And to know the place for the first time."

—T. S. Eliot

Intention: Do you sometimes feel like you need a miracle? Is there a dream in your heart you wish to come true? What about that goal you have set for yourself again and again? Take notice and you can begin to see the miracle you need come into being. Miracles happen in every moment that even one heart is open to receive. There is beauty, love, light, energy, joy, and all that is good all around you and within you. Take notice and begin to see all that is good manifest more fully in your life.

On the mat: Take notice by bringing your full attention to your practice. Notice the good work as you move in the exercises. Appreciate the miracle of being able to stand, move, breathe, and choose how to be. Be grounded, centered, and strong. Be open to receive this goodness. Feel energized by the heat generated by the working muscles. Focus your attention, and you can learn to direct this positive energy in ways that move you closer to your goals and dreams.

Off the mat: Your life itself is a miracle. Think for a minute about the amazing forces that came together to create you. In each moment of your life there are trillions of chemical and electrical messages being transmitted in your mind-body to sustain life. You do not have to think about a one. Take notice of this miracle. Take notice of the sunrise. Imagine the forces in place to maintain the order that allows us to predict the sunrise each and every day. Take notice of the beauty in a flower, a tree, or a dragonfly. Take notice of the good in others. Begin to see the miracle of life.

74. PRACTICE: Reach down deep

"Stability is achieved through perseverance, through holding on even under great strain, without weakening or trying to escape."

—Benedictine Rule

"Teach me to do your will, for you are my God, may your kind spirit guide me on ground that is level."

—Psalm 143:10

Intention: Roots must be established if optimal growth and full potential are to be reached. The depth of the root will predict the strength, stability, and height of the growth seen at the surface. Without depth, the root is superficial, and the slightest stress will result in the root being disconnected from its source of life. Reach down deep. Establish a root that is grounded deeply in the unseen.

On the mat: Reach down deep and draw your attention inward to be fully present in the body. Pay attention not only to the external, how the body looks, but also notice the feel of the body as it moves in the exercises. Feel your feet and legs grounding the body, feel your center, and feel your strength and stability in the work. Reach down deep and let it lift you. Let go of the need to prove your strength in the demonstration in the outer world. Believe in the strength within you, no matter what you see at the surface. Feel the strength within and you will see it grow.

Off the mat: The external world can demand our time and attention. Consider the time around Thanksgiving and Christmas. Reach down deep and remember the true meaning of the season. Let it be the foundation that provides you the strength and stamina to meet the external demands. With this root, you will be able to take on more with greater ease and remain centered and strong. This sense of being grounded and stable will allow you to enjoy this beautiful time of year rather than feel drained and overwhelmed by it. When you reach down deep, you will realize that you are far more capable than you once believed.

Remember that the root can only be established in the present moment. You cannot root yourself in the past or future. Be present, work in the now, and you will feel grounded and most able.

75. PRACTICE: To learn is to change

"You could not step twice into the same rivers; for other waters are ever flowing on to you."
—Heraclitus

"Do not conform yourselves to this age but be transformed by the renewal of your mind, that you may discern what is the will of God, what is good and pleasing and perfect."
—Romans 12:2

Intention: The mind is truly amazing. We have far-reaching potential, and we are capable of more than we can imagine. The brain alone contains 100 billion cells or neurons. We know that the mind is not confined to the brain alone but that intelligence exists in all cells of the body. Trusting a gut instinct is smart after all.

However, it is not the number of neurons that determines brain power or mental capacity; it is how the cells are connected to each other that matters most. How do we make connections, expand the neural network, and increase our mental capacity? We learn. Every time we learn, we make connections in the brain and the neural network expands and changes. New pathways are opened, and these pathways improve our ability to process information. To learn is to change. The key to learning is *new* experiences. We cannot learn something we already know. If we repeat the same activities with the same thoughts, we do not learn but continue to reinforce what we already know and believe. A willingness to change is essential to learning. Otherwise, we literally find ourselves in a rut. The same pathways are traveled again and again and we limit ourselves.

On the mat: The brain loves new. Learning is exciting. Bring a positive and open state of mind to change and learning will be enhanced. Every exercise, even those that have been repeated many times, can be new if you are fully present to the work. Moment to moment, every situation holds the promise of something new. Find the new and learn to love change.

Off the mat: Be willing to experience change and learn. Try new foods, music, activities, books, ideas, friends, and more. If you believe change is difficult, undesirable, or if you fear change, learning is impaired. The beauty here is that you can learn to enjoy change. Let go of the belief that change is difficult. You do not have to change everything in one day. There is plenty of time—a lifetime. Be open to the possibilities and the hope of something new.

76. PRACTICE: Your life is your message

"I call heaven and earth today to witness against you. I have set before you life and death, the blessing and the curse. Choose life . . ."

—Deuteronomy 30:19

A reporter approached Mahatma Gandhi as he was seated on a train to travel west and asked, "Before you leave, do you have a message for your people?" Gandhi wrote a few words on a scrap of paper and handed it to the reporter. It simply said, "My life is my message."

"Unless I am careful I am tempted to manipulate the people in my life. I find that I batter them with my demands, or force my own expectations upon them or so influence them that they feel bound to act in a way that they know will please me. I have in fact failed to accept them as they really are."

—Saint Benedict

Intention: As I read the words on this page as a message for the day, I remind myself that without action, the message is only words on a page, with no meaning and no life. Each day I bring the words to mind as my focus. I am amazed at how easily I can forget the words and therefore hinder my ability to bring the message to life in my thoughts, words, and actions. What messages do you hold in mind? What messages do you send each day to the people you touch? Do your thoughts, words, and actions convey a message of love and peace? Look within and begin to do the work that allows you to find the good within, and then in thought, word, and action, reflect that good to others.

On the mat: Devote time to your practice. You are investing in goodness. Can you expect yourself to perform good acts without practice? Our work on the mat is our practice time. We come and devote ourselves to the experience in mind-body of being vital, balanced, strong, enduring, flexible, focused, and coordinated. When doubt or fear arise in our awareness, our time on the mat can help us learn how to deal with these feelings effectively. We learn to respond to doubt and fear from a place within where faith and love abide.

Off the mat: Your life is your message. We do not always get to choose the circumstances, people, and events that come to us in life. Thank God for this. Can you imagine if you had to be responsible for orchestrating every detail of your entire life? Our minds could not process the amount of information necessary. We would literally lose our minds. Thank God also for freedom. He granted us free will, and in this we have the power within to choose how to respond to life. Our response to life, to others, is our message. Choose love and life.

77. PRACTICE: A price to pay

"Faith is the substance of things hoped for, the evidence of things not seen."

—Hebrews 11

"Twas grace that taught my heart to fear, and grace my fears relieved; how precious did that grace appear, the hour I first believed."

—"Amazing Grace" by John Newton

Intention: There is a price to pay for happiness, but it is not in dollars. Slow down, pause, take a deep breath in, exhale, and begin to let go. With each exhalation, feel the body letting go of unneeded tension. Let go of the past and the thoughts, feelings, and actions that are holding you back in the forms of regret and guilt. Let go of your worries over the future. Be here now. The health and happiness you seek can never be found in the past, and you will never know them if you insist on worrying over the future.

Happiness is here, now. What price do we have to pay?

The answer is within. Begin by asking yourself, "What am I fearful about?"

As an example, are you afraid the economy is failing? What is the economy? Does it have a life of its own? *No*—it has no life, no power over you except what you give it in your own mind. The economy has no life of its own. It is driven by our thoughts, words, and actions. *You*, on the other hand, have a life, a life that is a gift given to you, and you are called in turn to give this gift of self to others.

Are you waiting for the economy to get better? Will that lift you? Will you be happy then? You might be, but it won't last long because with your vision limited by seeing only what is on the surface in the outer world, there will always be something to fear around the next turn. If you are waiting for what is seen to lift you, you will most likely feel burdened and lacking life energy, like dead weight, without consciousness. *But that is not you.* You have a life, and you have much to offer. Raise your level of awareness, and begin to see more clearly. If you focus only on what is seen on the surface, you severely limit yourself, for things are not always as they appear. What is seen on the surface, in the outer world, is a small fraction of all that is. With limited vision, a full understanding of the truth is impossible, and this is why we fear. Human vision is limited, and we will never be able to see and understand all in life. We can learn to trust in the unseen and thus expand our vision and understanding.

If you feel afraid, you are human. Fear is essential for our survival. Being afraid to die helps us to live. We can learn to respond to our fears by remembering we are not only human, but we are also more than what is seen. God is within.

What is the price to pay for happiness? *Faith*—believe in the unseen. Believe that God's goodness and love is within. God reveals God to you, through you, in mind and body. See God in the vital energy that moves you—in the center that balances and stabilizes you, in the strength that gives you the discipline and courage to choose, in the open heart that lets you give and receive love, in the flow of the breath that comforts and guides you, in the eyes that see clearly—God is with you.

On the mat: Enough said. You do not have to wait. Stand up and be a part of the force that lifts and brings to life all that is good.

Off the mat: You are good, very good, because you are of God. Believe and remember in each moment to see God in you, in others, and in all that is. Have faith. Believe and see.

78. PRACTICE: Be willing

"The Advocate, the holy Spirit that the Father will send in my name—he will teach you everything and remind you of all that I told you. Peace I leave with you, my peace I give to you. Not as the world gives do I give it to you. Do not let your hearts be troubled or afraid."

—John 14:26

"When you encounter resistance, it means you are moving forward. When you come across a challenge, it means you have reached the point where you can successfully meet that challenge. Each new challenge is an opportunity to stretch beyond your previous limits."

—Ralph Marston

"Beloved, let us love one another, because love is of God; everyone who loves is begotten by God and knows God. Whoever is without love does not know God, for God is love."

—1 John 4:7

Intention: Be willing to move beyond your limitations. Whatever has stopped you in the past is in the past. Now, in this moment, you can choose to move beyond your past limitations. You have in mind a goal, a desire, a dream, and to move from that thought to action requires willingness. Be willing to act. In the moment of decision and as you progress along the way, you are certain to meet resistance. Expect it in many forms. Avoidance: "I can't do this. It's too hard." Distraction: "I've got too many other things to do." Perfection: "It's not good enough." Fear: "What if I fail? What if I succeed?" Self-centeredness: "This isn't fair." Procrastination: "I'm not ready or able now." Boredom: "I'm stuck in a rut." Whatever you meet in the form of resistance, remember, it is not there to stop you. It is there for you to overcome. *Honor the resistance, and be willing to act.*

On the mat: On the physical level, resistance is tension. As you move in the exercises, especially those that stretch you beyond your current level of flexibility, you are going to meet resistance. When you feel the tension in the muscle as tightness, honor the resistance. *Do not* try to push beyond this tightness until you honor it by moving gently to the edge of discomfort. You can judge this edge by the breath. You should be able to breathe easy. If the breathing is restricted or you notice you are holding your breath, you have pushed too far. Keeping your attention in the space of the body where you feel the tension, begin to follow the breath. Breathe in easy, and with each exhalation, notice the muscle softening as the tension eases. Use the mantra, "*Sustain in me, a mindful, willing spirit.*" Breathe in as you say, "*Sustain in me*" and on the exhale say, "*A mindful, willing spirit.*" Now, move beyond the limitation. Where there was once tension, there is now a greater sense of ease.

Off the mat: In order to be willing to act you must first remember what moves you. Spirit within is your sustenance and source of all movement. You are the one who must act. Be willing. The knots you feel in your gut, the tightness in your chest, are not there to stop you from moving forward. They are what you must move forward, through and beyond. Honor the resistance. The space in which you experience the resistance is also the space of release. Do not get stuck and focus on the resistance, move beyond it with a sense of ease. Remember, you are not alone. Let the breath comfort and guide you.

"Ask and it will be given to you; seek, and you will find; knock and the door will be opened to you."

—Matthew 7:7

"Come to me, all you who labor and are burdened, and I will give you rest."

—Matthew 11:28

79. PRACTICE: Find a way

"I sought the Lord and he answered me and delivered me from all my fears. Look to Him that you may be radiant with joy, and your face may not blush with shame."

—Psalm 34

"To learn, to raise new questions, explore new possibilities, to regard old problems from new angles, requires creative imagination with all the senses."

—Albert Einstein

"But if any of you lacks wisdom, he should ask God who gives to all generously and ungrudgingly, and he will be given it. But he should ask in faith, not doubting . . ."

—James 1:5

Intention: This week in your practice, explore the possibilities and find a way to see God in all things. Every moment holds a possibility. Choose to move in ways that help you recognize, nurture, and grow love and goodness. Be more and more able to see first in God all that is good. Remember, we cannot see God with the eyes. To see God is to see love, to see with the heart. God will then open your eyes, and you will begin to see this love and goodness manifest in your life.

On the mat: Find a way to come to your practice daily. There are an infinite number of possibilities. Find a way that works for you. We can come to love the work and come to it each day with renewed interest and positive energy. If you miss a few days, weeks, months, or years, do not let it matter. Begin again.

Off the mat: Your daily practice establishes a foundation for the work in mind-body that will not erode with added pressures or give way to the many distractions we face. All that you do with the intention to trust and love God, yourself, and others strengthens this foundation and brings stability, which allows you to endure.

"For stability says there must be no evasion; instead attend to the real, to the real necessity however uncomfortable that might be."

—Saint Benedict

80. PRACTICE: Come into being

"We lead a simple life when we do not pretend to be something we are not."

—Joan Chittister

"Now I saw that the principle of life, the secret to all successful living, was making God a part of my consciousness."

—Joel Goldsmith

"Yet for us there is one God, the Father, from whom are all things and for whom we exist . . ."

—1 Corinthians 8:6

Intention: Most of us feel we lead busy lives with many things to do. We can get so busy *doing* that we lose touch with our *being.* Come into being. Rather than focus on all that you have to do, pay attention to all that you can be. This week, give some time and attention to your being. As you come to all the things to do, remember, be happy, be peaceful, and be love. The more we are able to come into our being, all the doing will fall into place and we may experience a greater sense of being able.

On the mat: Begin with your exercise. Rather than coming to the work feeling like it is something to do (you might even believe it is something you have to do), let this be a space and time for you to *be.* Be fully present, centered, and strong. Be open to the experience; be flexible, and be focused on all that is good within. Be happy that you are able to be all this in whatever measure is possible today. Come into being by staying in touch with the body. The mind-body is your instrument of being in union with all that is good, with all that is God.

Off the mat: There will always be things to do, and doing is good. There is nothing wrong in thinking things through and coming up with our to-do list. I know, however, that I can think too much. I get caught up in my thoughts and believe if only I think harder I can find the answer. I may rethink and overanalyze. This is rarely productive. Sometimes in the space of no thinking, the answer is found. In the stillness and quiet, the answer emerges. Sometimes there is no answer—only peace. Maybe peace is the answer.

81. PRACTICE: Your best work

"Do more than belong: participate. Do more than care: help. Do more than believe: practice. Do more than be fair: be kind. Do more than forgive: forget. Do more than dream: work."

—William Arthur Ward

"For the one who is least among all of you is the one who is the greatest."

—Luke 9:48

Intention: When challenges arise and the going gets tough, you are called to do your best work. Your greatest challenges are also your biggest opportunities. My dad told me a story about his days playing football at the University of Cincinnati. One thing he remembers most is the short phrase he read posted on the wall as he left the locker room before every game. He said it has stayed with him his whole life and helped him achieve many great things. It said, "When the going gets tough, the tough get going." Try not to want something other than what is. Accept the challenge as it is and you will be best prepared to respond effectively. Wanting the challenge to go away is like wanting to win without ever playing the game. If things always went your way and you knew only success, one failure would be enough to bring you down. You must do the work, your best work, when the challenge is before you. Being willing and able to accept the low is precisely what is needed to reach the high.

On the mat: Be ready to do your best work, and be mindful of the factors that can improve your readiness. Consider the following:
1. Create a space and time to work.
2. Balance work with adequate rest.
3. Build discipline with structure and routine. Get in the good habit of doing your best work.
4. Stay with it. If you make a mistake or fail to get it done—do not delay. Begin again.
5. Relax. Believe in yourself, and let your best work flow from the positive thought, "I am willing and able."
6. Remember the many good works you have already done. Go forward now with this in mind.
7. Set yourself up to succeed. Be ready.

Off the mat: There are opportunities in each day to give of yourself and to do your best work. Opening the heart and opening the mind to recognize these opportunities is the key to fulfillment. An open heart is simply saying yes to all that is. Whatever arises in your awareness, be ready and willing to accept what is. From this space of open heart you are best able to choose a response. An open mind is a willingness to see the good in each moment. Old is good. New is good. Old is new with increased awareness. Recognize when the going gets tough, you are called to do your best work.

82. PRACTICE: Do it for love

"You shall love the Lord, your God, with all your heart, with all your being, with all your strength, and with all your mind, and your neighbor as yourself."

—Luke 10:27

"Respect those who labor among you . . . esteem them very highly in love because of their work. Be at peace among yourselves."

—1 Thessalonians 5:12

"We cannot do great things. We can only do little things with great love."

—Mother Teresa

"Work is love made visible."

—Kahlil Gibran

Intention: Some may think that taking time to care for you is selfish. It can be, depending on your intention and motivation. Whatever you do, if you do it for love, it can only be for the good of all. If fear is what drives you, then it's possible that your motives are selfish. If you exercise or work hard because you are afraid of what will happen if you don't, if you are afraid to fail, if you are afraid you're not good enough, these fear-based states of mind-body can lead to selfishness because fear becomes the driving force behind your choices. Love is not selfish. Let your love of God, love of self, and love of others be the driving force behind your thoughts, words, and actions.

On the mat: Do it for love. This work extends far beyond the physical movement and has the potential to awaken all that is good within. In the end, it will not matter nearly as much what you are doing but that you are doing it with great love.

Off the mat: Will you always be able to do it for love? No—not if you are human. We will all be motivated by fear at times. Fear is not bad; it is good if we can see fear as a messenger. Fear will always tell us where love is needed. If you are afraid of ill-health, love God, yourself, and others, and make the choices that lead to good health and well-being of mind-body. You are best able to serve others when you take care of yourself. If you are afraid to fail, learn to love the mistakes that teach you vital life lessons. If you are afraid you're not good enough, begin by loving yourself now just the way you are. If you are afraid of the future, love and live fully in each moment.

83. PRACTICE: Have fun

"Rejoice always . . ."

—1 Thessalonians 5:16

"Take courage, it is I, do not be afraid."

—Matthew 14:27

"Live and work but do not forget to play, to have fun in life and really enjoy it."

—Eileen Caddy

Intention: We each come to our work for our own reasons, and yet I feel certain that on some level we all have a shared purpose. Our work is good and productive. If our work feels like a burden, it may be that it is not the work but the lack of play that has created the imbalance. Work takes effort, but it can also be fun. The work can be fun when we are mindful to balance our work with play. Lighten up and let yourself move with greater ease. Have some fun. Trust others and work together. Your world will feel more balanced, and as a result of this balance, you will be more productive and creative.

On the mat: Remember the joy in playing as a child. Bring that playful spirit to your practice. Suddenly, everything is new.

Off the mat: Take time each week to have fun. Pause for a few minutes and remember the activities that are fun for you. Recall your childhood and remember some of the times in your young life that brought you joy. Share some of these stories with your family and friends. Bring that fun to life now. Add even more excitement, and try something new.

84. PRACTICE: Move with purpose

"There is an appointed time for everything, and a time for every affair under the heavens."

—Ecclesiastes 3:1

"The real purpose of teachers, books and teachings is to lead us back to the Kingdom of God within ourselves."

—Joel Goldsmith

"We know that all things work together for good to those who love God, who are called according to his purpose."

—Romans 8:28

Intention: Exercise can feel difficult at times. It can be hard to overcome inertia and get moving. Let go of the excuses—"I'm not able, I'm not disciplined, I don't have the time," etc. Most likely, none of these are true. If you want to be able to get going, find a reason to move. Ask yourself, "Why?" What is your purpose or reason for moving? Without a purpose, it can feel like trying to prepare for a trip with no place to go. Without a conscious decision to direct the movement, the mind-body may be idle or wander. This "mindless" movement will most likely be nonproductive and less than satisfying. In this state of mind-body, you are likely to feel a lack of energy, lack of desire, tired, unfulfilled, and bored. All these feelings are not because you don't like to move or are unable but because you lack a meaningful purpose, a direction that is consciously chosen. We learn to choose by being open to the information we need in order to make a good choice.

We are constantly taking in information from the outer world of our senses and the inner world of thought, feeling, imagination, and intuition. All this information is useless unless we are able to act on it. Without movement—the ability to act—the information becomes a burden, a heavy weight to carry. It would be similar to eating without being able to digest and assimilate the food into energy. Without proper digestion, the use of the food as energy to move the body would not be possible. The food would continue to pile up in the form of excess weight.

Knowledge without action becomes a burden. The stored information becomes the fuel of resentment, guilt, and anxiety. These are all signs the body needs to move with purpose. If you want to relieve this burden, find a reason to move. All movement is a form of giving and receiving. Give of yourself in ways that serve others. This is your purpose. Keep an open heart to receive their love in return.

On the mat: Why do you practice? Why do you want to be grounded, centered, and strong? Do you move for your benefit alone, or does your purpose extend beyond yourself to include others? Dedicate your time on the mat to becoming more able to move on purpose. To hold a thought, "I am going to balance on one leg," and to bring that thought to reality is purposeful movement. Feel the body in motion, and be conscious of all that comes into being as you move in the exercises. Remember the seven gifts: vitality, balance, strength, endurance, flexibility, focused attention, and coordination. These gifts are within. Move with purpose, and realize all that you are.

Off the mat: You definitely have what it takes. Take whatever time you need to identify your purpose. A meaningful purpose will move you beyond your current limitations. A purpose gives you something to move toward. It provides direction and can raise motivation to levels that will keep you moving even when challenges arise. Your purpose keeps you on track. Be decisive, and identify your purpose.

85. PRACTICE: Be ready

"Sometimes opportunities float right past your nose. Work hard, apply yourself, and be ready. When an opportunity comes you can grab it."

—Julie Andrews

"Before everything else, getting ready is the secret to success."

—Henry Ford

"Be dressed in readiness and keep your lamps lit."

—Luke 12:35

Intention: Being an observer is an important life skill. However, we cannot go through life as a spectator only. We are each called to be in the game. In life, it's not a question of whether you are good enough to play. You are in the game now. The question is, "Are you ready?" Are you ready to give it your best effort and make a difference?

Be ready on and off the mat. Readiness can be summed up in three basic steps:
1. Prepare
2. Receive
3. Respond

Try this exercise to ready yourself in a matter of seconds:

1. Prepare
- *Breathe:* Take a deep breath in and relax as you feel the exhale. Be fully present. You are most ready when the mind is fully present in the body here and now.
- *Believe:* Affirm your purpose. Believe in God. Believe in yourself and others. Work together.
- *Engage:* Engage the abdominal muscles and remember you are strong and you have the will to choose.

2. Receive:
- *Open:* Open the mind and open the heart. Try not to judge quickly. Leave a space for learning to occur. If you judge immediately, you only reinforce what you already know. Be open to receive new information.

3. Respond
- *Feel:* We feel with the body. Get in touch with your feelings and let them be a source of energy, drive, and motivation.

- *Think:* Once you identify the feeling, "I *feel* angry, I *feel* happy," remember you are *not* the feeling and dismiss the thoughts, "I *am* angry, I *am* happy." You are the one who is called to respond to that feeling. "I *feel* sad. How do I want to respond to the feeling of sadness?" Do not over-identify with the feeling. "I am sad" is simply not true. Feelings move through you, and when you learn how to respond to them, you can direct this energy in thought, word, and action. If you over-identify with the feeling, you have given it too much power, and it can move you seemingly against your will. This can lead you to feel a loss of control. The feeling has no power to take away your will and self-control. You have given it away when you believe you are the feeling rather than the one called to respond to it.
- *Act:* Choose to move in ways that are aligned to your purpose.

Use the key words for an easy reminder and be ready:

- Breathe
- Believe
- Engage
- Receive
- Feel
- Think
- Act

Breathe, believe, engage—this sets the foundation for all your movement in mind-body. You are now prepared. Receive the information from the outer and inner worlds by being open in mind and body. Feel, think, and act grounded in the present moment with the heart and mind open and your responses will move you forward confidently in the direction of your dreams.

86. PRACTICE: You give it meaning

"Men are disturbed not by things, but by the view which they take of them."

—Epictetus

"See God in all things."

—Thomas Merton

"For everything, absolutely everything, above and below, visible and invisible . . . everything got started in him and finds its purpose in him."

—Colossians 1:16

Intention: As you read the words on the page, as you take in life, remember that you give it meaning. The words on the page mean nothing until you receive them and give them meaning. Life's events are the same. You give them meaning. The beauty is that we can choose. We can choose the meaning we give to the words on the page and to life.

Consider these views on everyday life events:

- Work:
   Work is burdensome, draining, an obligation, or
   Work is an opportunity, a privilege, sharing one's abilities and gifts with others.
- Time:
   There's never enough time, I am always busy with too much to do, or
   The natural cycle of day to night is perfect. There is plenty of time. Everything has its place and time. Accept what is given, and choose how to spend it.
- Weather:
   It's too cold, too hot, too humid, too dry, too wet, or
   It is all good. Be thankful and enjoy what each day brings. A cold day can warm the heart if you are able to see the beauty in it.
- Health:
   Injury, disease, and dysfunction mean suffering, pain, and punishment, or
   Illness can be the mind-body's natural way of restoring balance and equilibrium by releasing the unneeded tensions and toxins. I am able to be healed.
- Sin:
   Sin is evil and to be condemned. The absence of God, or
   Sin is a mistake to be forgiven, drawing us closer to God.

On the mat: You give the work meaning. What does your practice mean to you? Each exercise or pose, *poses* an opportunity. The variety of poses challenges the mind-body in ways that awaken our awareness of all that is good within. When we hold the mind-body in the pose, we can become the observer and become increasingly aware of the power within to choose our response. If you feel weak, remember that weak is only a feeling; it is not who you are. What meaning do you give to that feeling? Is weakness in your awareness to tear you down or lift you up? Look for the strength within. Stay with the pose and make the necessary adjustments that allow you to find strength as you are able.

Off the mat: Life presents opportunities daily for us to learn and grow. We are going to face situations that cause us to doubt our abilities. This is not necessarily a bad thing. You give it meaning. The situations come not to weaken us, beat us down, or cause us to falter and end there. The difficulties we face come as openings to experience our inner source of all that is good. It takes time and practice. We have no problem accepting that it takes time for a baby to learn to sit up, to crawl, to walk, and then to run. Be patient with yourself. Accept, understand, and embrace your human nature. Remember, you give meaning to being human.

87. PRACTICE: Connect with the vital energy within

"We shall be God's temples, and God will be the God within us."

—Saint Ignatius of Antioch

"Fix the eyes of your inward man on God, until you understand that your life is in God. God is your soul's home and only safe dwelling. In God you stand firm and unshakable."

—Julian of Norwich

Intention: Where do we find the energy to do the work we want and need to do? Food is our outer source. We need to take in a certain amount of food, which is converted by the body into the energy we use to move and grow. We maintain our ideal weight when we balance calorie intake (food consumption) with calorie output (the energy we expend). If we take more than we expend, we gain weight. If we take less, we lose weight. In balance, we realize our ideal weight.

Food, however, is not our only source. We have an inner source of energy we can learn to access. Without awareness of this inner source, we may rely so heavily on the outer source that an imbalance results. In our need to feel vital, if we lack awareness of our inner source, we may overeat to compensate. *Try these suggestions to increase you awareness of the inner source of vital energy.*

1. *Early to bed*: When we sleep, we unconsciously reconnect with the vital energy within—God within. Sleep deprivation can lead to various states of imbalance in mind and body. Hormonal balances that control appetite, wakefulness, and metabolism can be altered. Most adults need seven to eight hours of sleep, while teenagers and children need more. Sleep renews, revitalizes, and readies us for the next day. Improve the quality of your sleep by keeping artificial lighting to a minimum after dark, keep the television out of your bedroom and shut it off one hour before bedtime, slow down toward bedtime, and do the heavy work early in the day. Refrain from eating two to three hours prior to sleep, read a book that relaxes you, pray, or meditate. Most importantly, *let go. Briefly* think over your day. Be thankful for all that you were able to do. Let go, and let the mind rest wholly in the body. Take a couple of deep breaths, and feel the body relax. Trust that everything will work out. Put your trust in God. You will sleep easy and wake up feeling refreshed.

2. *Early to rise:* Follow the natural cycle of day and night as much as possible. When it gets dark, go to sleep, and when the sun rises, rise with it. Start your day with prayer or meditation. The intention connects you immediately to the vital energy within. Remember to eat breakfast. Without "break fast," your body continues in the slowed metabolism of fasting that you experience at night during sleep. Eating breakfast gets your metabolism going again and can give you a lift. If you don't feel hungry in the morning, it is possible that you ate

too much the evening before. Consider exercise in the morning. It gets the mind and body warmed, energized, and ready to go.

3. *Move throughout the day:* Take time throughout the day to move. Take the stairs, walk from the parking lot, carry your groceries, get up from your desk and take a few deep breaths, pace when you are on the phone—the possibilities are endless. Do as much as you can for yourself.

4. *Eat smaller frequent meals:* Rather than three large meals, choose smaller portions and have high-protein snacks between meals. Choose whole foods as close to their natural state as possible.

5. *Drink plenty of water:* Drink eight glasses of water a day, more if you are exercising. Our body composition is 65 to 75 percent water. When you are dehydrated, you are really not your best self. Imagine a wilted flower. When you feel hungry, before you reach for food, drink a glass of water and wait ten minutes. You may have been thirsty, not hungry at all.

6. *Spice up your life:* Hot and spicy foods can have a positive effect on your metabolism. Find other ways to spice up your life.

7. *Adequate calcium intake:* Calcium is one essential mineral that keeps the mind-body functioning optimally. Good sources of calcium include low-fat dairy products, green leafy vegetables, and sesame seeds. Whole foods are best and more readily absorbed. Take a supplement if you cannot add these foods to your diet. A calcium supplement should also include magnesium to aid in absorption.

8. *Get some sun:* The skin is made to absorb sun rays and provide the body with adequate Vitamin D. Deficiency of this essential vitamin can lead to many ailments, including muscle weakness, bone pain, increased risk of death from cardiovascular disease, cognitive impairment in older adults, and rickets. Research suggests that Vitamin D could play a role in the prevention and treatment of conditions such as type 1 and type 2 diabetes, hypertension, glucose intolerance, multiple sclerosis, severe asthma in children, depression, and cancer. The body can produce adequate Vitamin D with fifteen to thirty minutes of unprotected exposure to the sun a few times a week for most people. Do not be afraid of the sun. The sun is life-giving. Everything in moderation is the key. Obviously, protect yourself from overexposure and burning of the skin. Other sources of Vitamin D include salmon, eggs, fortified milk, fortified cereals, and supplements.

88. PRACTICE: Try easy

"When you are inspired . . . dormant forces, faculties and talents become alive, and you discover yourself to be a greater person by far than you ever dreamed yourself to be."

—Patanjali

"I am the vine, you are the branches. Whoever remains in me and I in him will bear much fruit, because without me you can do nothing."

—John 15:5

Intention: We have all heard someone say to us, "Try hard." Trying hard is a good thing in balance with trying easy. Trying hard is of the ego, and it is important to develop a strong sense of self, a strong-minded will, and self-discipline. Our will and discipline can move us toward our goals, and we can achieve good things. We must also remember that we are more than just the ego. Ego is our identification with our human being. We are first a spiritual being, and if we want to experience our true and whole self, not just the ego, we have to give energy and attention to the spirit within.

Giving attention to the spirit within is being able to surrender to a power higher than the ego. To try easy, we let go of the idea or belief that we have to do it all by ourselves. Overworking is not a testimony to our true nature or a reflection of our awareness that God is within. It is a testimony to ego alone. Let God be a part of your life and your work. Try easy, knowing that all energy, strength, love, and goodness come from God.

On the mat: Try easy by allowing yourself to simply enjoy the work. You might think, "But I can't enjoy something that is difficult or hard for me." Practice bringing to mind the thoughts and beliefs that you are able to feel a sense of ease even in difficult situations. Come to the breath. Breathe easy, and try easy. Become the observer, and notice how your practice feels when you do not have to try hard but try easy.

Off the mat: Bring yourself to a situation that in the past you have found challenging. Remind yourself that God is with you. Take a deep breath, feel inspired, and try easy.

89. PRACTICE: Be what you want

"We ought to thank God always for you . . . because your faith flourished ever more, and the love of every one of you for one another grows ever greater."

—2 Thessalonians 1:3

"Nothing happens unless first a dream."

—Carl Sandburg

"Follow your dreams for they are the hope of the future."

—From a placard in Saint Mary's Cathedral in Sydney, Australia

Intention: What do you want? Take a few minutes and write down your response to this question. Make a list. Look over your list, and reflect for a few minutes. Does the list reflect the things in life that you value most? Maybe your list includes:

- I want to be happy.
- I want to be healthy.
- I want to know peace.
- I want to feel loved and connected with family and friends.
- I want to be appreciated and respected.

If it's things you want—that is real also:

- I want a home.
- I want good food for myself and family.
- I want a car.
- I want beautiful things in my life, such as: clean water, clean air, nature, art, music, pets . . .

Look over your list again. Are these wants within your reach? Do you have the ability to *get* what you want? You may. However, what is most definitely possible is that now in this moment you can choose any want on your list and *be what you want*. Not *get*, but *be*. It is already within you.

- If you want happiness, be happy now.
- If you want health, be healthy now by being able to think and act in healthy ways.
- If you want love, be love for others.
- If you want a car, be the person who is able to own that car.
- If you want beautiful things in your life, be that beauty and see it in others.

Be what you want. You may want peace. You may even pray for peace, but are you willing and able to be peace? Begin with a thought. Let your thoughts be peace. Focus your attention, and be the peace you want.

On the mat: Being what you want takes practice. Use the exercises to help you feel more able. If you come to the exercises thinking, "I want to be strong," in each movement ask yourself, "What does strong look like in me, here and now?" Be that. Be strong.

Off the mat: Be all that you can imagine you want to be.

"The future starts today, not tomorrow."

—Pope John Paul II

90. PRACTICE: When you are ready

"When the student is ready, the teacher appears."

—Buddhist proverb

"Whatever you ask for in prayer with faith, you will receive."

—Matthew 21:22

Intention: Everything, literally every particle in the universe, has its place and time. There is a beautiful and perfect order. This order is not for us to try and re-create or duplicate. To experience this order, to feel like everything is as it should be, we only have to begin to see the order and align ourselves with it. We see the order by recognizing the good in all things, the good in ourselves and each other. We are among the particles of the universe, and there is a time and place for each of us.

On the mat: Be fully present to the body and its alignment in space and time. Look, listen, and feel as you process the information that allows you to position yourself in the exercises. When you are ready, you will be able to process the information in such a way as to bring the physical body into alignment. The mind-body must be ready to perceive. It is possible to feel grounded, centered, strong, open, flexible, and focused even in the most awkward positions.

Off the mat: No matter how many times you practice a pose, no matter how many times you hear or read the words—the practice and the words will have meaning only when you are ready to receive them. We must not only hear and practice but also bring them to life. It will happen when you are ready.

91. PRACTICE: Victory over defeat

"Pursue righteousness, devotion, faith, love, patience and gentleness. Compete well in the faith."

—2 Timothy 6:11

"I am eager to encourage you in your faith, but I also want to be encouraged by yours. In this way, each of us will be a blessing to the other."

—Romans 1:12

"Nothing is stronger than gentleness."

—John Wooden, Hall of Fame basketball coach

Wooden said he learned this from his dad: "We had a team of mules named Jack and Kate on our farm. Kate would often get stubborn and lie down on me when I was plowing. I couldn't get her up no matter how roughly I treated her. Dad would see my predicament and walk across the field until he was close enough to say 'Kate.' Then she'd get up and start working again. He never touched her in anger. It took me a long time to understand that even a stubborn mule responds to gentleness."

Intention: We all want to win. The thrill of victory drives us to compete and to be enthusiastic spectators wanting to know what it feels like to be the best, the strongest, or the fastest. One way our family has known the thrill of victory is in the game of football. For generations, grandfathers, fathers, uncles, husbands, brothers, and sons have played the game. They play hard, sacrifice, and dedicate themselves to the game, the team, and their family. It is in the movement before, during, and after the game that brings us together with a common purpose—*victory!* Growing up with the game, you come to understand that you do not have to be on the field to be a part of the team. My mother taught me this lesson. When my dad played, she worked hard doing her part, and I never heard her complain. No spotlight, no glory—only love and dedication to her family. They both did their part.

Victory over defeat does not mean victory without defeat. Both have their place. It's easy to get wrapped up in the game and lose sight of your purpose. True victory is freedom from the opposition and cannot be achieved without facing the opposition with respect. We need each other to know the joy of victory. Winning the game alone does not set us free, because we are not always going to win. The game simply provides an opportunity for us to remember what is possible when we realize we are already free. There is no opposition trying to destroy or defeat us. Whatever opposition we meet is to lift us. Free yourself from having to prove you are the best or having to lift yourself above others. You and your opponent are just as good now and always because you are of God, not because you are stronger, bigger, or faster than someone else. If you play the game of having to be bigger, stronger, or faster than others, tomorrow someone will be bigger, faster, or stronger than you.

Play by the rules or laws of God, including the law of gravity. We cannot lift ourselves. Someone has to be on the bottom to lift the other. Someone has to lose so the other can win. Your hard work has not been wasted in defeat because you have been a part of lifting the other. Your effort, not lack of it, even in defeat, lays the foundation for the thrill of victory. *If you want to be a winner, you must be able to accept defeat.*

When the game is over, it's not really over. Opposing teams line up and face each other to shake hands. Players circle together on the field to pray, and families join them in a display of unity. This unity extends beyond what is seen on the field. Whether you came out on top or bottom on this particular day does not matter nearly as much as the fact that you recognize it was a team effort—one game, one team, and one victory.

On the mat: Come together and work together. Meet any opposition knowing that if you are willing to face it with respect, it can lift and strengthen all involved. If you find yourself down, you may be in a position to lift another. Stay in the game. We are not better than anyone else but no worse either. We are all just as good. We each have to begin to do our part.

Off the mat: Play a good game. I asked members of my family what it takes to play a good game. This message is a team effort:

- Be prepared and ready: train, practice, and have a game plan.
- Understand the opposition so you know what to expect.
- Be able to adjust and adapt to the movement of the game. Learn from your mistakes.
- Do your job, give your best effort, and trust others to do the same.
- See yourself making the plays, and be confident in your ability to get the job done.
- Play with integrity and respect your opponent.
- Accept defeat: make no excuses and blame no one.
- When the going gets tough, the tough get going. Persevere.

92. PRACTICE: Something light

"We are all meant to shine as children do. It's not just in some of us, it is in everyone."

—Nelson Mandela

"We were made for happiness . . . we can only discern our true condition before God in faith."

—Julian of Norwich

"We do not quit playing because we grow old, we grow old because we quit playing."

—Oliver Wendell Holmes

Intention: On occasion I say to my husband and adult children, "Let's do something fun together." We are all up for it, but sometimes we cannot think of anything to do. When the children were young, we had family fun night on Fridays. We would play games, build forts, run relay races, create obstacle courses, read books, tell stories, make ice cream sundaes, listen to music and sing, and sit outside and watch for falling stars. It is always wonderful to be together and find the time for something light and fun. Sometimes it comes together with little or no effort. Sometimes we have to put forth the effort to make room for something light in our lives.

On the mat: Let your movements in the exercises feel light and fun. Give your best effort and attention to the work, and be willing to feel the light and joy in it. If you give it too much weight by neglecting other aspects of your life, or taking the work too seriously, the work can feel more like a burden. In this state of mind-body you take away the light and lift that is yours to experience if you will only allow it. Remember the balance.

Off the mat: Let's get back to family fun nights. Get together with family and friends and remember the joy in something light and fun. It does not have to be a major event that requires a lot of thought and planning. It does not have to be something you do every week. Go for the simple things. Sometimes all you need is a deck of cards. The game is a time to be together.

93. PRACTICE: The flow of emotion

"Each emotion offers a distinct readiness to act, each points us in a direction that has worked well to handle recurring challenges of human life."

—Daniel Goleman

"I have learned the secret of being well fed and of going hungry, of living in abundance and of being in need. I have the strength for everything through him who empowers me."

—Philippians 4:12

Intention: Our emotions can carry us away like a torrent if we lose touch with the instrument that allows us to direct the flow of that energy. The mind-body is that instrument, and to stay in touch means to be grounded in the present moment. Without emotion we would not be human, and so we must learn to go with the flow of emotion, positive and negative. Do not attempt to rid yourself of every negative thought or emotion. It is not possible or desirable. The effort to do so will tear you apart. The thoughts and emotions we label as negative can work for us if we see clearly the negative in balance as part of the positive. Both negative and positive are essential parts of our experience. They move us in different ways and directions for a purpose.

When negative thoughts and feelings arise, it is easy to be tempted to think, "What's wrong? This is not good." We think "not good" because we feel a certain level of discomfort, uneasiness, and tension. When you feel this, do not worry or fret. Simply *take notice*. Identify the feeling. Do you feel heavy (burdened, sad)? Do you feel light (relaxed, happy)? Do you feel tight (anxious, fearful)? Do you feel soft and warm (trusting, open)? Do you feel heated (angry, frustrated)? Do you feel cool (flexible, focused)?

Once you identify the feeling, the key now is to remember—you are not this feeling. You are the one called to respond to the feeling as it arises in you. The negative as well as the positive emotions are meant to move you. You can choose how to direct the energy that arises from within. Which direction are you going to take? Turn to God. Dismiss the thoughts that lead you to believe you are "bad" or something is wrong with you because you feel discomfort or a negative emotion. Instead, recognize that the emotion can move you to action in a way that is intended to restore equilibrium. When you are uncertain what action to take, ask God, for He is ever-present and a very real source of guidance and help when in trouble. Remember, it is far more difficult to communicate with God when you perceive Him to be a distant God in heaven. Speak to God through His Son, Jesus Christ, who is present here with us now in every man, woman, and child through the Holy Spirit from the beginning and without end. Whether you are speaking to yourself or others, the question is the same. Simply ask, "How can I love you?" The answer you hear is your guidance.

On the mat: Whatever thoughts and feelings arise as you practice, take notice. Negative and positive can both work for you. Be mindful, and as you decide to take action, sort out the negative thinking and emotion. The negative thoughts and feelings can move us in creative and productive ways when we realize they can indicate a change of direction is needed. When you feel the negative emotion, pause and take a deep breath. Feel the emotion moving within you, and with each exhalation, let it go. Remember, God is within. Think now, how do you want to respond to this emotion? Ask, "What does love look like here and now?" Wait for the answer, and then act accordingly. For example, if you falter in an exercise and feel frustrated, notice the feeling and ask yourself, "How do I want to respond to this feeling of frustration?" Be willing and able to falter and experience the frustration. Change direction now, and focus on all that is good within. Stand strong and steadfast on both feet. Begin to let go of the frustration. Feel it lose its grip on you. If you are faltering today, maybe accepting and overcoming the frustration is exactly what you need to restore balance. This movement from frustration to acceptance is transformative. You will feel moved by the experience in a way that lifts and energizes you.

Off the mat: The energy generated from emotion is a powerful force to move us. If we refuse to feel and act on the emotion, to let it flow through us, that energy can be turned inward and leave us feeling restless, distracted, uneasy, and anxious. It becomes bottled up inside of us. This in itself may seem undesirable, but it does not have to be. See it as potential energy we can learn to use productively. The key is in our ability to respond and give direction to this flow of energy. Begin to see clearly that negative thinking and emotions do not have to keep you down. See the good, and use the flow of emotion to move you in the direction of all that is life-giving.

94. PRACTICE: Make a change

"I am told that the clinical definition of insanity is the tendency to do the same thing over and over again and expect different results."

—Albert Einstein

"Behold, God's dwelling is with the human race. He will dwell with them and they will be his people and God himself will always be with them as their God. He will wipe away every tear from their eyes, and there shall be no more death or mourning, wailing or pain, for the old order has passed away."

—Revelation 21:3

"Where the Spirit of the Lord is, there is freedom. All of us, gazing with unveiled face on the glory of the Lord, are being transformed into the same image from glory to glory, as from the Lord who is the Spirit."

—2 Corinthians 3:17

"Change alone is unchanging."

—Heraclitus

Intention: We have heard it said about our universe that the only constant is change. The entire visible universe is made up of the same ninety-two natural elements, and that includes us. Everything we see is made up of different combinations of these elements in varying states of matter and energy. A law of physics states that matter and energy can neither be created nor destroyed. They can only be transformed.

We change constantly. Our mind-body and the environment we live in are transformed not only year to year, but day to day and moment to moment. The mind-body, the world, and the universe are in a constant state of change in order to maintain equilibrium. Given that change is the natural order of the universe, it makes sense that we can improve the quality of our lives by learning to embrace change and direct those changes, when possible, through conscious choices.

Make a change today. Even a random change can be good for the system. Try a new food, new book, new music, new exercise, new place, new seat in church, new friends, and new thoughts. Change stimulates us and helps us be resilient. Small changes can help us let go of the fear of change and learn to embrace it.

On the mat: Sometimes we want to change but don't know how or think we are not capable. Our practice on the mat can prepare us and make us more able to face change with equanimity. Wanting to change but feeling unable to take the necessary action may lead to frustration, depression, and in extreme situations, aggression and hostility. Use your time on the mat to practice dealing with change. Every exercise places demands on you that increase your ability to adapt and respond to stress and change. Come to any new exercise or even the old exercise in a new way and make a change. You will be better prepared to live in this universe.

Off the mat: Change and adapt. Be able to take a trial and transform it into a tribulation. The opportunities will present themselves to you daily. Consider the common forms of stress listed below and think about how you might make a change. These signals of distress can be an awakening. If you refuse to change, do not expect an outcome any different from what you have right now.

Signals of distress:

- **Time urgency:** Trying to do more and more in less time and falling behind, chronically gazing at your watch, becoming angry when other people seem too slow, and feeling locked in a struggle with the clock.
  Make a change: Take a deep breath and slow down. Take your time. There will always be twenty-four hours in a day. Stop rushing yourself and others. Move with greater ease.
- **Tension:** Noticing your muscles tightening, your posture drooping, and/or the feeling of wanting to move and stretch, fidgeting.
  Make a change: Change your routine. Allow a space to take a breather. Try a few deep breaths, a breath of fresh air, a short walk, or five minutes in a rocking chair or swing.
- **Tiredness:** Feeling increasingly fatigued in mind and body.
  Make a change: Be sure to get adequate amounts of sleep. Sleeplessness can induce varying states of mental and physical illness. Sleep deprivation is cumulative. The good news is you can catch up by getting adequate rest. Take a nap and restore the balance.
- **Mistakes:** Noticing a drop in your performance.
  Make a change: A mistake is not necessarily a bad thing. See yours and others' mistakes as opportunities to learn and grow. A mistake can help us identify a point of weakness or ignorance—not to judge harshly but as a way to strengthen us in mind-body. Address the weakness, and learn from your mistakes. Forgiveness and patience are the keys to this change.
- **Irritability:** Feeling a rise in frustration, pessimism, impatience, hostility, or wanting to distance oneself from other people or events.
  Make a change: These feelings can build and cause us to act unknowingly *only* if we are unable to act effectively in the moment we feel them. When you feel these sensations, you will be prepared to respond if you take a moment to remember,

"I am grounded, centered, and strong. I am open, at ease, and focused." Focus on where you want to go, and then take action. Take the first step. You may need to step away. Distance can work for you when you know you can come back when you are ready.

- **Distractions:** When you find your mind wandering, have difficulty concentrating, and experience forgetfulness and procrastination.

  Make a change: Every distraction is an opportunity to focus. Draw your attention back and you strengthen your ability to attend to the things that matter most. It is like working a muscle. Every time you use it, you build strength.

- **Hunger or thirst:** Sensing the first deep pangs of hunger or thirst.

  Make a change: Take small portions more regularly rather than waiting until you feel starved or deprived. You will be less likely to overeat or drink in excess.

- **Feeling blue:** Feeling down, empty, despairing, or pessimistic or having a heightened sense of vulnerability.

  Make a change: Rather than seeing being low as something terrible to be avoided, accept the lows as a natural part of the cycle of being human. When you accept the lows in life, they can be the springboard for the next high or lift. It is coming. Be patient and have faith. Make a choice to *move* in ways that lift your spirits. Be with somebody. Watch a funny movie, call a close friend, walk in nature, listen to music, dance, read, write, and/or draw.

- **Aggression or hostility:** Feeling a surge of anger at other people, accompanied by an urge to harm them or wish that they be harmed or "taught a lesson."

  Make a change: Aggression and hostility are heightened states of frustration. Prevent these states and deal with them more effectively by acting in a productive way when the frustration arises rather than letting it build. Identify the source of frustration. It can never be another person or event. The source is within you. It is your thoughts and your feelings that you must learn to act on. If you are unsure of what action is necessary, go to the mat and practice. Let the movement awaken in you the answer. The answer is within. Do not blame others. Do not hold others accountable for your thoughts and feelings. This is your responsibility. Be "response-able."

95. PRACTICE: Read

"To read well, that is, to read true books in a true spirit, is a noble exercise, and one that will task the reader more than any other exercise which the current customs of the day esteem. It requires training such as the athletes underwent, the steady intention almost of the whole life to this object."

—Henry David Thoreau

"Saint Benedict assumes that the whole of the body and thus the whole of the person is engaged in the act of reading. So the Scriptures are mouthed by the lips, understood by the intelligence, fixed by the memory, and finally the will comes into play and what has been read is also put into practice. The act of reading makes the reader become a different person; reading cannot be separated from living."

—Esther de Waal

"He shall keep it with him and read it all the days of his life that he may learn to fear the Lord, his God, and to heed and fulfill all the words of this law and these statutes."

—Deuteronomy 17:19

Intention: Reading is food for thought. It is a powerful tool to train the mind-body to receive, assimilate, integrate, and respond to information. When we read, we receive information from two equally important sources. We take in information from the outer world of what is seen with the eyes as words on the page, and we take in information from the inner world, behind the eyes, the world of thought, feeling, imagination, and intuition. To read, to understand, and to act on what is read require an integration and balance of attention between these two sources. This cannot be taught but occurs naturally by being read to from infancy and by reading aloud and silently to oneself in a state of mind that is relaxed and receptive so that the spoken and/or written word flows easily. No other instruction is necessary.

When too much attention is placed on the outer world, the words on the page, the flow of reading will be interrupted and comprehension will suffer. When attention is overly drawn inward, daydreaming and loss of focus will make reading difficult. Consider the following suggestions to improve your reading:

- From the beginning, pair reading with relaxation and enjoyment. Read to your children every day from infancy. Let reading be a time of warmth, closeness, and comfort. Hold your children and read to them stories they enjoy. Let them read aloud with you. When they get old enough, let them choose their own books. Bedtime reading can help ease the tensions of the day and prepare the mind-body for a restful sleep. It can be continued into adulthood.

- Do not try to memorize the material when reading. This inhibits rather than improves comprehension. Memory will follow with greater ease from repetition and rhythm.
- Scan the written word in a flowing motion rather than trying to read every word in isolation.
- Link hand and eye movements by moving the hand along the written word in a flowing motion as you read.
- Increase the light in the room.
- Consider your posture and position. Upright posture is most conducive to effective reading and is less strenuous on the eyes.
- Take time for mental rest after intensive reading or learning.
- Consider what you choose to read. Words are to the mind what food is to the body. The daily intake of information from newspapers, magazines, Internet, television, video games, and other sources can consume the mind with images and messages that do not contribute to our learning and growth and can be overwhelming. When the mind-body feels overwhelmed, its natural tendency is to shut down. This will inhibit reading because the mind-body is no longer open to receive the incoming information.

On the mat: Bring a few words from your favorite passage, poem, or song to your practice. Let it be a point of focus for you to draw your attention to the present moment. Choose words that lift and inspire you in your work.

Off the mat: Read every day. Expand your vocabulary by reading new and different material. Stephen D. Krashen (2004) in his book *The Power of Reading: Insights from the Research* explains that "Free voluntary reading (henceforth FVR) means reading because you want to: no book reports, no questions at the end of the chapter . . . FVR is one of the most powerful tools we have in language development . . . it provides a foundation so that higher levels of profiency may be reached" (p.1).

Read the Bible and other sources of inspiration each morning and before going to sleep at night. After reading, take time and allow a space of silence. In the space of silence, new and creative thoughts arise that expand our vision of what is possible. You will feel lifted in no time.

96. PRACTICE: Work together

"Love one another as I love you."

—John 15:12

"So that we may no longer be infants . . . Rather, living the truth in love, we should grow in every way into him, who is the head, Christ, from whom the whole body, joined and held together by every supporting ligament, with the proper functioning of each part, bring about the Body's growth and build itself up in love."

—Ephesians 4:14-16

Intention: Vital families are the foundation for love in this world. Stay together, pray together, work together, and spend time together in ways that unite and strengthen. Draw those in who need you. Let everyone belong. Honor all living things because God made them.

On the mat: If you are here on earth, you have been given a body as an amazing gift with a purpose. You have been called by God to be love in this world. God has chosen each of us for love. We are here through Him alone. In your practice on the mat, remember your purpose. Prepare yourself to be open to fulfill this purpose, which is to love one another.

Off the mat: Do those things that unite and strengthen family, the most vital team:

- Stay together. Make a commitment and honor it. Marriage is a sacred union. Nourish and sustain it. Keep it alive and well.
- Pray together. Make prayer a part of your family life. Go to church weekly, and let God strengthen you in faith and love. Be a part of a larger community of faith.
- Work together. We share a common purpose. Let each person contribute in his or her unique way.
- Spend time together. Nothing shows love more clearly than giving your time and attention to someone. Devote yourself to God and family before all other things.
- Love one another. More than riches, love is the greatest gift. Honor the other. Remember the goodness and love within, especially when what is seen outwardly tempts us to doubt and fear.

97. PRACTICE: See clearly

"Forgiveness is the greatest factor of growth for any human being. It is demanding; it is an exercise which asks of us honesty and love."

—Saint Benedict

"Stop judging, that you may not be judged . . . Why do you notice the splinter in your brother's eye, but do not perceive the wooden beam in your own eye? How can you say to your brother, 'Let me remove the splinter from your eye,' while the wooden beam is in your eye? You hypocrite, remove the wooden beam from your eye first; then you will see clearly to remove the splinter from your brother's eye."

—Matthew 7:1-5

"Go first and be reconciled with your brother, and then come and offer your gift."

—Matthew 5:24

Intention: When we are grounded in God and rooted in our family, we can begin to expand our vision of "family" to include all of God's children. We can see more clearly that we are brothers and sisters and God is father and mother to us all. God created each of us in God's own image and likeness. To see each other clearly is to see God in the other. The only way we can possibly do this is to believe that our sins have been forgiven and remember that we are asked to forgive others as God has forgiven us.

"Let the one among you who is without sin be the first to throw a stone at her."

—John 8:7

On the mat: Look beyond the imperfections that are seen with the eyes. God did not allow imperfections in us as judgment or punishment against us. The imperfections remind us of our human nature and our need for God. They open the mind and heart so we can realize God is with us. God does not want us to suffer, nor does God ask us to suffer. We suffer because it is hard for us to believe in our goodness. When we look and see imperfections, mistakes, weaknesses, and failures, it is tempting to believe the body is a heavy burden. We think something is wrong with us or that we are not good. It is not meant to be this way. The mind-body is a gift that we are most definitely meant to carry—not in sorrow and pain, but in joy. The exercises are purposeful stress, and they awaken all that is good within us when the mind and body are one in the present moment. If the mind is not present in the body, the exercises will feel like a burden, and rather than being lifted by your work, you will feel drained and depleted. *When is the mind not present in the body? It is very easy to tell. In truth, the mind is always present, one with the body. We only think, believe, and feel separated, distant, and alone. The mind is truly present. We cannot separate the mind from the body. It is our thoughts alone that* *keep us stuck in the past with regret, remorse, or guilt, wanting things to be different than they are now. Our fearful thoughts over the future can immobilize us and prevent us from moving forward in love. We must remember that we are not our thoughts. We are God's love manifest in this world. God is ever-present. We will feel God's presence when we realize we are already home. The mind is home, fully present in the body. God is with us always. We only have to believe.*

Off the mat: Focus on all that is good in yourself and others. Try not to judge harshly. When human imperfections arise, respond with acceptance, understanding, compassion, and love. We make a mistake, but we are not a mistake. We have faults and failings, but we are not a failure. God is love—only love. God does not judge, condemn, and sentence us because of our failings. We judge, condemn, and sentence ourselves and each other because we fail to clearly see the truth. We forget who we are. Remember, we are all of God, and God is love. Believe in God's unending and unfailing love. It is within us.

"Asked by the Pharisees when the kingdom of God would come, he said in reply, "The coming of the kingdom of God cannot be observed, and no one will announce, 'Look, here it is,' or, "There it is.' For behold, the kingdom of God is among you."

—Luke 17:21

"He has bestowed on us the precious and very great promises, so that through them you may come to share in the divine nature, after escaping from the corruption that is in the world because of evil desire. For this very reason, make every effort to supplement your faith with virtue; virtue with knowledge, knowledge with self-control, self-control with endurance, endurance with devotion, devotion with mutual affection, mutual affection with love."

—2 Peter 1:4

"He took away our infirmities and bore our diseases."

—Matthew 8:17

98. PRACTICE: Come home

"Love the Lord your God with all your heart, with all your being, with all your strength, and with all your mind; and love your neighbor as yourself."

—Luke 10:27

"This is what gives us strength and certainty—when we come to trust God with our whole being."

—Julian of Norwich

"Blessed are the poor in spirit, for theirs is the kingdom of heaven."

—Matthew 5:3

Intention: God is both the space and substance of our being. In Him we breathe and move and have our being. God comes to earth not to break the law but to fulfill and sustain it through us. As God does works here on earth, the law must be fulfilled in every thought, word, and action. God will not break the law to conform to our will. For although we may benefit in the short term, breaking the law would ultimately result in chaos and confusion. Therefore, God fulfills the law in all things and all people. And God's law is love. God's love and goodness are infinite and everlasting, and His goodness and love abound. It is through faith that the law is carried out. As you believe, so be it done unto you.

"The only thing that counts is faith working through love."

—Galatians 5:6

When we come to this earth, every one of us, we come *poor in spirit*. We come in body as an infant with no conscious awareness that God's Holy Spirit is within us. Our parents and others may see pure love in us but may not truly know we are a gift from God. But God blesses us and leads us home. God wants us to come to know love and to consciously choose love—to love God with our whole being. If you try to know God through spiritual training alone, ignoring the body and your humanness, then you will have to leave this earth, leave this body, the dwelling place, and meet God in heaven. For God in heaven is infinite and pure spirit and cannot be comprehended with a finite human mind-body.

The only way to know God here on earth is through the mind-body. God came to this earth in human form through Jesus that we might know Him and believe in Him. That is, we can only know God, here on earth, through the body of Christ, which is within us. Our body, both individually and collectively as one, is the dwelling place of God. God is with us here and now. The desire in your heart to know love and peace here on earth is your desire to know God through Jesus. The mind-body is the instrument of knowing and experiencing God's presence.

Jesus showed us how God is within us through the power of the Holy Spirit. We can train the mind-body to be open to perceive the Holy Spirit within. The work must become a part of our whole being, bringing God's love to life. If we focus only on the spiritual training, the body is likely to feel burdened in some way, and we may feel heavy or uncomfortable. This heaviness is not a punishment for our mistakes or misunderstanding. God is simply trying to bring our attention to the space where God resides within. He wants us to come home. Your father and mother want you to know you are loved. God wants you to feel His warm embrace, His soft touch, and His gentle voice to soothe, comfort, and heal you. We have to stay in touch with the mind-body to know and feel God within us and with us. We need each other. Rather than transcend, punish, abandon, scorn, ignore, or judge the body, come home. Let the mind come home and abide in God, who is within. Abide in God, and let God who is love abide in you.

On the mat: I get frustrated, even angry sometimes, when I try to hold a posture and I fall out of it. What do I expect? Do I expect that the law of gravity should not apply to me in this situation? When I fall out of a pose, rather than asking God to conform the law to my will so the pose will be as I desire it, I must stay grounded and feel the sense of center that allows me to reconcile my will to the law. I learn to accept the fall not with resignation but with a spirit of determination to get up and try again so I might understand. I can learn and grow when I accept the fall, knowing that God wants me to turn to Him when I need help getting up. Take a deep breath in and feel the breath lift you. With the exhalation, let go and feel the weight of the body. Every breath can be a reminder. The in-breath is the lift of spirit, the weightless that is the one source of all life. The out-breath reminds us to let go, to feel our humanness, to be weighted on this earth by the force of gravity, and to love being human.

Off the mat: We are the body of Christ, not alone, but together, as one. God's Holy Spirit moves within us to energize, lift, and inspire us. We can feel this presence with each in-breath. With the out-breath, we let go into our humanness and feel at home in the body, grounded and relaxed. The truth of your being will never change or cease to be. God is within you, and God is love and all that is good. How you choose to show yourself in this life is ultimately up to you. Choose love and be true to yourself and others.

A song can bring the message home beautifully. This is the "Song of the Body of Christ":

We come to share our story, we come to break the bread,
We come to know our rising from the dead.
We come as your people, we come as your own, united with each other, love finds a home.
We are called to heal the broken, to be hope for the poor, we are called to feed the hungry at our door.
Bread of life and cup of promise, in this meal we all are one,
In our dying and our rising may your kingdom come.
You will lead and we shall follow, you will be the breath of life,
Living water, we are thirsting for your light.
We will live and sing your praises, Alleluia is our song,
May we live in love and peace our whole life long.

Song lyrics by David Haas. GIA Publishers Inc., Chicago 1989.

99. PRACTICE: Be the one who follows

"As Jesus passed on from there, he saw a man named Matthew sitting at the customs post. He said to him, 'Follow me.' And he got up and followed him."

—Matthew 9:9

"While he was still speaking, behold, a bright cloud cast a shadow over them, then from the cloud came a voice that said, 'This is my beloved Son, with whom I am well pleased; listen to him.' When the disciples heard this, they fell prostrate and were very much afraid. But Jesus came and touched them, saying, 'Rise, and do not be afraid.' And when the disciples raised their eyes, they saw no one else but Jesus alone."

—Matthew 17:5-8

"The Lord is my shepherd, there is nothing I lack."

—Psalm 23:1

Intention: It can be hard to follow. If you do not pay attention, you can easily lose sight of the one you are following and lose your way. Imagine trying to follow someone you cannot see. I feel this way sometimes when I try to follow Jesus. I cannot see Him here with me now. And so, we are told to listen. Listen to the Word of God in Jesus. When Jesus says, "Follow Me," He speaks in the present tense. If we believe that Jesus is with us here today, then we are called to follow Jesus now in this day and in this moment. "Follow me" does not mean try to do what He did. It means, "Listen now to My voice, feel My touch, and know that I am with you. I will lead and guide you. I will show you the truth."

We can know Jesus, hear His voice, and feel His presence in and through the mind-body. We are afraid at times to stay fully present to the body because we think that to pick up our cross and follow Jesus means that we have to suffer. Most of us want to avoid suffering. The cross becomes a symbol of suffering and death that we are afraid of, and so we avoid it. While it is true that the body is the cross, when Jesus says, "Pick up your cross and follow Me," remember that He is speaking to us now in the present moment. Through the resurrection of Jesus, God has shown us that death, sin, and all suffering have been overcome. And while we must remember that the body is weighted and we must rise and move it, we must also remember that when Jesus asks you to pick up your cross, He is asking you to come into your being, your body, and live in the joy of the resurrection. God is asking you to see with the eyes of faith and follow. If we believe in a loving and compassionate God, then we must let go of our fear that God has put us on this earth to suffer and die for Him. No. This is not true. What is true is that He died for us out of His great and unending love. Our human love is finite, and our human bodies are frail, and God does not expect us to bear that burden alone. Through Jesus our sins are forgiven and our bodies are redeemed. The body is a cross to bear—not to follow in death but to live in the life of the resurrection. We do not have to do what Jesus did.

We only have to believe what He did. Believe that He is raised. If we believe in death and suffering alone, we leave Him hanging. When we believe in the life and joy of the resurrection, we become grounded in the truth of God's promise in the risen Christ. This does not mean we will never suffer. We are still young and learning. We are going to make mistakes and suffer because of our human nature. When we believe in God, when we believe in Jesus, our suffering will not be a burden but a blessing because we will not be overcome when we believe God is with us. God will sustain us. We will be transformed, and we will know love and peace, on earth as it is in heaven.

On the mat: Our work is a moving meditation. We train the mind to stay wholly present in the body to become conscious of God within. Jesus has shown us what God is like, and we are called to see this good within ourselves and others. When you practice, remember that God is the space and substance of your being. Know what God is like, and begin to see God's goodness and love in all things. Feel the breath and know that God is the inspiration for all things—the source of life. Feel both feet on the ground and remember that you are here on earth for God's purpose, which is love. Engage the core to connect with your inner source of strength and stability. Open the heart, and begin to let the love and light within be seen in this world. When the heart is open, love will flow. Give direction to this flow of life energy by focusing on all that is good within you, others, and all that is. It all comes back to the beginning. Remember who you are.

Off the mat: A very interesting thing happened as I sat to write this passage one morning sitting in the sunroom of our home. I lifted my gaze from the computer screen, and as I looked out the window, I saw a chipmunk running across the deck, and it jumped straight into the pool. It was fall, and the water was shockingly cold. I jumped up thinking, "Oh my God, he's going to die." I ran outside and grabbed the net, ready to save this little creature. I got the net under it, and the chipmunk jumped up and out of the net. Twice more I tried to scoop it out of the water and he jumped out, all the while swimming the width of the pool. On my last attempt, standing from the rocks on the edge of the pool, I stumbled and almost fell in. That did not stop me. I rushed around to the other side of the pool to reach him. But he was not in the pool. How could he possibly have gotten up and over the pool edge? I asked myself, "Am I seeing clearly?" I stood there for a moment in disbelief. And then I laughed out loud. Maybe he was going just for a morning swim. He did not need me to save him. Things are not always as they appear.

I learned a valuable lesson that morning, and I have learned it before in other ways, many times. I think I can save others. I think I know what I'm doing. I think I am strong. I am well-intentioned, and I think I know what others need. I have to remind myself again and again. When I look out and see others and even as I see myself, I have to remember we are already saved through Jesus. God does not expect or ask us to bear the burden of salvation, but I take it on myself when I forget who I am and see the world in disbelief. God only asks that we believe, trust, and love God, ourselves, and each other. Believe in the good news of the gospel. Stay present to God. Listen and follow. In this way, we become the good news in thought, word, and action.

We do not have to save others or make any effort to save this world. We only have to believe that we are already saved and begin to move like we believe. When we believe in God, we believe in love. When we believe in Jesus, we are able to act in love by seeing God present in each of us and in all things. Let go of trying to fix and save this world, and as a friend reminded me this morning, live and love in each moment.

100. PRACTICE: Believe and you will see

"As he passed by he saw a man blind from birth. His disciples asked him, 'Rabbi, who sinned, this man or his parents, that he was born blind?' Jesus answered, 'Neither he nor his parents sinned, it is so that the works of God might be made visible through him . . . he spat on the ground and made clay with the saliva and smeared the clay on his eyes, and said to him, 'Go wash in the Pool of Siloam (which means Sent). So he went and washed and came back able to see."

—John 9:1-7

"But he said to the woman, 'Your faith has saved you; go in peace.'"

—Luke 7:50

"Let us ask Mary to teach us how to become like her; inwardly free, so that in openness to God we may find true freedom, true life, genuine and lasting joy."

—Pope Benedict xVI

"Wherever you turn, there is the face of God."

—Mohammed

Intention: God does not make mistakes. People make mistakes, and I make plenty of them every day. I sin mostly when I forget that I need God and that God also needs me. I need God, for without God there is no life. God needs me to bring this life to life. Do not be afraid to reach out a hand to others. They do need you. They need to be loved. They need you to see their goodness. They need to grow to be responsible for themselves. We need each other to know God's love. When you extend a hand to others, remember whose hand it is. It is not your own. You belong to God. Remember who it is you are reaching out to. To touch another in love is to touch God.

God sent Jesus to us by the message of an angel through Mary. Mary, the Mother of God, did not have any position or title. We know very little about her for a reason. None of the details about her outward life make her who she is to God. He accepts and loves her just as she is. God sees in her an opening for His Holy Spirit to grow and to be born into this world. Mary's pure, open heart and open mind were all God needed.

I remember years ago watching the movie *The Nativity Story* at Christmastime. One scene showed Mary with child walking with Joseph through the desert on the way to Bethlehem. They sat down on some rocks to rest and share a morsel of food. They looked tired and hungry. In the quiet stillness of the desert, Joseph raised his head and looked at Mary. "Are you afraid?" he asked her. I was surprised at her answer. I thought she would say, "No, I'm not afraid. I have faith that God is with us." She did not say that. She only said, "Yes I am." Joseph said, "I am afraid too." They stood up and continued on together. Like Mary and Joseph, we are human, and we are going to feel afraid and have thoughts that cause us to doubt and worry. God understands when we feel fear and doubt. God asks that we continue on in faith rather than allowing our fears and doubts to stop us from knowing and feeling His loving presence.

On the mat: We have a mind-body as an amazing gift to know and feel the loving presence of God within. We are asked to share this gift of self with others so God's love is made visible in this world. Use your time on the mat to remind yourself, again and again, to stay present to the presence of God within. See the Good Within. See growing within you and expressed outwardly through the seven gifts of God's goodness: *vitality, balance, strength, endurance, flexibility, focused attention, and coordination.* When you feel discomfort, it is human to be afraid. It does not mean something is wrong. Continue on. Move in ways that allow God's love to be made visible through you.

Off the mat: Love manifests in an infinite number of forms. See God in all beings and all things. Every person, every religion has its place in God. We each come to the body through our birth in a unique yet universal way. Do not be afraid to let others be as they are. When you feel afraid, remember God is within, and continue on. In every thought, word, and action, demonstrate that you believe in love. And not only believe, but feel it within you and extend it to others. Be an opening, like Mary, the mother of God, and let love grow within and through you.

"This is the work of God, that you believe in the one he sent . . . I am the bread of life; whoever comes to me will never hunger, and whoever believes in me will never thirst."
—John 6:29-35

"Amen, I say to you, whatever you did for one of these least brothers of mine, you did for me."
—Matthew 25:40

If you are a sister, do not be offended by the use of the word "brother" or "he" as God. Jesus came through Mary. God needs a body and a mind as one in each of us to do good works and to bring love to this world. Be happy with who you are, brothers and sisters.

101. PRACTICE: A beautiful thing

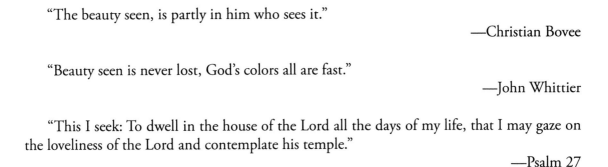

"The beauty seen, is partly in him who sees it."

—Christian Bovee

"Beauty seen is never lost, God's colors all are fast."

—John Whittier

"This I seek: To dwell in the house of the Lord all the days of my life, that I may gaze on the loveliness of the Lord and contemplate his temple."

—Psalm 27

"There is nothing in a caterpillar that tells you it's going to be a butterfly."

—Richard Fuller

Intention: There is beauty and goodness in all beings and in all things. It is not a beauty or peace you can gain for yourself or others no matter what you do. It cannot be achieved no matter how hard you try, for it is already given. It resides within. You can experience this beauty and peace by coming to the temple and being present in the body, remembering the infinite source of love and goodness within. Without God, beauty and peace can be elusive and fleeting, for they become dependent on man and circumstance. Depend on God and you will begin to see that all life is a beautiful thing.

On the mat: It is a beautiful thing that we can work together to know goodness and love. We have an opportunity in each and every day to begin to recognize and realize the beauty that is within us and all around us. As you practice, look for the seven gifts of God's goodness—vitality, balance, strength, endurance, flexibility, focused attention, and coordination. You are beautiful as you are.

Off the mat: This week behold a beautiful thing and give thanks.

102. PRACTICE: Wake-up call

"We must consider how to rouse one another to love and good works."

—Hebrews 10:24

"You need endurance to do the will of God and receive what he has promised."

—Hebrews 10:36

"It is important for everyone to move every day, and what I prescribe is daily aerobic exercise of about an hour. Everyone says they don't have time for that. Even retired people say that. It doesn't change the fact that we need it. The body's got to move. If we don't move, that's when we get in trouble."

—Dr. Klauer

Intention: There is no other single factor that promotes health and happiness more than an open heart. On the physical level, an open heart is a strong heart and one that can endure. We build endurance through aerobic exercise in some form. There is no other way. The body must move daily, and we must sustain an elevated heart rate for a period of thirty minutes or more. All the yoga, core work, and strength training will lead nowhere if you do not have an open heart. It is through an open heart that we can begin to feel lifted, energized, inspired, and moved to realize our potential. Mentally, an open heart is a willingness to go the distance.

On the mat: If you have found the way to make aerobic exercise a part of your life—keep up the good work. If not, begin today. Make a commitment to thirty minutes of aerobic exercise every day. Let go of the idea that you don't have time or that it's too hard or no fun. Focus on all the positive possibilities before you when you begin to feel your heart open. Start slow and easy and you will gain momentum, strength, and endurance as you learn to move with greater ease.

Off the mat: Put first things first. Aerobic exercise keeps our heart open and strong. It promotes endurance on the physical level. Mentally, endurance equates with love, patience, and perseverance. Make the choices that allow you the space and time to experience an aerobic workout for thirty minutes every day. Walking is a good start.

"If I speak in human and angelic tongues but do not have love, I am a resounding gong or a clashing cymbal. And if I have the gift of prophecy and comprehend all mysteries and all knowledge; if I have all faith so as to move mountains, but do not have love, I am nothing. If I give away everything I own, and if I hand my body over so that I may boast but do not have love, I gain nothing . . . Love bears all things, believes all things, hopes all things, endures all things. Love never fails."

—1 Corinthians 12:31

A Song:
"How Can I Keep from Singing?"

My life flows on in endless song, above earth's lamentation.
I hear the real though far off hymn that hails a new creation.
No storm can shake my inmost calm, while to that rock I'm clinging:
Since love is Lord of heaven and earth,
How can I keep from singing?
Through all the tumult and the strife, I hear that music ringing;
It sounds and echoes in my soul;
How can I keep from singing?
What through the tempest 'round me roar, I hear the truth it liveth,
What through the darkness 'round me close, songs in the night it giveth.
When tyrants tremble, sick with fear, and hear their death knells ringing;
When friends rejoice both far and near,
How can I keep from singing?
The peace of Christ makes fresh my heart, a fountain ever springing.
All things are mine since I am his;
How can I keep from singing?

Song lyrics by Robert Lowry. Sanga Music Inc., 1957, 1964.

103. PRACTICE: Be Warm

"Would not the child's heart break in despair when the first cold storm of the world sweeps over it, if the warm sunlight of love from the eyes of mother and father did not shine upon him like the soft reflection of divine light and love."

—Max Muller

"Cold hands, warm heart."

—Proverb

"Do not neglect to show hospitality to strangers, for by this some have entertained angels without knowing it."

—Hebrews 13:2

"The only way to have a friend is to be one."

—Ralph Waldo Emerson

Intention: No matter how cold it is outside, be warm of heart and your light and love will comfort others and keep you warm. Winter can be harsh and cold. We may see things we have never seen before. I saw another "first" for me that seemed to be a sign of warmth to come. In a tree nearby, covered with red buds, I saw robins perched on the branches. There were so many robins they looked like ornaments on a Christmas tree. It was a beautiful sight. Be warm this week and feel the light of sunshine lift you.

On the mat: Cardio exercise is one of the best ways to be warm. It raises your body temperature and can keep you warm for hours after a workout. It also gives you a nice lift and opens the heart. All good things come when the heart is open and warm. Come to the work, and you will reap the many benefits of an open heart. This work is not only for you. Imagine all those you can touch with light and love when your heart is open.

Off the mat: Be warm to others. Renew your love, and be the touch of warm sunlight for a spouse, a parent, a child, a friend, or a stranger this week. Be warm. Be a friend.

"Say nothing harmful, small or great: be not a foe, instead a friend . . . A faithful friend is a sturdy shelter, he who finds one finds a treasure."

—Sirach 6:1, 14

A Prayer:
The Angelus

"The angel Gabriel was sent from God to a town of Galilee called Nazareth, to a virgin betrothed to a man named Joseph, of the house of David, and the virgin's name was Mary. And coming to her, he said, 'Hail favored one! The Lord is with you.' But she was greatly troubled at what was said and pondered what sort of greeting this might be. Then the angel said to her, "Do not be afraid, Mary, for you have found favor with God. Behold, you will conceive in your womb and bear a son, and you shall name him Jesus. He will be great and will be called Son of the Most High . . . for nothing will be impossible for God."

—Luke 1: 26-37

The Angel of the Lord declared unto Mary.
And she conceived by the Holy Spirit.
Hail Mary, full of grace, the Lord is with you. Blessed are you among women and blessed is the fruit of your womb, Jesus. Holy Mary, Mother of God, pray for us sinners, now and at the hour of our death, Amen.
Behold the handmaid of the Lord.
Be it done unto me according to your word. Hail Mary, full of grace . . . Amen.
And the Word was made flesh.
And dwelt among us. Hail Mary, full of grace . . . Amen.
Pray for us, O holy Mother of God.
That we may be made worthy of the promise of Christ.

Let us pray

Pour forth, we beseech You, O Lord, Your grace into our hearts; that as we have known the Incarnation of Christ Your Son by the message of an Angel, so, by His Passion and Cross, may we be brought to the glory of His Resurrection, through Christ our Lord, Amen.

The Greatest Love

"You shall love the Lord your God with all your heart . . . This is the greatest and first commandment. The second is like it: You shall love your neighbor as yourself."

—Matthew 22:37-38

"And that Christ may dwell in your hearts through faith; that you, rooted and grounded in love, may have strength to comprehend with all the holy ones what is the breadth and length and height and depth of Christ's love, and to know it even though it is beyond all knowledge, so that you may be filled with all the fullness of God.

—Ephesians 3:17-19

"Inside the heart of each and every one of us is a longing to be understood by someone who really cares. When a person is understood, he or she can put up with almost anything in the world."

—Ed Hird

To come home now, just as you are, and to be welcomed with open arms by the most loving and forgiving father and mother is not a dream. It is the absolute truth of your being. Here, now in this instant, you can begin to feel this great love. This love is being poured out to you abundantly and with no end. Feel your feet on the ground. You are here on earth with a purpose. Be strong and brave enough to open your heart and mind. Take a deep breath in, and let go as you feel the exhalation. The breath is the touch of God's Holy Spirit within. Let it comfort and guide you. Believe and feel this life and goodness and remember you are loved.

Whatever the circumstances of your birth and young life, honor and love your earthly father and mother, for they loved you in their hearts and acted outwardly in accordance with their beliefs. No matter what they believed, however, cannot change who you are or who they are. We are all of God, and by this one cause we are created inherently, equally, and infinitely Good Within. This goodness and love that is God is unchanging and everlasting and is our true nature. What we believe cannot change who we are inwardly. Our beliefs can change and determine how we appear and act outwardly. The key to love, peace, and happiness here on earth is to align our beliefs and outward actions with the truth of our inward being. In other words, believe and act both knowing (of the mind) and feeling (of the body) the presence of a loving God who is both distant and within, both far and near.

"For you love all things that are and loathe nothing that you have made . . . You spare all things because they are yours. For your imperishable spirit is in all things."

—Wisdom 11:22

Your human parents cannot, nor were they meant to, provide you with perfect love. If you looked to them alone, your vision of love would be severely limited. No human being can love us as God loves us. Parents, family, friends, and strangers can be an opening for us to come to know and feel love in this world, but we must each find the glory, majesty, and fullness of the Kingdom of God within ourselves and in each other if we are to experience our true nature. If we focus on only what is seen with our human eyes, we will not understand the fullness of God's love. Begin to see beyond the façade, the barriers and veils we mistake for the truth of our being. Believe that God is infinite love and goodness within and you will begin to see, hear, taste, smell, and touch the goodness and love of God in all beings and in all things. This is the greatest love.

During the writing of this book, two of our closest friends, our golden retrievers, Chessa and Cody, died within weeks of each other. When we lost them, it was like losing a touch of goodness and love in our lives. There were times when I was close to either dog and I could feel their breath on my face. It was so tender and pure. It soothed me and made me smile. I miss their touch, their smell, their movement around the house, and their companionship and love. My husband and I talked it over with our two adult children, and we decided to get another dog. Brody joined us four months later. This little pup is another story.

His presence in our home gave us all a lift and brought the four of us together to pay attention and care for him. In time, most of the training fell into my hands because I work at home more than the others. The first few sessions went smoothly, and then Brody started behaving in ways I never remember seeing in the other dogs. For a little pup, he was very feisty, and it seemed to me, at the time, almost defiant. Some might say he had the "devil" in him. There were moments when he was completely out of control. I hate to admit it, but in a moment of shear frustration, I actually thought, "I can't keep this dog. He is not like Chessa and Cody."

Not only did I have the thought, but I also said something to my family about it. We talked for a few minutes, and I concluded that there was nothing wrong with the dog; it must be me. My daughter kindly asked me, "Mom, do you think when any child has a problem, the parents are to blame?" I responded, "No, I don't think they are to blame, but they must be able to respond to the problem with love rather than anger or frustration." I did not realize it then, but I see now that my frustration and anger were understandable feelings given the situation. The problem was not in the feelings but in my beliefs and actions. In other words, anger and frustration are not problems when I can learn to respond in love. I can feel frustrated with the dog's behavior and still act with love when I am able to see the dog's goodness and understand his behavior rather than jumping to the conclusion that something is wrong or bad in him or me. The dog can only be true to himself. He cannot be anything other than what he is. I must accept him as he is in this moment and respond from a place of love rather than fear and ignorance.

I was afraid because I believed that his behavior was a big problem, and even more frightening for me was that I did not know how to deal with it. I felt out of control as I watched him spin out of control. I was also ignorant. I did not know or understand him. I was stuck in the past with thoughts of how he was not like our other dogs. I was also worried about the future and how much time and trouble this dog was going to cost me. I believed I had so many important things to do and I was not going to get any of them done with this little creature around.

I needed some answers. The breeder was unavailable that day, so I called our friend Patty, who sold us Chessa and Cody. She offered sound advice and assured me things would work out fine. I listened carefully as she reminded me to be patient, set firm boundaries, and be consistent. I knew this, but I needed constant reminders when it came time to act. In fact, what I thought I knew was part of the problem. I was so sure I knew how to raise this puppy. Only he wasn't the puppy I was expecting. Patty talked about how the puppy will learn from how you respond to him. When he is belligerent, unless you want to teach belligerence, respond in a calm manner and show him how to behave by your example. My son understood this. I heard him saying to the dog as he corrected him calmly, "I'm not mad at you. I am showing you how to behave." He might have said this more for my benefit than the dog's.

I sat down that night and reread the book *The Art of Raising a Puppy* by the Monks of New Skete. I had read this book twelve years before when we got Chessa. With Patty's advice in mind, I searched the pages for the answers to our little pup's behavior. What was he trying to tell me? Two passages stood out for me, and I include them here because they speak volumes about love and its power to overcome fear. You do not have to own a pet to learn from this lesson.

"In dog training, most people conceive of obedience simply as something the dog does in response to his handler: the dog is the one who is obedient or not."(p.136). This is only half of what real obedience is. Obedience comes from the Latin word *oboedire*, which in turn is cognate to "ob-audire," meaning "to listen, to hear"; by extension, this always implies acting on what is heard. Contrary to popular thought, obedience is as much your responsibility as it is your dog's—even more so, since you are responsible for shaping your dog's behavior to fit your living circumstances. The problem with many dog owners is that they fail to listen and respond to the real needs of their dogs, and unknowingly, they are disobedient.

To be a good companion to your dog, *you* must be obedient, that is, fully alert and focused on your dog, flexible enough to adapt your approach instantly to his needs . . . Brother Thomas had this insight into obedience:

> *Learning the value of silence is learning to listen to, instead of screaming at, reality: opening your mind to find what the end of someone else's sentence sounds like, or listening to a dog until you discover what is needed instead of imposing yourself in the name of training* (p. 137)

> The trainer must himself be a psychologist, he must learn to read the soul of the dog, *and his own too.* He must observe himself closely so that he shall not only be prevented from underestimating the dog in human arrogance, but also that he may be able to give the dog suggestions and help in an intelligent way.

This approach "has the potential to teach you as much about yourself as it does about your dog" (p. 142). Allow an opening in mind and heart. Allow a quiet space to listen and hear the voice of God, sometimes in unexpected places. Make every effort to understand and act on what is heard. Here, in obedience, is the opening to love and peace on earth.

Jesus said to his disciples:
"Not everyone who says to me, 'Lord, Lord,'
will enter the Kingdom of heaven,
but only the one who does the will of my Father in heaven.

"Everyone who listens to these words of mine and acts on them
will be like a wise man who built his house on rock.
The rain fell, the floods came,
and the winds blew and buffeted the house.
But it did not collapse; it had been set solidly on rock.
And everyone who listens to these words of mine
but does not act on them
will be like a fool who built his house on sand.
The rain fell, the floods came,
and the winds blew and buffeted the house.
And it collapsed and was completely ruined."

—Matthew 7:21, 24-27

This new perspective on obedience changed everything in an instant. I realized I was so absorbed in my own wants that I was unable to listen to the other and act on what was heard. I was not aware of my roots in the solid ground of God's unending and unfailing love.

Rather than feeling grounded and centered, I felt tossed about by the negative emotions. The discomfort I felt in the form of frustration and anger was not wrong but misdirected. I tried to blame the dog, believing it was his behavior that caused me to feel frustrated. It was not. The emotion arises out of my thoughts and from within me. It is my responsibility. And this is perfect because when I understand I am responsible for responding to my feelings in thought, word, and action, I gain access to my free will and the power to choose. When I choose to stay grounded in God, to stay present, I realize that the love of God also arises from within. When I believe God's love is most powerful, I begin to find ways to respond to the negative feelings in love.

When I feel discomfort, then I realize that this discomfort arises from a part of me that knows my behavior is not aligned to my purpose, which is love. I am uncomfortable with my outward self and with good reason. I do not feel grounded and aligned to my true self. Thank goodness for the uncomfortable feeling. Thank goodness for the dog that can only respond in alignment to its true nature. Hopefully, it gets my attention and I learn to listen and I listen to learn. If and when I listen and align myself to the truth, I will act in ways that bring love and goodness to life.

The dog is biting this paper as I write and reminding me that my purpose in life is not about how many things I have to get done. It is about being the presence of understanding and love for the other. No matter what you are doing or who you are with, in your heart believe, "I am here to understand and love you." I was very short-sighted and selfish in that moment of frustration. But the experience opened my eyes. What was I thinking? Did I expect to have complete control and have the dog behave according to my will? He could not give that to me, not because he was defiant but because he was obedient. He was obedient to his true nature. In a very real way, he was being obedient to God who made him a dog. I only have to do the same—be obedient to God who made me. I must be myself, but unlike the dog, I have free will. The dog can only behave according to God's will. I must make the choice.

I must remember that even though I do not always *feel* grounded, I *am* grounded. As long as I am here on earth, I cannot defy the law of gravity. We are grounded. We are grounded in God's love the moment our soul enters the body with mass and weight whether we realize it or not. When we realize it, a whole new world opens to us.

In this case we have to remember that we took a pup, new to this world, from his mother and his pack, and he is counting on us to show him what this world is about and how to belong in this family. If we want him to be a vital part of our family, we have to show him that he belongs by accepting him as he is rather than wanting him to be different or trying to fix him according to our will. His behavior was not bad. He was only acting in accordance with his true nature. We have to be able to honor that truth and respond to him in a way that he can understand.

When we encounter misbehavior, it gets our attention. If we are willing to listen, we come to understand the behavior rather than judge the dog as bad. When we listen, he will reveal to us what he needs. We are all both teacher and student. Our purpose is to teach and learn how to love. The Latin word to teach or educate is *educare*. It means to draw forth, to bring out from within. Draw forth the goodness and love within yourself and others by seeing the truth in all beings. Rather than seeking perfection in the outer world, remember to trust and have faith that all God made is good within. Listen to others and be willing and able to respond in love to their needs. Put aside harsh judgments based solely on what is seen on the surface. Be obedient to God and to each other. Listen and give the other what they need most—love in its infinite number of forms. God is love. God is within all that is. Begin to recognize God in all beings and all things and you will learn to respond in a way that brings love and goodness to your life and to the lives of those you touch.

When I changed my perspective and remembered to see myself and the pup through the eyes of love, he responded immediately and became obedient to the one who demonstrated obedience to him. He learned self-control from the one who demonstrated it for him. He reflected back to me my way of being with him. He can only reflect back to me the truth. Instinctively he knows that his survival depends on me. He will cry, bite, and bark to get my attention if he senses I do not understand him. He is afraid because he senses my fear and lack of leadership. I am afraid because I believe that he is a bad dog and/or I am a bad owner. When I see the truth and act accordingly, he stops crying, biting, and barking because he trusts I will love and care for him. His purpose is love, and he will fulfill his purpose and love obediently through anyone who is able to see him as he truly is. This all takes time and patience, for no matter how hard we try, we will continue to make mistakes.

When I stopped to listen, rather than blindly imparting my will on him, I discovered that I was trying to do too much, too soon. I was trying too hard to train him to my liking without the balance of letting him be himself. He needed more downtime, more time to sleep, and more time to take in this new environment. When I put him in his crate, I was not trying to push him away or punish him. I was allowing a space for him away from me for him to know that even though he cannot see me, he can be fine on his own, trusting that I am there when he needs me. He must learn to feel at ease in this space, not trapped but free from the fear that he is alone and cannot survive. I have to believe that he can do this on his own or I would not be able to separate myself from him. When I listened and remembered, I began to understand, and I was more able to respond in ways that were good for all of us. Thank God He did not listen to me until I listened and learned my lesson. I am humbly reminded of my place and purpose by a little pup that wags his tail when he is happy.

Clearly, we can see how this applies to our human condition. We are all born into this world of one God. As infants, we are obedient to God and our true nature, for we have no sense of ourselves as an individual with choice. As infants we can only be as God made us. We cry, we protest, we fail and falter as we must in order to learn of our unique place in space and time. Hopefully, we laugh, celebrate, and continue to listen and learn as we grow. We develop a sense of separateness so we can learn to relate to our environment and the people in our world. We are one with God but not conscious of this oneness.

We have to know and feel our separateness before we can know and choose our belonging in oneness with God and others. Ego development and a strong sense of self are necessary conditions for healthy, loving relationships. As we mature and understand our unique place and purpose, we must then remember our beginnings in God so we can consciously choose to take our place in relationship to God through others. Remembering our beginning in God is like coming home and knowing you are loved.

We can remember by letting the mind take its place in the body as the opening to know and feel God's love. When we know who we are, we can begin to reach out and build relationships with others. I learn to listen so I have a chance to understand the needs of others rather than trying to impose my will on them. When I remember that my purpose is to both learn and teach *being in love,* everything changes in an instant. I feel sad and happy at the same time. I feel sad and sorry for all the times in the past I have failed to listen to those closest because I was preoccupied with my own needs and wants. I feel happy and hopeful for a bright future in the light of truth. I am not called to make others like me. I am called to love them just as they are. Imagine what is possible when we learn to listen to each other, especially those with the meekest voices.

"Whoever says he is in the light, yet hates his brother, is still in the darkness. Whoever loves his brother remains in the light, and there is nothing in him to cause a fall. Whoever hates his brother is in darkness; he walks in darkness and does not know where he is going because the darkness has blinded his eyes."

—1 John 2:9

I am reminded of a piece from *The Prophet* by Kahlil Gibran on children:

And a woman who held a babe against her bosom said, Speak to us of Children. And he said: Your children are not your children. They are the sons and daughters of Life's longing for itself. They come through you but not from you, And though they are with you yet they belong not to you.
You may give them your love but not your thoughts, For they have their own thoughts. You may house their bodies but not their souls, For their souls dwell in the house of tomorrow, which you cannot visit, not even in your dreams. You may strive to be like them, but seek not to make them like you. For life goes not backward nor tarries with yesterday.

You are the bows from which your children as living arrows are sent forth. The archer sees the mark upon the path of the infinite, and He bends you with His might that His arrows may go swift and far. Let your bending in the archer's hand be for gladness; For even as He loves the arrow that flies, so He loves also the bow that is stable.(p.17).

I came upon this verse when our children were little. I cried as I read it. I think it touched my heart with the truth in these beautiful words. I realized how many times I had forgotten to live this truth. The words reminded me to exercise my will to serve God, not myself, to be the steady bow that bends gladly in the archer's hands. I have read the verse many times to help me remember. Yet no matter how hard I try, I cannot hold onto the truth, and therefore, there are times when I forget to live it. I am so thankful to my family for their patience, forgiveness, and love. I will keep trying to remember in each moment. I will continue to invite the ego to take its place among the wholeness, the oneness that is God. What this means is that I can no longer see my needs as separate from the other. Rather than basing my actions on what is good for me, I begin to ask, "How do I act for the highest good, the good of all?"

Only God knows what is good for all. So in order to act for the highest good, I must act according to the Word of God. I cannot rely solely on myself and other human beings with finite vision because it seems that sometimes I act even against my own will when I say and do things I do not intend to do. How do I tame this ego, so to speak, to act in accordance with the will of God? I have heard some say that the ego must be overcome, subdued, even destroyed in order to know God. I cannot believe this. I cannot believe that God wills us to destroy what He made as beautiful and good.

I imagine the ego not as an evil enemy but as a little child who does not feel, hear, or understand. I wonder if this little child would willingly follow once it felt embraced and loved.

Maybe the ego does not need to be subdued as much as it needs to remember that it is understood and loved. Ego is essential to ensure our survival. At its basic root, it teaches us to avoid pain and seek pleasure. However, if we live under the rule of ego alone, if we fail to mature into our whole being, we will experience a constant struggle to avoid what is bad and seek what is good for us from our limited perspective. The ego is like the young child who fears separation yet wants to be free. Imagine happy children when they realize they are free but never alone. When we learn to see beyond our own needs and wants and trust in a loving God who cares for all beings and all things, we can gladly accept, embrace, and endure the limitations of our humanness in ourselves and others. We can feel more at home here on earth.

"So that we may no longer be infants . . . Rather, living the truth in love, we should grow in every way into him who is the head, Christ, from when the whole Body, joined and held together by every supporting ligament, with the proper functioning of each part, bring about the Body's growth and build itself up in love."

—Ephesians 7:16

Take a moment and bring to mind a picture of the earth from space. This is how God sees us. See the earth's amazing beauty and place among the stars and realize that we are in this together. In the end, what is good for one is good for all. It cannot be any other way, for all beings are created by God, and all that God made is good. Every thought, word, and action is upheld in the law of love. When we believe this, we will begin to understand more fully the greatest love, which is God's love for us revealed in all of Creation.

"Open my eyes that I may see wonderful things in your law."

—Psalm 119:18

This view helps us to see a most important point. It is not enough to be *reminded* of our place and purpose in thought and knowledge. What is also vital is that when it comes time to act, we must *remember our place and purpose in and through our movements in body.* The thought is transmitted in mind while memory is primarily of the body. We remember by making a connection, a thought with an experience. We have been given the mind-body as an amazing and wondrous gift. It is our touch point for all memories, including the memory of our beginning in God. The seven gifts of God's goodness within can be touch points to help us remember. The gifts do not embody all we are but provide points of awareness to help us remember our true nature and act accordingly.

When it comes time to act, we can remind ourselves in thought and remember the feeling in body. In this moment of union, mind, and body, the seven gifts of God's goodness come to bear.

We are grounded now, here by the touch of our feet to the earth and the weight of our bodies. We are not alone. God is present. God is the vital energy that moves us and every being and particle in the universe. Begin to see God in all beings and all things and experience the gift of vitality as an inner source of boundless energy.

We are centered. Feel the balance between the opposite aspects of your physical self, right/left, front/back, and top/bottom. Acknowledge the dual nature of our earthly existence and the desire for union. Remember, we know God in relationship. In relationship there is a union or coming together, a giver and receiver to bring love into this world. Let both have their place. Respect and love all life. Speak less and listen more, and recognize the gift of balance.

We are strong. Engage the muscles of the core, and remember that we have the ability to discipline the mind to stay fully present. We can choose freely to see God in self, others, and all things. Be humble, not proud, and exercise the gift of strength to develop discipline and self-control.

We are open. From our foundation, which is grounded, centered, and strong, lengthen the spine and lift into the heart center. Open the heart to both give and receive love. What do others need? Stay with them, listen until you understand, and unleash the gift of endurance in thought, word, and action.

We are at ease. Feel the flow of the breath within. Let it comfort and guide us. Do not be afraid. Feel the flow of emotion, and be willing and able to let go. Stay in the space of open heart, and open the mind. Practice forgiveness. Be at ease when things do not go your way, and enjoy the gift of flexibility.

We are focused. Let us keep our attention one-pointed. See clearly God's goodness and love in all of Creation, and call on the gift of focused attention to bring love and peace to earth.

We are fulfilled. Be aware of the amazing gift of mind-body. Let us act now like we believe and celebrate the gift of coordination as all the parts come together in perfect unity. What a difference we can make in this new life in God.

Begin now. Look out into the world and look within yourself and others and see God's love and goodness. Reflect on the possibility of living your life in love. The power you seek to transform a burden into a blessing, sickness into well-being, and sin to forgiveness is given to you by God through Christ in the Holy Spirit. It is already yours. It is love, and faith will make it visible. God is counting on you—not to prevent suffering, not to heal yourself or save the world. God is counting on you to count on Him and to believe and trust in His great love. God wants you to remember that you are never alone, you are loved, and with God all things are possible.

Our doubts and fears are understandable when we experience the evil and suffering in our world. Be comforted by a most loving God who understands our fears and wants to help us overcome undue fear and know love, peace, and happiness. God allows evil and suffering not to punish or destroy us but as an opening to transform and heal us through God's unending and great love. The opening is in our hearts and minds. When you believe you see evil in the world, do not be tempted to blame yourself or others. This embodies fear of evil and gives it a space to grow. Pause—take a deep breath in, and on the exhalation, let go of the blame and guilt and ask out loud, "How can I embody God's love to be made visible here in this moment?"

Let go of the belief that your body, others' bodies, our churches, and our world are not good, not of God. Remind yourself that this can never be true. God is infinite and eternal love. God is all that is. Every being and every thing exists as part of God's creation. No human being has the power or authority to declare what God made as good and holy to be evil or separate. Any such declaration is a non-truth and should be regarded as such. We do not have the power to change God's law of love and its effect anymore than we can change the laws of physics. We do have the power, however, granted to us by God through our consciousness and the gift of free will, to come to understand the law and abide in love. We can choose to see the good, to see God in all beings and things, and to act in accordance with God's law of love.

When we see evil or suffering, we can be sure God is calling us to love. We will be most able to choose love when we realize that suffering is not a force meant to punish, destroy, or separate us from God or each other but an opening to bring God's love here on earth as it is in heaven. We can choose to expand our vision, open our mind and heart, and see beyond our humanness alone and begin to feel the presence of God's goodness and love within ourselves and each other. In this way, we will realize that God has kept His promise of peace in and through us.

Nothing can separate us from God. He will never abandon us or stop loving us. Without awareness of God's presence, however, our suffering and pain may feel unbearable. Without love, what is inwardly good and pure becomes distorted and disfigured by our false perceptions that we are alone and that no good is in our lives. When we feel pain, we may conclude, then, that there is no God, no love for us in this world. On the other hand, when we feel pleasure or happiness, we might believe that God favors us and those who are suffering are not of God or they are being punished by an angry God. Neither of these beliefs can be true. We are not the cause of our suffering or happiness anymore than we are the cause of gravity. God is the one cause, and we are all under the same effect. We are simply under the effect of God's law of love as we are under the effect of gravity.

Suffering, like gravity, is an experience we bear as a result of our humanness. It is not a punishment for our wrongness or weakness. By our humanness, our mass and weight, gravity keeps us on the earth. When we fall, do we believe gravity is evil? It was the cause of our fall. Without it, we could never fall. But living here on earth without gravity is not possible, so we learn to accept and understand the law and live by it. We learn to get back up. Fear of falling is our only inherent fear. All other fears are learned. We cannot nor should we try to rid ourselves of our fear of falling. We must accept it, for this fear is essential to live. We must, however, learn to overcome the fear of getting back up. We must be willing and able to accept the fall and get back up because we remember we are meant for love and goodness.

God does not want or ask us to suffer anymore than He created the body to be a burden under the force of gravity. He created us so we might know love and joy. He asks of us that we believe in love and call on love to transform evil and suffering. When we experience tension, anxiety, pain, or suffering, if we focus on the discomfort alone and see it as punishment for being no good, the discomfort or pain will grow and may overcome us, not because we are bad or good but as a result of where we have placed our attention. Turn your attention to God. Do not hold onto suffering as if it is your purpose. It is not. Let go of this belief. Be cleansed and purified of the false beliefs, and remember your purpose is love.

Gravity holds us here on earth, but that does not necessarily mean it draws us away from God in heaven unless we fail to see that God is also here on earth among us. God came to earth through Mary, the mother of God, in Jesus. If we believe in Jesus, if we believe that it is possible for God to be here on earth with us, then when we feel the weight of the body, we can bear joyfully our humanness, knowing that through Jesus and God's unending love all burden is transformed into blessing. In Jesus, through the power of the Holy Spirit, lies our freedom from sin and suffering. When we realize our freedom, we fulfill our purpose, which is to choose to be in love, to abide in God. We learn to face our fears together and remember a loving God who is with us always. Begin to imagine living a life in love.

Love can relieve our fears and change our perceptions in an instant. I remember when I first began the practice of meditation over twenty years ago I awoke one night from a bad dream. It was as if every fear in my mind and heart was revealed to me. In the dream I experienced loss, darkness, separation, pain, falling, and loss of control. The next day I thought, "Meditation is not for me." I quit my practice. I thought it was taking me someplace I did not want to go. I stayed with my faith, continued to pray, and God brought me back. I have practiced prayer and meditation ever since. The practice has helped me to face these fears with greater awareness. I try to see the world believing that it is all of God, all of God's goodness and love. Is it possible that the things we fear the most are the openings in mind and heart to know God more fully?

Is it possible that cancer cells serve a vital function in keeping us alive rather than the feared enemy that is trying to kill us? The cancer cell has qualities such as immortalization, which means they can grow indefinitely. This could be a highly adaptive mechanism to sustain life if we could understand why the cancer cells become disconnected from the whole, lose all sense of boundaries, and invade other tissues and organs. It is as if the cells forget their place and purpose. The cancer cell itself is not evil and something to fear and fight but a form of life to understand; an understanding that can lead to healing.

Rather than bombard these cells with radiation and bathe them in poison with the intention to destroy, what if we tried instead to bathe the cells in love. Maybe oxytocin, a natural mammalian hormone, is worth a try as a chemical equivalent of love. We could redirect our efforts at helping the cells remember their place and purpose.

In the cancer treatments we both give and receive, we can begin to see anew. See the radiation as a powerful "light" that can guide the cancer cells to see their place and purpose. See the chemotherapy as a cleansing agent to wash away cells that are no longer vital and needed. It is not the surgeon's knife or the medicine alone that heals but faith in the surgeon and faith in the human hands that form and deliver the medicine with the intention to heal. We each have the potential to be a touch of God's love here on earth. We can actualize this potential and make it real when we believe it is love that heals. It is this love within that opens us to the many positive possibilities.

Is it possible that ticks and mosquitoes rather than being dreaded carriers of disease could just as easily transmit goodness? When the mind-body is in a receptive and balanced state, the bite that introduces a small dose of bacteria could act as an inoculation similar to a vaccine that establishes in the host immunity to the disease. When the mind-body is unduly stressed, fear can become the breeding ground for the overgrowth of bacteria that lead to disease. Maybe all bacteria have a place and purpose that benefits the whole organism in a balanced and healthy environment.

Is it possible that the men and women incarcerated in our prisons can reveal to us the true meaning of freedom? To the same degree and intensity they directed their energy and attention away from God, not realizing the truth of their being, they can choose to redirect that energy and turn to God. In God and through love they are set free from the false beliefs that got them into prison in the first place. With a new direction in God, they can in equal and opposite measure bring good into this world.

Is it possible that the homeless can teach us what it means to come home? Home is not measured in dollars, square feet, or the quantity of possessions. Home is where the heart is. Remember to love God, self, others, and all that is and you will begin to feel at home wherever you are.

Is it possible that attention deficit disorders are not deficits or disorders at all but powerful adaptations to an environment in which the perceived stress load is high? The brain is not in a state of disorder but perfectly ordered for that individual's place and purpose. Observe and listen to those who seem distracted rather than trying to get them to listen to you. They want to be heard and understood. They are feeling stressed, possibly to the point of fear—maybe with good reason, maybe with no apparent reason at all. In any case, when the mind-body perceives a threat, it is essential for survival that one is on the lookout. This means the individual must constantly divert his or her attention from one thing to the next, all around him or her, to react to the perceived threat. To focus on one thing in this moment is physiologically impossible. The mind-body is wired to react to fear in just this way. The key to focused attention then is to remember to stay present. Stay in touch with the body, for the body grounds us in the here and now, the present moment. When we stay present, we can learn to respond to our fears in ways that build confidence, discipline, self-control, and focused attention.

Is it possible that our heart could work twice as long if we saw that the heart's pumping action is not all work but equal parts work and rest? The heart pumps blood through the body by the alternating contraction and relaxation of the heart muscle. Contraction is the muscle at work while relaxation is the muscle at rest. Other muscles of the body work in a similar flow from work to rest. When we do a leg lift, one muscle contracts as the complementary muscle relaxes. One shortens as the other lengthens. We cannot change the action of the heart or other muscles. We can learn to see more clearly that there are two sides to every equation. The key is in understanding the relationship between the two.

Is it possible that the weakest can show us the true meaning of strength? And is it possible that those who are most feared hold the answer to peace?

"For behold, some are last who will be first; and some are first who will be last."

—Luke 13:30

In the equation that is life, we can recognize the dual nature of our earthly existence as the two sides of the equation: day/night, up/down, good/bad, male/female, empty/full, rich/poor, etc. What is not as apparent is that God is the center and space where every opposite comes together and each understands its place and purpose in relationship to the other in love. God is the bridge, the equalizer that brings opposites together in harmony when the lion will lay down with the lamb.

With awareness that God is center, our life can change in an instant. When *I try to change myself outwardly according to my will*, lacking an awareness of God's love within, I am living in a state of imbalance that leads to mounting tension, and change can seem difficult. I have placed too much attention on the human being side of the equation or I have mistakenly put myself, others, or something other than God at center. *God is center in a balanced world.* My attempts to change myself may or may not be successful and can potentially bring on undue suffering and pain because I am misaligned and out of balance. I have forgotten that God is center, and I have tried to do it on my own. The consequences of this misalignment or imbalance are essential for me to perceive so I can continue to make choices that help me realize center and feel balance and equilibrium restored. This is possible when I am present, attentive, and open to receive this information. This is possible when I believe that equilibrium is my natural state.

God created us human. God did not make us human and then ask us to be perfect like God. We are made of the same matter that comprises the entire visible universe. Matter is dense, and it takes energy and time to change. We must learn to accept and embrace our human limitations as we work patiently to understand more fully God's great love. Take, for example, the struggle many of us face with our humanness in the form of our weight. We cannot lose ten pounds in an instant. We have to exert a certain amount of energy over a period of time to lose the weight. Some of us struggle for a lifetime with this aspect of our humanness. However, in love we can be transformed in an instant. Thought has no mass and can change instantly. By changing our thoughts and aligning our beliefs to the truth about ourselves and others, we can feel ten pounds lighter in an instant. Love yourself and others now, knowing that it is God's perfect love that sustains us. Let go of having to be perfect in your humanness. Choose to love life and the gift of mind-body. The beauty here is that if you remain in this state of mind that embodies love and lightness, if you choose the present moment to act, you will lose the ten pounds as balance is restored because balance is your natural state.

The present moment is center where mind and body unite to be most able to respond. Rather than looking out into the world and trying to judge "what is good for me or what is bad for me," when we look out, let us develop the discipline to see what is and accept it. By accepting what is, we bring our consciousness to the present moment. The present moment is the point of balance, which is center, which is also where we meet God. God is ever-present. If we believe this, we can learn to accept what comes our way because we know God is with us. We can learn to face our fears in love.

Remember the equation of life: good on one side, bad on the other. God is center of this equation. Our awareness of God's goodness and love as center bridges the gap, brings opposites to touch, and restores balance. God is not singularly on either side of the equation but holds both sides in the balance. God holds the place where every opposite can come together in relationship and understand how they are indeed one. God reveals to us that although we appear outwardly separate and very different, we are inwardly one in and through God.

"For you were once darkness, but now you are light in the Lord. Live as children of light, for light produces every kind of goodness and righteousness and truth."
—Ephesians 5:8

I had another dream more recently that like the dream of darkness became a turning point in my life. This dream was of great love. It came at a particularly challenging time when I held many doubts and fears in my mind and heart. I felt a growing anxiety but could not identify the cause.

In the dream, I was in distress. I felt bound and scared. I was wrapped in layers of clothing like sheets. Then He was with me. I never saw His face. I only felt His presence. I felt His gentle embrace and a voice that said, "I am with you." He carefully began to unravel the layers of clothing. He spoke softly, reassuring me that I was okay. I could feel the soft touch of His breath in His closeness. I trusted Him. He knew it.

He held me very gently as some skin was finally exposed from beneath the wrappings. He held me like He was holding something precious. He whispered, "I love you." I responded, "I love You," and I awoke. The feeling was so overwhelming and lovely that I got out of bed to write down all I could remember. I did not want to let this feeling ever leave me. It lifted and filled me.

The next morning I saw things in a new light. The doubts and fears had faded. I felt energized. I vowed to let go of criticisms, harsh judgments, and unreasonable demands. I promised to be gentle, loving, and humble and to honor and respect others. In a few days, the feeling of great love started to fade. As much as I try, I cannot hold onto the love I felt in the dream. I can only try to be that love in each moment by remembering the great love that was shown to me. I will always remember the love dream even though I sometimes forget to act in remembrance of that love, but I will never stop trying.

"God created man in his image; in the divine image he created him; male and female he created them . . . God looked at everything he had made, and he found it very good."
—Genesis 1:27, 31

"The Lord loves justice and right and fills the earth with goodness."
—Psalm 33:5

God did not create us to deny our human being. God created us to love and embrace our being. We are meant for love, and our purpose is to love and be loved. We can fulfill our purpose in love in mind-body by remembering God is center and holds in that present moment all that ever was, all that is, and all that will be. We are all children of God, fallen angels who have come from God to this earth. We are not disgraced or banished in our coming but granted freedom by God out of a deep and everlasting love for us. God allowed us to leave home trusting and knowing that in time we will return to God by our free will when we realize the truth. We will take our place in love.

We did not fall to disgrace Him or flee God to escape His will and His law of love. No, we came to be a part of its fulfillment.

Remember God is all. Remember the departed, all those who have gone before us. Remember those who walk beside us and those who will follow. All are waiting now in God to be reunited in mind-body. Imagine the joy when we are all united in love to embrace and feel the love and peace of God, here on earth as it is in heaven.

The Cathollic prayer Glory Be echoes a most profound truth and is the basis of our faith in a loving God, our Creator. In the beginning, is God only and God is love. This love is unchanging and eternal. No matter the external circumstances of our lives we must hold fast to the belief that love never fails. Nothing can alter this truth. We must remember our beginning in God and His promise of love and joy. In this memory we can begin to love and live in truth.

"Glory be to the Father, and to the Son, and to the Holy Spirit, as it was in the beginning, is now, and will be forever., Amen." (The Catholic Faith Handbook, 2004, p.382).

Pope John Paul II in *Man and Woman He Created Them: A Theology of the Body* states "we draw a first hope already from the mystery of creation: namely, that the fruit of the divine economy of truth and love, which revealed itself 'at the beginning,' is not Death, but Life, and not so much the destruction of the body <of man made 'in the image>' of God, but rather the 'call to glory' (Rom 8:30)."

Conclusion

Remember as you work, that there is no effort that can add to the Infinite life energy that is God within. As you come to the exercises keep in mind that the movement itself is not nearly as important as what that movement awakens in you and others. Let all you do be for God's glory.

PRACTICE: The long haul

"When you get into a tight place and everything goes against you, till it seems as though you could not hold on a minute longer, never give up then, for that is just the place and time that the tide will turn.

—Harriet Beecher Stowe

"Acceptance of what has happened is the first step to overcoming the consequences of any misfortune."

—William James

"God is now my strength."

—Isaiah 49:5

Intention: We all find ourselves at one time or another in a place where everything seems to be going against us. Try to let go of the belief that things never go your way and choose instead to see that the difficulty is indeed the opportunity to overcome and free yourself of the burden you feel. The challenges we face are not before us to make life miserable or bring us down. They call us to respond in a way that builds inner strength and self-confidence. They are not repeated again and again to wear us down but to continue to put before us another chance to overcome and be set free. Make a commitment and stay with it for the long haul. Expect to falter. We are all human, and we are going to experience failure. Be ready, willing, and able to get back up and go again.

On the mat: It is not easy to go the long haul, and that is exactly why we must. It is the difficulty that we overcome that awakens in us strength and endurance. Give yourself the best chance to succeed. Support your efforts with life-giving nutrition. Carbohydrates alone are fast, fun fuel. They are not enough to hold you for the long run. Be sure to include protein and healthy fats in your diet for sustenance. Good sources include eggs, Canadian bacon, lean meats, fish, chicken, turkey, nut butters, raw and unsalted nuts, and seeds, low-fat dairy products (milk, cheese and yogurt), unsaturated vegetable oils (olive, sunflower, safflower, canola), and beans.

Off the mat: You do not have to change who you are to be able to endure for the long haul. You only have to believe and be true to yourself. You were made to go the distance.

PRACTICE: Come home to peace and love

"This is my body that is for you. Do this in remembrance of me."

—1 Corinthians 11:24

"A heart that loves is always young."

—Greek proverb

"For behold, the kingdom of God is among you."

—Luke 17:21

"But seek first the kingdom of God and his righteousness, and all these things will be given you besides. Do not worry about tomorrow; tomorrow will take care of itself."

—Matthew:33

Intention: We are meant for love and goodness. We are made for joy and peace. The mind-body is home to the living God. Come to abide in this truth and to rest in God by remembering the good within. See God in all beings and all that is and you will most certainly know and feel this love that is yours to behold.

On and off the mat—remember:

- Let God be your root to the present moment and your one source of vital energy that conceives, nurtures, and sustains life.
- Embrace God, yourself, and others in loving relationship. Love being human, and feel God's love and peace as a part of you, others, and all that is.
- Be strong. Practice every day so you may discipline yourself in mind-body and align your will to the most beautiful, loving, and perfect will of God.
- Open your heart and believe that love endures all things. Love God, yourself, others, and all that is. Be patient, listen, and learn.
- Be at ease. Feel the flow of God's grace as the life energy that inspires and moves you. You are forgiven. Forgive others as God has forgiven you.
- Stay focused. See God in all beings and all things. Direct your attention and energy and move toward this goodness, love, and light.
- Know and feel peace, love, and happiness now. It is given as a gift. It is yours to behold.

"Ask and it will be given to you, seek and you will find, knock and the door will be opened to you."

—Matthew 7:7

Appendix A

Suggested Exercise Routines

Series 1: Warm-up energy series
1. Deep breathing exercises x 3
2. Postural pose x 3
3. Knee-up R/L (right and left sides)
4. Standing crunch alternate R/L x 8
5. Open heart 4R/4L or 4L/4R
6. Woodcutter 4C/2L/2R (center, left, and right)
7. Forward warrior with deep breathing exercises
8. Deep breathing x 3

Series 2: Cardio/Core/Yoga
1. Deep-breathing exercises x 3
2. Forward bend
3. Backward bend
4. Forward warrior R/L
5. Open heart 4L/4R
6. Dancer's pose R/L
7. Walk for thirty minutes
8. Bicep curl with overhead press 2 x 8 (two sets of eight repetitions)
9. Back lunge with twist 2 x 8 alternate R/L then 4R/4L
10. Chest press 2 x 8
11. Lateral raise 2 x 8
12. Triceps extension 2 x 8

Series 3: Cardio/Yoga
1. Warm-up series
2. Walk for thirty to forty minutes
3. Sun salutation x 2 R/L

Series 4: Cardio/Core/Yoga
1. Deep-breathing exercises x 3
2. Postural pose x 3
3. Sun salutation x 2 R/L
4. Walk at a brisk pace (fifteen-minute miles for thirty minutes or two miles)
5. Sit-ups 3 x 8 to C/R/L
6. Boat x 3
7. Child
8. Up dog
9. Reclining pigeon
10. Knee down twist

Series 5: Cardio/Yoga
1. Warm-up series
2. Walk at a brisk pace (fifteen-minute miles for forty-five minutes or three miles)
3. Forward bend from straddle position
4. Backward bend
5. Open heart
6. Lunge R/L
7. Dancer's pose
8. Reclining pigeon
9. Knee down twist
10. Psoas stretch/compression/release

Series 6: Cardio/Yoga
1. Warm-up series
2. Walk/run for thirty to forty minutes. Run when you feel able for short intervals (one to five minutes) and return to your walking pace. Remember the talk test. You should be able to talk while running. If you are out of breath, slow it down and walk.
3. Lunge/bicep curl 3 x 8
4. Back lunge/twist 3 x 8
5. Upright row/back lunge 3 x 8
6. Chest press/leg press 3 x 8
7. Lateral raise with alternating knee-up 2 x 8 R/L
8. Triceps extension 3 x 8

9. Sun salutation x 2

Series 7: Cardio/Yoga
1. Warm-up series
2. Walk/run for thirty to forty minutes
3. Side warrior, lateral angle, exalted warrior series R/L
4. Tree
5. Triangle
6. Standing forward bend
7. Cross bar
8. Boat
9. Cat/cow
10. Child
11. Pigeon
12. Seated twist
13. Seated forward bend
14. Psoas stretch
15. Knee down twist

Series 8: Cardio/Core/Yoga: On this series you decide how many sets and repetitions. Work as you are able.
1. Warm-up series
2. Walk/run for thirty to forty minutes
3. Lightning bolt with step and touch
4. Lunge/overhead press
5. Back lunge with twist alternate
6. Back lunge with upright row
7. Lightning bolt with double squat
8. Lightning bolt with triceps extension
9. Leg press with chest press
10. Knee-up with lateral raise
11. Full body extensions with squats
12. Knee-up with back lunge
13. Leg press from table top
14. Pelvic lift
15. Sit-ups C/R/L
15. Abdominal rock with half shoulder stand/leg straddle/scissor
16. Sun salutation

List of exercises and postures

1. Mountain pose
2. Deep-breathing exercises
3. Knee-up/Dancer's pose
4. Standing crunch
5. Open heart
6. Woodcutter
7. Forward warrior/Side warrior
8. Warm-up energy series
9. Lightning bolt/step and touch
10. Warrior lunge/ bicep curl/overhead press
11. Back lunge/twist
12. Upright row/back lunge
13. Lightning bolt/double squat
14. Lightning bolt/triceps extension
15. Leg press from straddle position/chest press
16. Lateral raise/knee-up
17. Full body extensions/squats
18. Knee-up/back lunge
19. Knee lifts/leg extension
20. Leg press
21. Iliopsoas extension/flexion
22. Pelvic lift
23. Sit-ups
24. Leg pump
25. Sun salutation

26. Side warrior/lateral angle/exalted warrior series
27. Tree
28. Triangle/Half moon
29. Standing forward bend
30. Cross bar
31. Boat
32. Cat/cow
33. Child/Up dog
34. Pigeon series
35. Reclining pigeon
36. Seated twist
37. Seated forward bend
38. Abdominal rock/half shoulder stand
39. Knee down twist
40. Iliopsoas stretch/compression/release

See the Good Within

Gifts of God's Goodness	Embodied As: The Primary System	The Focus of Our Practice	The Results in Mind-Body
Vitality: Our root, our connection to God and to each other	Skeletal system and blood	Being grounded, rooted in the present moment in mind-body, establishing the foundation	Feeling vital, lifted, energized, and inspired
Balance: The union of duality as a creative and productive force	Reproductive and excretory systems, including the skin	Being able to see opposing forces as essential parts of one whole	A sense of center and stability. A state of balance and equilibrium. Peace.
Strength: A well-trained and disciplined mind, self-control	Digestive (processing) and endocrine (self-regulating) systems	Being responsible for our thoughts, words, and actions; Being "response-able"	Disciplined thought and action, self-confidence, and faith
Endurance: An open heart	Cardiovascular system	Being open-hearted. Being able to go the distance. Open to give and receive love and say yes to life	Perseverance, patience, forgiveness, and a willingness to meet challenges with confidence and faith

Flexibility: A state of flow, grace, and ease of movement	Muscular, respiratory, and lymph systems	Being flexible in mind-body, going with the flow by aligning movement with the flow of the breath	Feeling a sense of ease in mind-body and being able to respond to life's challenges by taking action
Focused Attention: Purposeful movement and responsible choices.	Nervous system	Being able to identify your purpose, passion, principles, and practice	Seeing clearly the truth of being human. Achievement of goals and success
Coordination: Let it all come together: A harmonious interaction in the present moment	The whole self	Being your best self and letting the Good Within flow out into the world with direction and purpose	Everything has its place and your life feels ordered. You feel fulfilled, peaceful, and happy

Additional Readings

Turn to the Bible first

Barry, W. (2008). *Finding God in All Things: A Companion to the Spiritual Exercises of St. Ignatius.* Notre Dame, IN: Ave Maria Press.

Benson, H. (1984). The *Relaxation Response.* New York: Times Books.

Camerson, J. (1992). *The Artist's Way.* New York: Penguin Putman.

Campbell, J. (1991). *Reflections of the Art of Living: A Joseph Campbell Companion.* New York: Harper Collins.

Chittister, J. (2009). The *Breath of the Soul: Reflections on Prayer.* New London, CT: Twenty-Third Publications.

Chittister, J. (2005). *Becoming Fully Human: The Greatest Glory of God.* Lanham, MD: Roman & Littlefield Publishers.

Chittister, J. (1996). *The Psalms: Meditations for Every Day of the Year.* New York: The Cross Road Publishing Company.

Colledge, E. & Walsh, J. (1978). *Julian of Norwich Showings.* Mahwah, NJ: Paulist Press.

DeStefano, R., Kelly, B., & Hooper, J. (2009). *Muscle Medicine: The Revolutionary Approach to Maintainig, Strengthening, and Repairing Your Muslces and Joints.* New York:Simon and Schuster.

De Waal, E. (2001). *Seeking God: The Way of St. Benedict.* Collegeville, MD: The Liturgical Press.

Dossey, L. (2006). *The Extraordinary Healing Power of Ordinary Things: Fourteen Natural Steps to Health and Happiness.* New York: Random House.

Dyer, W. (2006). *Inspiration: Your Ultimate Calling.* Carlsbad, CA: Hay Books.

Flynn, Vinny (2006). *7 Secrets of the Eucharist. Stockbridge, MA: MercySong, Inc.*

Gershon, M. (1998). *The Second Brain.* New York: Harper Collins.

Gibran, K. (1994). *The Prophet.* New York: Alfred Knoff.

Goldsmith, J. (1986). *Practicing the Presence.* New York: Harper Collins.

Goleman, D. (1995). *Emotional Intelligence.* New York: Bantam Books.

Goodman, S. (1993). *Amazing Biofacts.* New York: Peter Bedrick Books.

Hahn, T. (2007). *Living Buddha, Living Christ.* New York: Riverhead Books.

Hazard, D. (1995). *I Promise You A Crown: A 40-Day Journey in the Company of Julian of Norwich.* Minneapolis, MN: Bethany House.

Howard, P. (2000). *The Owner's Manual for the Brain.* Marietta, CA: Bard Press.

John Paul II (2006). *Man and Woman He Created Them: A Theology of the Body.* Boston, MA: Pauline Books and Media.

John Paul II (1995). *The Gospel of Life.* Boston, MA: Pauline Books and Media.

John Paul II (1993). *The Splendor of Truth.* Boston, MA: Pauline Books and Media.

Keller, T. (2008). *The Prodigal God: Recovering the Heart of the Christian Faith.* New York: Penguin Group.

Kowalska, Saint Maria Faustina (2010). *Divine Mercy in My Soul: Diary of Saint Maria Faustina Kowallska.* Stockbridge, MA: Marian Press.

Kushner, H. (2003). *The Lord is My Shepherd.* New York: Random House.

Lucado, M. (2007). *Grace for the Moment.* Nashville, TN: Thomas Merton, Inc.

Martin, J. (2006). *Becoming Who You Are.* Mahwah, NJ: Paulist Press.

Merton, T. (1987). *Spiritual Direction and Meditation.* Collegeville, PA: The Liturgical Press.

Merton, T. (1962). *New Seeds of Contemplation.* New York: New Directions Books.

Patel, N. (2008). *Total Yoga.* San Diego, CA: Thunder Bay Press.

Peck. M. (1978). *The Road Less Traveled.* New York: Simon & Schuster.

Pert, C. (1999). *Molecules of Emotion: Why You Feel the Way You Feel.* New York: Simon and Schuster.

Ruiz, D. (1997). *The Four Agreements.* San Rafael, CA: Amber Allen Publishing.

Rupp, J. (2001). *Inviting God In: Spiritual Reflections and Prayers Throughout the Year.* Notre Dame, IN: Ave Maria Press.

Singer-Towns, B. (2004). *The Catholic Faith Handbook: For Youth.* Winona, MN: Saint Mary's Press.

Warren, R. (2002). *The Purpose Driven Life: What on Earth am I Here For?* Grand Rapids: Zondervan.

Winter, A & Winter, R. (1986). *Build Your Brain Power.* New York: St. Martin's.

Wojtyla, H. (1993). *Love and Responsibility.* San Francisco, CA: Ignatius Press.

Van De Putte. W. (1990). *Following the Holy Spirit. New Jersey: Catholic Book Publishing Corp.*

Yogananda, P. (1981). *Autobiography of a Yogi.* Los Angeles: Self-Realization Fellowship.

Zapolsky, R. (1996). *Why Zebras Don't Get Ulcers.* New York: Henry Holt & Company.

CPSIA information can be obtained at www.ICGtesting.com
Printed in the USA
BVOW081656221111

276654BV00003B/1/P